Multinationals, Technology and Localization in Automotive Firms in Asia

East Asia has led rapid economic growth in the last few decades with India joining them over the last five years. Automotive parts manufacturers have been an important component of domestic production in all these economies. Experts with several years of multi-disciplinary research experience on the field examine the actual and potential technological and localization implications of MNC operations in East Asia and India. The rich collection of country experiences are both original and incisive.

This volume includes:

- Case studies from China, Japan, India, Thailand and Malaysia
- A study of the role of multinationals in Asian technology building
- An examination of the growing Chinese automobile sector

Featuring leading academics from across Asia, this title is essential reading for those studying industrial growth in the continent's major economies.

This book was previously published as a special issue of *Asia Pacific Business Review*

Rajah Rasiah currently works as professor of technology and innovation policy at University of Malaya. He has undertaken research and consultancy as well as published extensively in the fields of multinationals, technology, innovation, competitiveness and development.

Yuri Sadoi is associate professor of Faculty of Economics at Meijo University, Japan. She obtained her PhD in Human and Environmental Studies from Kyoto University in 1999. She has published in the fields of skill formation and technology transfer.

Rogier Busser studied at Leiden University and Kyoto University. His research interests are primarily in industrial organization, technological upgrading and business-government relations in East Asia. He currently serves as director for International Relations at the Faculty of Arts of Leiden University.

Multinationals, Technology and Localization in Automotive Firms in Asia

Edited by
Rajah Rasiah, Yuri Sadoi and Rogier Busser

Routledge
Taylor & Francis Group
LONDON AND NEW YORK

First published 2008 by Routledge
2 Park Square, Milton Park, Abingdon, Oxon, OX14 4RN

Simultaneously published in the USA and Canada
by Routledge
270 Madison Avenue, New York, NY 10016

Routledge is an imprint of the Taylor & Francis Group, an informa business

Typeset in Times 11/12pt by Alden Group, Oxfordshire
Printed and bound in Great Britain by MPG Books Ltd, Bodmin, Cornwall

British Library Cataloguing in Publication Data
A catalogue record for this book is available from the British Library

ISBN 10: 0-415-44067-X
ISBN 13: 978-0-415-44067-7

CONTENTS

Acknowledgements

This publication comprises papers from the conference, 'Foreign Direct Investment and Technology: A Study of Automotive and Electronics Industries in Asia' held at the University of Malaya, Kuala Lumpur on 1–3 September 2005. We wish to take this opportunity to offer thanks for the generous financial support of the Asia Europe Foundation, Meijo University Research Foundation, International Institute for Asian Studies and Institute for Industrial District which made it possible to finance the flights and accommodation of the foreign participants, and the Faculty of Economics and Administration, University of Malaya for other organizational costs involved in hosting the conference. Professors Takahiro Fujimoto (Tokyo University) and Rajneesh Narula (Reading University) provided us with incisive keynote speeches in the field, while Fatimah Kari managed the day-to-day running of the conference extremely well.

We are also grateful to the following people who contributed in various different ways to make the publication a success: Chris Rowley, Malcolm Warner, Norma Mansor, Wendy Smith, Laurids Lauridssen, Ad Notten, Yeo Lin, Nungsari Razi Ahmad, Geoffrey Gachino, Paulo Figeiredo, Banji Oyeyingka, Mako Yoshimura, Kamaruding Abdulsomad, Madeline Berma, Tham Siew Yean, Sandra Kumar, Ahmad Farid Osman, Amien Jamaluddin, Chong Chin Seng, Evelyn Shyamala Devadason, Hanira Hanapi, Mior Ibrahim Mior Norahan, Mohd Haizal Ismail, M. Krishnasamy, Nurul Huda Mohd. Satar, Noor Hasniah Kasim, Nur Diyana Mohd Saifuddin, Razak Darus, Yong Sook Lu and the general and graduate supporting staff of the Faculty of Economics and Administration, University of Malaya. However, the errors that remain are ours.

Rajah Rasiah, Yuri Sadoi and Rogier Busser

Introduction: Critical Issues on Multinational-driven Technological Capability Building and Localization

RAJAH RASIAH

Introduction

Multinational corporations (MNCs) have continued to remain a critical channel for the transmission of knowledge to latecomer firms in developing economies. Japan (see Johnson, 1982; Freeman, 1987; Fukasaku, 1992), Korea (Edquist & Jacobssen, 1987; Amsden, 1989; Kim, 1997) and Taiwan (Hamilton, 1983; Fransman, 1985) enjoyed little FDI but accessed extensively technology from MNCs through licensing and imitation. Singapore and Malaysia have enjoyed direct participation of MNCs. Although FDI levels were low in Thailand, Indonesia and Philippines until the 1990s MNCs have been dominant in export manufacturing (see Pongpaichit & Baker, 1995; Rasiah 1998; 2003, 2005; Thee, 2005). China enjoys strong FDI levels in export-oriented manufacturing industries (see Rasiah, 2005).

Given the importance of MNCs as a critical source of foreign knowledge in latecomer development – indirectly (as in Japan, Korea and Taiwan) and directly (as in Singapore and Malaysia) - this contribution seeks to examine technology diffusion potential to local firms, the extent of techonology diffusion and its channels in the automotive industry in East, South East and South Asia. The Japanese experience has become interesting following mergers and acquisitions that have taken place since the late 1990s.

Automotive manufacturing is an important economic activity in Japan, China, India, Korea, Malaysia, Philippines, Taiwan and Thailand. Japan and the rest of Asia accounted for 22.1 per cent and 16.7 per cent respectively of global automobile production in 2004.[1] The essays in this publication deal with technological capabilities and localization implications – potential and actual – from the direct operations of MNCs.

Multinationals on Technology and Localization

The impact of MNCs on technology and localization vary across economies and industries. Existing work points to initial conditions (including demand-supply conditions), government policy (some as stimulators while others as creators of unproductive distortions), institutional coordination, size of domestic markets, human capital and nature of supply chains as drivers of spillover from MNCs to local firms (see Dunning, 1958, 1974; Lall & Streeten, 1977; Rasiah, 2004a). Foreign MNC affiliates' intensity of participation in technological and localization activities to tap host-site institutions and human capital capabilities is often conditioned by the location of the sites in the technology ladder (see Dunning & Narula, 2000; Cantwell, 1995; Cantwell & Mudambi, 2001; Narula, 2003; Rasiah, 2004a). Host governments sometimes impose conditions to stimulate (for example, financial incentives such as tax breaks for R&D activities) or pressure (for example, R&D activities as a condition to sell in domestic markets) foreign MNCs to participate in technology-intensive and localization activities (see Mathew & Cho, 2000; Mathew, 2001; Wong, 2001). Foreign firms also sometimes relocate aspects of R&D in fairly developed locations such as Taiwan to tap specialized knowledge (see Ernst, 2006).

Nevertheless, whatever the reasons for relocation, the participation of foreign firms offers host-sites the potential for knowledge spillovers. Local firms in some developing economies seek from abroad knowledge through imports, training of personnel abroad, licensing and subcontract deals (Freeman, 1987; 1989; Rasiah & Lin, 2005). MNCs still play a major role involving this channel, albeit indirectly as imitation and arms length transactions figure prominently. Countries such as Japan, South Korea and Taiwan generally imported foreign technology through imitation and licensing from MNCs (Freeman, 1987, 1989; Fukasaku, 1992; Kim, 1997; Amsden, 1989). Others such as Singapore and Ireland have relied extensively on MNCs' foreign direct investment (FDI) to stimulate learning and innovation (UNCTAD, 2002). Clearly, both strategies – learning and innovating to compete, using MNCs both directly and indirectly – are embedded in national economic policies (Rasiah, 2004a). Hence, discussions relating to the role of FDI on technology cannot be detached from the conditions prevailing and economic policies pursued at host-sites.

Because the focus of assessment in this publication is on both the actual and potential benefits brought by foreign MNCs, stand alone foreign firms were excluded from analysis. A number of factors influence the development of technological capabilities, localization and competitiveness. Typical industrial organisation exponents argue that the embedding environment (structure) influences the conduct of firms, which then influences the performance of firms

(Bain, 1978; Scherer, 1985). Public policy recommendations from this perspective often target structural conditions (including institutions) to influence the conduct and performance of firms and these elements transcend economics to include the political sphere (see Nelson & Winter, 1982b; North, 1994). Chandler (1962) articulated an historical account of the origin and growth of national corporations in the United States, which explains the early business understanding of the role of multi-divisional firms.

Drawing from the ownership, location and internalization (OLI) framework of motives by Dunning (1974), Narula & Dunning (2000) explain the potential implications of MNC relocations in developing economies. Hence, efforts to understand the technological impact of foreign MNCs at host-sites require at least some knowledge of the motives and characteristics of the foreign firms involved. Natural resources (for example, oil in Indonesia and Malaysia), large reserves of literate labour (for example, China, Philippines and Vietnam), domestic markets (for example, China and India) special trading spheres (for example, the Association of South East Asian Nations (ASEAN) Free Trade Area), the strength of the local and national innovation systems (for example, Singapore, Taiwan and Korea) have been important in attracting foreign firms – especially when accompanied by political stability and bureaucratic efficiency (see Narula & Dunning, 2000; Rasiah, 2002; Rasiah, 2004b).

Apart from oligopolistic advantages driving the expansion of national firms to MNCs (see Hymer, 1960) the growth in the number of cross-border subsidiaries is also driven by efforts to internalize intangible assets – embodied and disembodied knowledge – and to appropriate the relative benefits offered by host-sites (see Dunning, 1958; 1974, 2003). The social dimension used in the business school in the activities of MNCs was advanced by Dunning (2003: 1–21) who introduced the concept of relational assets, which are intangible assets that are either internalized directly or indirectly through alliances. Relational assets are human-intensive – though they may be embedded or articulated by individuals or organizations (Dunning, 2003: 4). Subsumed in this concept are the elements of economic transactions influenced by social relationships, which is referred to as social capital. Relational assets are internalized or appropriated directly or indirectly through participation in business networks – a two-way process of fostering intra-network and inter-firm relational capital (Dunning, 2003: 9). These relationships also help enrich human capital, but the diffusion of both codified and tacit and experiential knowledge from foreign firms to the local economy is likely to be strong only when the systemic conditions – institutional, density of firms and systemic links (including elements of trust) – are strong.

A firm's conduct (strategy) and performance are influenced by its own endowments, the nature and degree of coordination with other economic agents (including the structure). Industrial organization typically expounds that firms' performance is determined by the structure (or environment, including other economic agents in factor and final markets) in which the firm is located and its conduct (see Bain, 1968; Scherer, 1973; 1980; Greer, 1992). Five related and overlapping approaches – National Innovation System (NIS), Industrial Policy (IP), institutional economics, Industrial Organisation and the Business School (BS) – discuss the policy and institutional environment necessary to stimulate learning, innovations and firm-level performance. Business School exponents such as Prahalad & Doz (1987), Bartlett & Ghoshal (1989), Andersson *et al.* (2002), Birkinshaw *et al.* (1998) and Cantwell & Mudambi (2001) discussed local integration, embeddedness and differentiated subsidiaries on the basis of competence creating and competence exploiting conduct of MNCs.

The earliest IP argument in economic literature can be traced to Smith (1776), Hamilton (1791), Mill (1848) and List (1885). However, the earliest application of IP in driving industrial upgrading and exports can be traced to Henry VII in 1485 in Great Britain, which was followed later by government-led efforts in continental Europe well before its use in the United States and Germany (Reinert, 1994: 175). The national innovation system approach examines knowledge production, flows and diffusion involving learning and innovation, which provides a systemic dimension to firms' conduct and performance (Freeman, 1989; Lundvall, 1992; Nelson, 1993; Nelson & Winter, 1982a, 1982b; Dosi, 1982; Pavitt, 1984; Freeman, 1989). The concept of knowledge flows within industrial districts was articulated lucidly by A. Marshall (1890). Industrial policy approaches typically prescribe a regulated trade environment to nurture infant firms to competitive status (see Lewis, 1955; Myrdal, 1957; Kaldor, 1957). The institutional embeddedness of learning, innovation and knowledge flows can be viewed better by integrating the value chains (Gereffi, 2002; 2003) and the national innovation systems approaches (see also Rasiah, 2007). The Business School and institutional economics approaches offer a broader exposition of the environment – socio-political and cultural, conduct of affiliates, and the importance of social capital – in explaining the operations of firms (see Coase, 1992; North, 1994; Williamson, 1985; Dunning, 2003).

Figure 1 shown below attempts a synthesis of the five approaches above to synthesize the nature of technological and localization linkages that can be expected in host-site locations in Asia. Technological capabilities of firms are often conditioned by the environment they embed: they vary from high levels in locations where strong high- tech support institutions (for example, human capital, R&D laboratories and intermediary organizations) and network cohesion exists, and low levels in locations where the commensurate institutions and networks are weak. Firms' demand and supply for high- tech capabilities increase as the embedding high-tech infrastructure rises (see Dosi, 1982; Pavitt, 1984). High-tech infrastructure is essential to stimulate firms' participation in product and process technology development (for example, R&D support). Foreign firms are generally able to access high-tech support in locations where such institutional support exists, and hence seldom perform R&D activities in underdeveloped locations. In addition to seeking technology through various learning activities and licensing, local firms invest more in R&D activities than foreign firms initially since they do not have the option of accessing know-how from superior affiliates overseas. Foreign firms generally participate more in R&D activities at host-sites once the embedding environment becomes conducive. However, the depth of engagement of foreign firms in R&D activities at host-sites is also conditioned by industry type, network strength and cohesion, nature of local government policy instruments and local market structure.

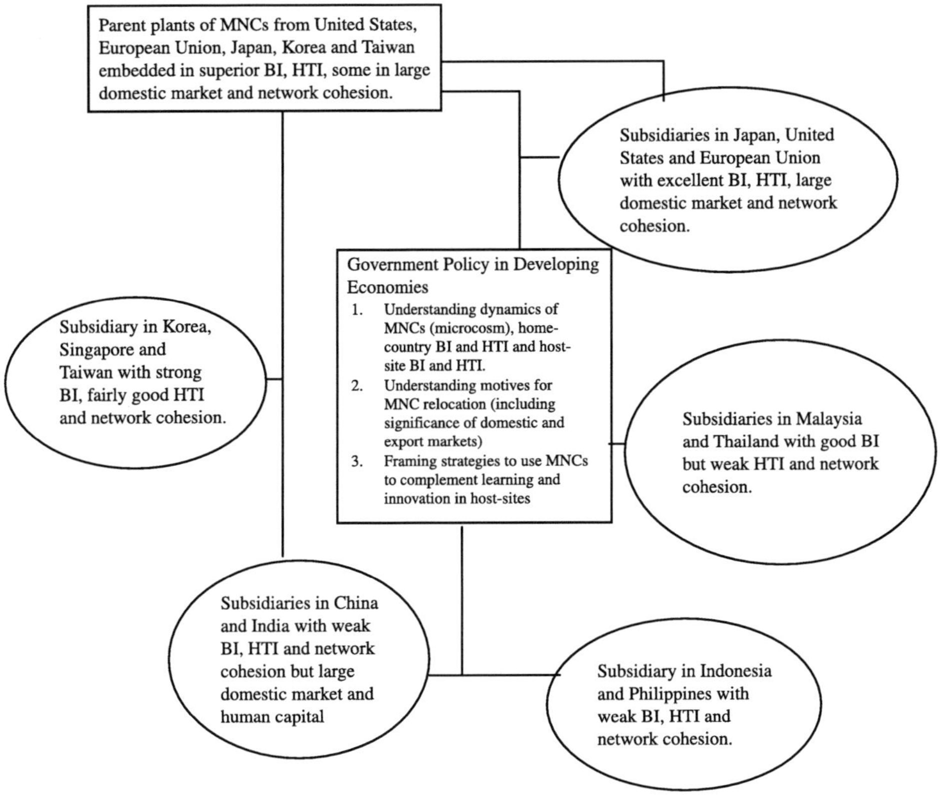

Figure 1. A model of multinationals, technological capabilities and localization. *Source*: Adapted from Rasiah (2004a).

The Automotive Industry in Asia

Given the focus in this publication on examining the influence of multinationals on technology and localization in local firms and how it varied across economies with different institutional strength, the countries were selected on the basis of strong participation of multinationals – both through direct investment as well as through technology tie-ups and varying strength of the embedding infrastructure. Whereas direct MNC participation through FDI is high in Malaysia, Thailand, China and Philippines, it is high through joint-venture and licensing tie-ups with local firms in (especially in automotives) in India, China, Japan, Korea and Malaysia.

Net FDI inflows in these economies varied strongly. Despite the removal of all controls on ownership in the manufacturing sector in 1971, net FDI in gross fixed capital formation (GFCF) has remained extremely low in Japan – not exceeding 1 per cent. Among the remaining economies examined in this publication Korea (3.1 per cent), India (3.5 per cent) and Thailand (3.7 per cent) had the lowest net FDI levels in GFCF in 2005 (see Table 1). Malaysia (15.2 per cent) had the highest levels followed by China (9.2 per cent) and the Philippines (7.5 per cent) in 2005.

Japan enjoys by far the strongest institutions and firms at the technology frontier followed by Korea (and Taiwan). Malaysia and Thailand enjoy good basic infrastructure but fairly weak high-tech infrastructure. The Philippines, India and China offer good basic infrastructure in special industrial districts. India and China in addition enjoy enormous domestic markets, and human capital to drive upgrading. Government support was instrumental in the emergence of automotive assembly at least in the initial stages in all these economies. Policies to develop national cars were also important at some point in history in Japan, Korea, China, Malaysia, India, Indonesia and the Philippines.

East Asian economies figure prominently in global trade involving automotives and the industry has undergone increasing integration and globalization. The former constitutes a significant part of inward- and export-oriented manufacturing activity in all the selected economies while the latter dominates manufactured exports in China, Malaysia, the Philippines and Thailand. Japan is still a major exporter of automotive products though its share in world exports has fallen over the period 1990–2005 (see Table 2). Korea, China and Thailand continued to expand their shares in world exports of automotives over the period 1980–2005. China's share in world automotive imports has also risen though it only accounted for 1.5 per cent in 2005. Also, the automotive industry enjoys synergizing or clustering properties (including through increased modularization (see Gereffi *et al.*, 2005)) that help industrial expansion faster than others such as steel and leather products.

Automotives once enjoyed natural insulation owing to distance but increasing globalization arising from both the development of capabilities in many parts of the world (often through inward-oriented government policy), differentiation and modularization has removed such advantages so that Taiwan has become an important exporter of automotive parts. Automotive manufacturing has experienced a decentralization of production since the 1990s as MNCs are increasingly seeking to internationalize operations to take advantage of low-wage literate labour and special pools of human capital emerging in particular locations and region-specific customer tastes (see Rasiah, 2002). However, while manufacturing is increasingly relocated out of major assembly sites in the developed world, automotive manufacturing has also begun to face integration in particular locations since the 1990s so that key component production sites have had to upgrade to remain in their value chains (see also Ofreneo, 2003; Prasada, 2003; Quadros, 2003; Veloso & Kumar, 2003).

Aims and Objectives

The central task of this publication is to assemble a set of contributions to provide a good understanding of the nature, extent and depth of technological and localization linkages – actual and potential – that have, and are likely, to evolve from foreign MNCs in selected Asian economies in the automotive industry. Given the importance of governments the publication also discusses the impact of policies on the development of technological capabilities in local firms.

Although it is impossible to produce a cohesive collection of works in such a complex field as technology and localization this publication provides interesting

Table 1. Share of Net FDI in GCF, 1990–2005 (%)

	1990	1991	1992	1993	1994	1995	1996	1997	1998	1999	2000	2001	2002	2003	2004	2005
China	3.5	3.9	7.3	12.2	17.3	15.4	14.9	14.9	13.6	11.3	10.3	10.5	10.4	8.6	8.1	9.2
India	0.3	0.1	0.4	0.9	1.4	2.4	2.9	4.0	2.9	2.2	3.5	5.2	4.9	3.4	3.1	3.5
Korea	0.8	0.9	0.5	0.4	0.5	0.7	1.0	1.4	4.8	7.3	5.4	2.7	1.9	2.1	3.9	3.1
Malaysia	18.0	22.6	23.7	22.1	15.3	15.0	17.0	14.6	14.0	22.5	16.4	2.5	14.5	10.8	19.1	15.2
Philippines	5.4	6.1	7.0	9.6	10.5	8.9	7.8	6.2	12.7	8.6	13.9	1.5	11.4	3.7	4.8	7.5
Taiwan	3.7	3.2	1.8	1.6	2.3	2.4	3.0	3.4	0.4	4.2	6.4	7.3	2.7	0.8	2.8	2.3
Thailand	7.5	5.0	4.9	3.7	2.4	3.0	3.1	7.6	29.9	23.9	12.4	14.6	3.3	5.7	3.4	3.7

Source: Compiled from World Bank (2006)

Table 2. World's leading exporters and importers, automotives, 1980–2005

	Value	Share in world exports/imports				Average annual growth (%)			
	2005	1980	1990	2000	2005	2000–05	2003	2004	2005
Exporters									
European Union (25)	486.83	–	–	49.8	53.3	11	22	18	2
Japan	122.90	19.8	20.8	15.3	13.5	7	11	13	6
United States	85.99	11.9	10.2	11.6	9.4	5	3	10	13
Canada	66.75	6.9	8.9	10.5	7.3	2	1	12	5
Korea, Republic of	37.75	0.1	0.7	2.6	4.1	20	33	40	17
Mexico a	35.38	0.3	1.4	5.3	3.9	3	–3	6	11
Brazil	11.97	1.1	0.6	0.8	1.3	21	33	33	38
China a	9.96	0.0	0.1	0.3	1.1	44	33	76	59
Turkey	9.36	0.0	0.0	0.3	1.0	43	57	59	16
Thailand	7.98	0.0	0.0	0.4	0.9	27	22	40	44
South Africa	4.35	0.1	0.1	0.3	0.5	21	29	19	18
Taiwan	3.82	...	0.3	0.4	0.4	11	22	23	2
Australia	3.52	0.2	0.2	0.4	0.4	10	18	12	14
Argentina	3.05	0.1	0.1	0.4	0.3	8	–9	44	39
United Arab Emirates b, c	2.97	...	0.0	0.2	0.3	...	14	31	...
Above 15	892.60	...	...	98.6	97.7	–	–	–	–
Importers									
European Union (25)	407.54	–	–	41.8	44.1	11	24	17	1
Extra-EU (25) imports	54.91	–	–	5.4	5.9	11	27	20	5
United States	205.45	20.3	24.7	28.8	22.2	4	3	9	4
Canada d	57.61	8.7	7.7	7.8	6.2	4	5	8	9
Mexico a, d	25.14	1.8	0.3	3.4	2.7	5	–5	8	16
Australia d	15.19	1.3	1.2	1.4	1.6	12	30	20	14
China a	13.55	0.6	0.6	0.6	1.5	29	84	13	–6
Japan	13.17	0.5	2.3	1.7	1.4	6	13	15	3
Russia	12.90	–	–	0.4	1.4	40	35	50	42
Turkey	11.96	...	0.4	1.0	1.3	15	122	85	4
Saudi Arabia b	11.64	2.7	0.9	0.6	1.3	25	11	24	55
South Africa d	9.27	...	...	0.4	1.0	31	41	45	30
Switzerland	8.52	1.8	1.9	1.1	0.9	6	12	11	2
United Arab Emirates b, c	6.05	0.4	0.3	0.4	0.7	...	32	36	...
Norway	5.25	0.6	0.4	0.4	0.6	15	18	32	15
Brazil	4.51	0.3	0.2	0.7	0.5	1	–5	16	30
Above 15	807.72	...	...	90.7	87.5	–	–	–	–

Note: a: includes significant shipments through processing zones; b: includes Secretariat estimates; c: 2004 instead of 2005; d: imports are valued f.o.b.
Source: WTO (2006: Table IV.66).

analysis of a range of critical issues that are important to the automotive industry in general, and to Asia in particular. The volume focuses on the flow of financial, managerial, and technological benefits from foreign MNCs to local firms under different embedding environments. Critical issues examined include government policies, alliances, upgrading, localization, company strategies, and differences in technological intensities and economic performance in the automotive industry.

Note

[1] Computed from SurfIndia: Web Directory of India, available at: http://www.surfindia.com/automobile/production.html

References

Amsden, A. (1989) *Asia's Next Giant: South Korea and Late Industrialization* (New York: Oxford University Press).

Andersson, U., Forgren, M. & Holm, U. (2002) The strategic impact of external networks: subsidiary roles in multinational corporations, *Strategic Management Journal*, 23, pp. 979–996.

Bain, J. (1988) *Industrial Organization* (New York: John Wiley).

Bartlett, C. A. & Ghoshal, S. (1989) *Managing Across Borders: The Transnational Solution* (Boston, MA: Harvard Business School Press).

Birkinshaw, J., Hood, N. & Jonsson, S. (1998) Building firm-specific advantages in multinational corporations: the role of subsidiary initiative, *Strategic Management Journal*, 19, pp. 221–241.

Cantwell, J. (1995) The globalization of technology: what remains of the product cycle model, *Cambridge Journal of Economics*, 19, pp. 155–174.

Cantwell, J. & Mudambi, R. (2001) MNE competence-creating subsidiary mandates: an empirical investigation. International Investment and Management Discussion Paper, No. 285, Reading University.

Chandler, A. (1962) *Strategy and Structure: Chapters in the History of the American Industrial Enterprise* (New York: Doubleday).

Coase, R. (1992) The institutional structure of production, *American Economic Review*, 82, pp. 713–719.

Dosi, G. (1982) Technological paradigms and technological trajectories, *Research Policy*, 11(3), pp. 147–162.

Dunning, J. H. (1958) *American Investment in British Manufacturing Industry* (London: Allen & Unwin).

Dunning, J. H. (1974) *Economic Analysis and the Multinational Enterprise* (London: Allen & Unwin).

Dunning, J. H. (2003) Relational assets, networks and international business activity, in: J. H. Dunning & G. Boyd (Eds) *Alliance Capitalism and Corporate Management: Entrepreneurial Cooperation in Knowledge Based Economies* (Cheltenham: Edward Elgar).

Dunning, J. & Narula, R. (2000) Globalization and multinational enterprises: new realities, *Oxford Development Studies*, 28(2), pp. 141–167.

Edquist, C. & Jacobssen, S. (1987) The integrated circuit industries in India and South Korea in an international techno-economic context, *Industry and Development*, 21, pp. 1–62.

Ernst, D. (2006) Innovation offshoring: Asia's emerging role in global innovation networks. East-West Center Special Report 10, East-West Center, Hawaii.

Fransman, M. (1985) International competitiveness, technical change and the state: the machine tool industries in Taiwan and Japan, *World Development*, 14(12), pp. 1375–1396.

Freeman, C. (1987) *Technology Policy and Economic Performance: Lessons from Japan* (London: Frances Pinter).

Freeman, C. (1989) New technology and catching-up, *European Journal of Development Research*, 1(1) pp. 85–99.

Fukasaku, Y. (1992) *Technology Development in Pre-War Japan: Mitsubishi Nagasaki Shipyard* (London: Routledge).

Gereffi, G. (2002) Prospects for industrial upgrading by developing countries in the global apparel commodity chain, *International Journal of Business and Society*, 3(1), pp. 27–60.

Gereffi, G. (2003) International competitiveness of Asian firms in the global apparel commodity chain, *International Journal of Business Society*, 4(2), pp. 71–110.

Gereffi, G., Humphrey, J. & Sturgeon, T. (2005) The governance of global value chains, *Review of International Political Economy*, 12, pp. 78–104.

Greer, D. (1992) *Industrial Organization and Public Policy* (New York: Macmillan).

Hamilton, A. (1791) Report on manufactures, 5 December. Available at: http://www.oberlin.edu/~gkornbl/Hist258/ReportMfres.html (accessed on 13 December 2005).

Hamilton, C. (1983) Capitalist industrialization in East Asia's four little tigers, *Journal of Contemporary Asia*, 13(1), pp. 35–73.

Hymer, S. (1960) *International Operations of National Firms* (doctoral thesis published in 1976) (Cambridge, MA: MIT Press).

SurfIndia (2006) Industry: production. Available at http://www.surfindia.com/automobile/production.htmlAutomobile (accessed on 27 December 2006).

Johnson, C. (1982) *MITI and the Japanese Miracle* (Stanford, CA: Stanford University Press).

Kaldor, N. (1957) A model of economic growth, *Economic Journal*, 67, pp. 591–624.

Kim, L. (1997) *From Imitation to Innovation* (Cambridge, MA: Harvard Business School Press).

Lall, S. & Streeten, P. (1977) *Foreign Investment, Transnationals and Developing Countries* (London: Macmillan).

Lewis, A. (1955) *The Theory of Economic Growth* (London: Allen & Unwin).

List, F. (1885) *The National System of Political Economy* (London: Longmans, Green & Company).

Lundvall, B. A. (1992) *National Systems of Innovation. Towards a Theory of Innovation and Interactive Learning* (London: Frances Pinter).

Marshall, A. (1890) *Principles of Economics* (London: Macmillan).

Mathew, J. (2001) *The Asian Multinational* (Oxford: Oxford University Press).

Mathew, J. & Cho, D. S. (2000) *Tiger Technology* (Cambridge: Cambridge University Press).

Mill, J. S. (1848) *The Principles of Political Economic with Some of Their Applications to Social Policy* (London: John Parker and West Strand).

Myrdal, G. (1957) *Economic Theory and Underdeveloped Regions* (New York: Methuen).

Narula, R. (2003) *Globalisation and Technology: Interdependence, Innovation Systems and Industrial Policy* (Cambridge: Polity Press).

Narula, R. & Dunning, J. (2000) Industrial development, globalization and multinational enterprises: new realities for developing countries, *Oxford Development Studies*, 28(2), pp. 141–167.

Nelson, R. R. (Ed.) (1993) *National Innovation Systems* (New York: Oxford University Press).

Nelson, R. R. & Winter, S. G. (1982a) The Schumpeterian tradeoff revisited, *American Economic Review*, 72(1), pp. 114–132.

Nelson, R. R. & Winter, S. G. (1982b) *An Evolutionary Theory of Economic Change* (Cambridge, MA: Harvard University Press).

North, D. (1994) Economic performance through time, *American Economic Review*, 84(3), pp. 359–368.

Ofreneo, R. E. (2003) TRIMs and the automobile industry in Philippines, in: R. Rasiah (Ed.) *Transnational Corporations, Learning and Innovation* (Maastricht: UNU-INTECH).

Pavitt, K. (1984) Sectoral patterns of technical change: towards a taxonomy and a theory, *Research Policy*, 13(6), pp. 343–373.

Pongpaichit, P. & Baker, C. (1995) *Thailand: Economy and Politics* (Kuala Lumpur: Oxford University Press).

Prahalad, C. K. & Doz, Y. L. (1987) *The Multinational Mission: Balancing Local Demands and Global Vision* (New York: Free Press).

Prasada, R. (2003) TRIMs and Technological Capacity Building, in: R. Rasiah (Ed.) *Transnational Corporations, Learning and Innovation* (Maastricht: INTECH).

Quadros, R. (2003) TRIMs, TNCs, Technology Policy and the Brazilian Automobile Industry, in: R. Rasiah (Ed.) *Transnational Corporations, Learning and Innovation* (Maastricht: INTECH).

Rasiah, R. (1998) Relocation of the electronics, textile and garment industries in Malaysia, in: A. Y. Hing, E. Chang & R. Lansbury (Eds) *Work, Organisation and Industry* (Singapore: Armour Press).

Rasiah, R. (2002) Systemic coordination and the knowledge economy: human capital development in MNC-driven electronics clusters in Malaysia, *Transnational Corporations*, 11(3), pp. 89–p129.

Rasiah, R. (2003) Industrial Technology Transition in Malaysia, in: S. Lall & S. Urata (Eds) *Technology Development in East Asia* (Cheltenham: Edward Elgar).

Rasiah, R. (2004a) *Foreign Firms, Technological Capabilities and Economic Performance: Evidence from Africa, Asia and Latin America* (Cheltenham: Edward Elgar).

Rasiah, R. (2004b) Technological capabilities in East and Southeast Asian electronics firms: does network strength matter?, *Oxford Development Studies*, 32(3), pp. 433–454.

Rasiah, R. (2005) Foreign ownership, technological intensity and export incidence: a study of auto parts, electronics and garment firms in Indonesia, *International Journal of High Technology and Globalization*, 1(3/4), pp. 361–380.

Rasiah, R. (2007) Human capital and cluster synergies: the case of Penang and Jalisco, in: A. J. Scott & G. Garofoli (Eds) *Development on the Ground: Clusters, Networks and Regions in Emerging Economies* (London: Routledge).

Rasiah, R. & Lin, Y. (2005) Learning and innovation in the information hardware industry in Taiwan: the role of markets, government and trust, *International Journal of Technology and Globalization*, 1(3/4), pp. 400–432.

Reinert, E. S. (1994) 'Catching-up from way behind': a Third World perspective on First World history, in: J. Fagerberg, B. Verspagen & N. V. Tunzelmann (Eds) *The Dynamics of Technology, Trade and Growth* (Aldershot: Hassocks).

Scherer, F. (1973) The determinants of industry plant sizes in six nations, *Review of Economics and Statistics*, 55(2), pp. 135–175.

Scherer, F. M. (1980) *Industrial Market Structure and Economic Performance* (Chicago, IL: Rand McNally).

Scherer, F. M. (1985) *Industrial Market Structure and Economic Performance* (Chicago: Rand McNally).

Smith, A. (1776) *Wealth of Nations* (London: Strahan & Cadell).

Thee, K. W. (2005) Technology and Indonesia's industrial competitiveness, Asian Development Bank Institute (ADBI) Working Paper, Tokyo.

UNCTAD (2002) *World Investment Report* (Geneva: United Nations Conference for Trade and Development).

Veloso, F. & Kumar, R. (2003) The automotive supply chain: global trends and the Importance of Asia, *International Journal of Business and Society*, 4(2), pp. 22–59.

Williamson, O. (1985) *The Economic Institutions of Capitalism* (New York: Free Press).

Wong, P. K. (2001) Leveraging multinational corporations, fostering technopreneurship: the changing role of S&T policy in Singapore, *International Journal of Technology Management*, 22(5/6), pp. 539–567.

World Bank (2006) *World Development Indicators* (Washington, DC: World Bank Institute).

WTO (World Trade Organization) (2006) *Trade Statistics* (Geneva: World Trade Organization).

Foreign Influences on the Japanese Automobile Industry: The Nissan-Renault Mutual Learning Alliance[1]

MERIEKE STEVENS

Introduction

The post-war Japanese economy is a much disputed topic. It is however generally agreed that more than in the United States or Europe the Japanese governmental bureaucracy protected the domestic market and interfered in the economy in a way that was effective in reaching certain national goals (Van Wolferen, 1989). Governmental interference has played a crucial role in the initial stages of the development of Japan's automobile manufacturing industry, and it has been argued that without the protection they received Japanese carmakers would have been out-competed at their inception by their much more advanced American and European counterparts (Cusumano, 1989).

A shared domestic setting however did not give rise to a group of identical Japanese automobile producers and Nissan and Toyota to a certain degree exemplify two opposite types of large Japanese enterprises: the first intertwined with the governmental bureaucracy and partly dependent on governmental funding throughout much of its growth, and the second much more independent from these influences.

Drawing on literature research and case study interviews,[2] this essay seeks to examine the impact of foreign management practices on the Nissan-Renault alliance. In the first section of this contribution the common historical economic setting of Japanese automobile manufacturers is discussed, while section two pays attention to the differences between Nissan and Toyota. In the third section Nissan's alliance with Renault is discussed, and in the fourth section this alliance is placed within the broader framework of the mutual learning alliance. In the conclusion the wider applicability of lessons from the Nissan-Renault alliance is briefly addressed.

Build to Grow

Protection

It is widely recognized that interference by the governmental bureaucracy in Japan's economy has been successful in supporting Japan's rapid post-war economic growth (e.g., Johnson, 1998). However, once Japan joined the ranks of fully developed economies it became apparent that the system actually needed growth to function successfully and did not perform as well when expansion slowed down (van Wolferen, 1989), and therefore had to change. Pressure to change also came from abroad; Japan's economic partners became increasingly unwilling to allow Japan its exclusive position in the global trading arena, and they demanded more and more that if Japan wanted to hold on to its position of major player in the world economy it had to fully adapt – externally as well as internally – to the free market principles its trading partners abided by.

While external demands did not spur immediate revolutionary change in Japan, it seems that since the economic downturn of the 1990s – known as Japan's lost decade – at least some aspects of Japan's post-war economic growth model are slowly but steadily changing. Recent cross-*keiretsu* mergers in the banking system (for example, between the Industrial Bank of Japan, Dai-ichi Kangyo Bank, and Fuji Bank in 2000) and alliances between flagships of Japan's post-war economy and foreign companies (like the Nissan and Renault alliance) are notable examples. Another visible example of change is the new but spreading phenomenon of foreign corporate representatives on the managerial boards of large Japanese companies (e.g. Carlos Ghosn at Nissan and Howard Stringer at Sony); a phenomenon that initially met with great scepticism in Japan.

Because Japanese companies were closed for decades to managerial influence from abroad, the current presence of foreigners on their boards is followed with great interest in Japan. While it is beyond the scope of this contribution to discuss the underlying motivations and mechanisms of Japan's closed post-war economy, two important pillars of the post-war high growth system – the main bank system and the vertical *keiretsu* system of industrial relations – are briefly discussed because they had an important formative impact on developments at Nissan.

Main Bank System

Japan's economic growth model has its roots in the crisis era of the 1920s-1930s when factions of Japan's ruling bureaucracy became increasingly militaristic and attempted to persuade big business to participate in the achievement of national goals (van Wolferen, 1989; Noguchi, 1996). Companies were given financial incentives to support militarization and mobilization for war, and especially companies that were considered to be of direct military use like the automobile industry, were greatly supported by the army. Consequently, while on a global scale Japan's automobile companies were not yet competitive, and all Japanese automobile producers to some extent depended on technology imported from abroad at this time, governmental protection ensured their survival (Cusumano, 1989).

During the build-up for war, credit was relatively easily available for companies that were considered to be of national importance, and these companies did not need to worry about their profitability but instead could focus completely on growth and building world-class manufacturing systems; in line with national economic goals (van Wolferen, 1989). Not all companies however assisted voluntarily in building a wartime apparatus. One of the companies that did cooperate closely with the military was Nissan, whose founder was a cousin of an important wartime leader.

After the war, the American Occupiers attempted to democratize Japan's political structure and introduced free market mechanisms into the economy. However, the Occupiers left the Japanese wartime bureaucracy largely intact and the wartime ideal of a production-centred and highly government controlled economy continued to shape governmental policies (van Wolferen, 1989). And thus the belief that national goals were more important than profits of individual companies continued its legacy.

Post-war rebuilding was directed by a system of central credit allocation, based on wartime credit controls. As had been the case during the period of military mobilization, credit allocation was controlled in order to direct economic growth. In replication of the wartime system, different sectors were classified according to their presumed national importance, and funds were allocated accordingly. At the upper end of the scale of economic importance exporting companies like the automobile industry were placed because these could help increase Japan's economic wealth and contribute to rebuilding Japan's international image (van Wolferen, 1989).

Nissan's assistance to the military during the war gave it a favourable position in the post-war rebuilding period, and it became popularly known as the 'darling' of the Ministry of International Trade and Industry (MITI); a ministry that is recognized for being closely intertwined with the national effort to effectively support and direct economic growth (Johnson, 1998). As a consequence Nissan found itself close to the source of national rebuilding funds in the post-war period. One of the results of being in this position was that Nissan did not prioritize cost-competitiveness but instead focused on expansion and manufacturing excellence; an orientation that is believed to have contributed to the deterioration of Nissan's profit performance when markets contracted during the 1990s.

Keiretsu Supplying System

The Japanese *keiretsu* system of industrial relations consists of both a horizontal as well as a vertical structure. While the horizontal *keiretsu* system – which links large Japanese manufacturers to a main bank, insurance companies and trading companies – is one of the core characteristics of post-war Japanese business structures, here only the vertical *keiretsu* structure is discussed because it was targeted as one of the main areas for change when Nissan embarked on its restructuring process together with partner Renault.

The vertical *keiretsu* is a fairly rigid pyramidal system of parts supplying relationships between large Japanese companies and their suppliers. In general, these relations are hierarchically organized in a system that holds midway between competitive bidding on one side and vertical integration on the other; both of which are found in the American automotive industry. Effectively the prime contractor at the top of a *keiretsu* – which gives the *keiretsu* its name – only deals with a limited number of first tier suppliers from which it buys complete assemblies and system components (Nishiguchi, 1994). First tier suppliers are often large and well-established companies and most of them subcontract for more than one assembler. The first tier subcontractors are supplied by a group of second tier subcontractors from whom they buy specialized parts. The second tier suppliers buy parts from third tier subcontractors, and so on. Nishiguchi (1994) defined this subcontracting system in which parts for a certain product or component are purchased from a limited number of suppliers as the 'clustered control' system.

In the traditional vertical *keiretsu*, the close relationships between carmakers and first-tier suppliers are supported by financial ties (for example, mutual stockholding, or money loans to subcontractors), managerial ties (for example, the sending of executives from the parent to suppliers), technical assistance and the lending of equipment to subcontractors, and by purchasing the majority of a supplier's output for extended periods of time (Smitka, 1991; Nishiguchi, 1994; Dyer & Chu, 1997). In addition, personal ties between representatives of the companies mostly developed, as well as a more generally institutionalized perception of a social relationship between the 'parent' company and its suppliers.

Like the post-war credit allocations, the roots of the subcontracting system can be traced to regulations for wartime mobilization; in this case the National Mobilization Act of 1938 that was declared to rapidly increase production of wartime essentials like munitions (Noguchi, 1996). Nishiguchi argues that the wartime intervention by the government introduced the systematic pyramidal structure in which each keiretsu subcontractor was 'ordered to be as "dedicated" as possible to a designated customer' (1994: 119).

Diverging Paths

Learning from Abroad

As it was mentioned above, at their inception all Japanese automobile manufacturers relied heavily on imported technology (Cusumano, 1989). This was however especially the case for Nissan. Toyota engineers also studied American production techniques in the pre-war period but whenever possible tried to rely on internal technological strengths. Not only at its inception was Nissan strongly influenced by technology imported from the United States, in the post-war period Nissan continued to learn from American practices. By importing technology and equipment from abroad Nissan became more dependent on external know-how and less innovative in process development, production management and quality control in comparison with Toyota. This early dependence on technology from outside the company, together with the above-mentioned post-war governmental support Nissan received for assisting the military, shaped Nissan's organizational structure in a fundamental way.

Contrary to Nissan's founder of whom it has been said that he was more interested in building empires than in building automobiles (Cusumano, 1989), Toyota's founder is widely recognized as a genuine entrepreneur who built his company by relying completely on internal strengths. Both of these contrasting images are however exaggerated; if Nissan had not been run by capable entrepreneurs – like Toyota – it would not have existed at all, likewise, if Toyota had been completely left alone by the Japanese government it might not have existed today, as would Nissan. Instead, the differences between Toyota and Nissan can to a certain extent be attributed to path-dependency; it was mainly through family connections that Nissan came into contact with the military, which at the time gave the company a growth impulse and also after the war provided it with benefits like financial assistance.

Post-war Divergence

Because Toyota had not been voluntarily involved in the wartime industrial project and did not receive the favourable treatment Nissan received after the war, it had to be more self-reliant than Nissan; both technologically as well as financially. This however ensured that Toyota accumulated valuable organizational and manufacturing skills. Interviewees often portrayed the 1990s Nissan management as an aristocracy producing old-fashioned cars, while in popular opinion Toyota managers are believed to be very entrepreneurial and therefore able to communicate effectively with the entire production line. As was suggested above, these opposed images of Nissan as a dull bureaucratic entity and Toyota as an entrepreneurial pioneer are misleading. During most of the post-war period Nissan has been able to produce technologically innovative and attractive cars and its engineers were known for their originality and inventiveness.

Next to the relative freedom Toyota enjoyed because its ties with the bureaucracy were looser and it mainly relied on internal funding, Toyota also had more freedom in organizing its production line because of its location; Toyota has a single, large manufacturing plant in a rural area at some distance from the government in Tokyo. Nissan's main facilities on the contrary are dispersed throughout greater Tokyo where costs are higher than in the countryside and traffic is denser. In 2010 however Nissan headquarters are scheduled to be moved to Yokohama where there is a concentration of Nissan manufacturing facilities and which is nearer to Nissan's technological centre.

Toyota's favourable location entails the advantage of being able to keep a close watch on its suppliers; because of its physical proximity to suppliers Toyota has for example found it easier to ensure that its suppliers comply with its 'just in time' production process. Nevertheless, proximity to suppliers is not the main factor of Toyota's successful organization of its parts supplying network. As is the case between manufacturers in an alliance like that of Nissan and Renault, the most important aspect of successful ties between manufacturers and their suppliers is mutually beneficial cooperation; something that Toyota has proven to be especially skilful in realizing. As Dyer & Nobeoka for example argue, 'Toyota ... [has] developed bilateral and multilateral knowledge-sharing routines with suppliers that result in superior inter-organizational or network-level learning' (2000: 346). By exerting pressure while at the same time assisting suppliers, Toyota seems to have been able to correct negative sides of having long-term and close relationships with suppliers at an earlier stage and more incrementally than Nissan. Through a combination of these factors – early technological and financial independence, effective organization of suppliers – and general organizational and manufacturing effectiveness and excellence, Toyota has established itself as a leading company in the global automobile manufacturing industry.

Independence and Success

It could be argued that Nissan's reliance on governmental funds and Toyota's independence hold part of the explanation for their respective downturn and success. Because Nissan could count on financial support from the government, it was able to prioritize technological excellence over cost competitiveness; an orientation that Toyota could not permit. This arguably contributed to the fact that Toyota was more adapted to the rules of the increasingly globalizing market, in which profitability and operating costs take a more critical place then they did in Japan's post-war automotive industry. This is not to say however that Toyota has not consistently devoted its resources to R&D; on the contrary, Toyota is known as a strong R&D player, exemplified by its first-mover advantage in hybrid technology. Nissan on the other hand, while being known for its technological excellence throughout most of the post-war period, after the 1999 Nissan Revival Plan (NRP), was criticized for not investing enough in R&D (Fujimoto, 2004). It might therefore be argued that in the ever-progressing opening up of the Japanese market, Toyota was better prepared for global competition than Nissan. Inevitably, the differences between these two carmakers indicate that a shared domestic setting does not lead to a similar company structure.

Nissan-Renault Alliance

Problems at Nissan

Nissan was in a very bad shape during most of the 1990s. It had been losing global market share since 1991; its production had dropped with more than 600,000 cars; and seven out of the eight years before the alliance Nissan suffered serious financial losses and accumulated a debt of almost US$20 billion. Nissan first negotiated with Ford and DaimlerChrysler before signing a deal with Renault in the spring of 1999. Renault acquired 37 per cent of Nissan stock, which was increased to 44 per cent in 2001 when Nissan also acquired 15 per cent of Renault (see Table 1 for an overview of the main alliance events). The two brands retained their individual identities and brand names, but agreed to share what they did best: for Renault this was design and management, for Nissan manufacturing and engineering.

Table 1. Renault-Nissan Alliance highlights

1999	27 March	Louis Schweitzer and Yoshikazu Hanawa sign the Alliance agreement in Tokyo.
	28 May	Closing date of the agreement: Renault takes a 36.8 per cent equity stake in Nissan Motors, a 15.2 per cent equity stake in Nissan Diesel and acquires Nissan's five financial subsidiaries in Europe.
	9 June	First informal meeting of the Global Alliance Committee (GAC) in Paris, monthly meetings alternately in Paris and Tokyo follow.
	10 June	Yoshikazu Hanawa joins Renault Board of Directors.
	25 June	Carlos Ghosn (Chief Operating Officer), Patrick Pelata (Executive Vice-President, Product Planning and Corporate Strategy) and Thierry Moulonguet (Senior Vice-President, Deputy Chief Financial Officer) join Nissan Board of Directors.
	6 July	Renault and Nissan each take their stake in Nissan Diesel to 22.5 per cent.
2001	16 February	Renault and Nissan's new common commercial organizations in Europe, the first Single Legal Entities (SLEs), are established in Switzerland and the Netherlands. Germany (September 2002), Austria (May 2003), Slovenia (January 2004), Croatia (January 2004) and Portugal (January 2005), follow.
	2 April	Renault-Nissan Purchasing Organisation (RNPO), a joint purchasing company, is established.
	21 June	Carlos Ghosn is named President and Chief Executive Officer of Nissan by the Board of Directors.
	13 September	Renault and Nissan set up a common IS/IT organization.
2002	1 March	Renault increases its stake in Nissan to 44.4 per cent
	28 March	Renault and Nissan set up a common strategic management structure: Renault-Nissan BV.
	29 March	Nissan acquires a 13.5 per cent stake in Renault (increased to 15 percent on 28 May).
	May 29	The Alliance Board, replacing the Global Alliance Committee meets for the first time.
	1 July	Renault-Nissan Information Services (RNIS) is established
2003	27 November	Renault reduces its stake in Nissan Diesel from 22.5 per cent to 17.9 per cent, while Nissan increases its stake from 22.5 per cent to 23.9 per cent.
2004	January	RNPO Phase III, enlarging the scope of its activities and its geographic responsibilities, begins.
2005	21 February	Toshiyuki Shiga appointed as Nissan's Chief Operating Officer.
	8 March	Renault sells its 17.9 per cent stake in Nissan Diesel.
	29 April	Carlos Ghosn is appointed president and CEO of Renault. Louis Schweitzer is appointed chairman of the Board of Renault.
2006	30 January	The Renault-Nissan Alliance global market share comes to 9.8 per cent, ranking among the world's top four global carmakers in terms of unit sales.
2007	21 August	The Renault-Nissan Alliance global market share is announced to be 9 per cent.

Source: Official Press Releases Nissan Motors (2006), pp. 40–47.

Symbolic for the unprecedented changes that were taking place at Nissan, the 1999 NRP was not announced by a Japanese manager, but by Nissan's Renault-sent top manager Carlos Ghosn. This made clear very powerfully to everybody that a different turn had been taken at Nissan. In the history of global alliances it is unusual to have far-going managerial interference of a smaller partner with a minority stake in a bigger partner, as is the case in the Renault-Nissan alliance. Moreover, Nissan had been closely associated with powerful governmental institutions like the Ministry of International Trade and Industry (MITI), which were widely expected to assist Nissan at whatever costs. It has therefore been argued that the Nissan-Renault alliance was a 'humbling take-over by Renault [that] was [a] poignant testimony to how weak Japan had become' (Lincoln & Gerlach, 2004: 338). While this might have been the initial feeling of some in Japan, the success of the alliance between Nissan and Renault later changed this assessment into a much more positive one.

The five main causes for Nissan's state described in the NRP were:

(1) a lack of a clear profit orientation;
(2) an insufficient focus on customers and a misplaced preoccupation with chasing competitors;
(3) a lack of cross-functional, cross-border and intra-hierarchical lines in the company;[3]
(4) a lack of a sense of urgency;
(5) no shared vision or common long term plan.

The NRP proposed far-going restructuring measures to overcome these problems. Product development was placed at the heart of Nissan's revival and the main objective became freeing all capital resources from non-strategic, non-core assets and investing them in Nissan's core business, while at the same time reducing Nissan's debt. The timeframe that was set for achieving these considerable goals was three years.

The catchword of the NRP was 'reduction': it was planned to reduce purchasing costs by 20 per cent, lead time by 50 per cent, the number of vehicle platforms by 50 per cent, the number of manufacturing plants in Japan from seven to four, capacity by 30 per cent, administration and sales costs by 20 per cent, distribution subsidiaries by 20 per cent and total retail outlets by 10 per cent. Fixed overhead costs were reduced, financial operations centralized worldwide, 14,000 jobs cut in Japan, land, securities, and non-core assets were disposed of, and companies in which Nissan held shares were planned to be reduced from 1,394 to only 4.

Organizational Change

Nissan's problems which surfaced during the 1990s were mostly strategic and managerial and therefore the changes that occurred at Nissan as part of the alliance with Renault were mainly organizational; Nissan's productive capabilities as such were not in need of a drastic overhaul. Heller (2003) identified the following areas of change:

Corporate culture. One of the main problems that Ghosn focused on publicly is the above-mentioned lack of cross-functionality in Nissan's former management structure. With the instalment of cross-functional teams (CFTs) it was attempted to improve communication between the different departments of the company. For example, before the NRP the product development and purchasing departments were known for having divergent interests, but now that these departments are united in a cross-functional team, communication and cooperation has improved (Takeishi, 2003). Nissan is also increasingly managed from a global basis, while at the same time more bottom-up decisions are being taken. Speed and commitment are prioritized, and Ghosn himself committed to the NRP by promising he would resign if it failed.

Product development. Nissan and Renault are attempting to ultimately share ten vehicle platforms that will account for 90 per cent of their combined production volume. Nissan designers were requested to design more distinctive vehicles and Shiro Nakamura, known for his remarkable car designs, was recruited from Isuzu Motors.

Purchasing. As became clear from the above, Nissan's *keiretsu* system has arguably undergone the most drastic changes after the NRP. In 2001 the Renault–Nissan Purchasing Organization (RNPO) was founded, which started negotiations with car parts manufacturers on behalf of both carmakers. Starting with the initial aim of 30 per cent of commonly purchased parts, RNPO accounted for 75 per cent of parts purchased for both carmakers in 2006. Parts that Nissan and Renault still purchase individually include steel, exterior parts and some cockpit functions (Stevens, n.d.).

Production facility utilization. Above it was mentioned that in Japan three out of seven manufacturing plants were closed. Currently Renault and Nissan are sharing production facilities in Mexico, Brazil and Spain. Where possible, overlaps in production facilities, and sales and distribution networks are eliminated.

Marketing. Nissan's logo has been restyled and more attention is now given to brand management both domestically as well as globally. It is attempted to give Nissan a more unified and globally coherent image. Nissan's showroom in Tokyo underwent a metamorphosis and attracts more visitors than before the NRP.

Finance. As it was mentioned above, Nissan sold most of its shares in other companies. In addition, large sales of land holdings took place. Nissan's asset utilization greatly improved and Nissan's debt was eliminated by the end of fiscal year 2002.

Domestic market. Nissan's domestic market share had seen a long decline, and was given priority after the NRP. Ghosn himself took charge of domestic sales operations and extensive restructuring was undertaken in the dealer network. This part of the restructuring however is not as successful as hoped for yet (Heller, 2003). Nissan's domestic market share (excluding minicars) was 23.4 per cent in

1990 but steadily declined to an all-time low of 17.8 per cent in 2000. After rising to 19.4 per cent in 2003, domestic market share (excluding minicars) was down again to 16.6 per cent in 2006.

Gaiatsu

Reflecting on Renault-sent manager Carlos Ghosn's role, interviewees often mentioned *gaiatsu*, or foreign pressure, which has a long tradition of being seen by Japanese as an effective way to shake Japan, willingly or unwillingly, out of its fixed patterns. In this light interviewees compared Ghosn to American Commodore Perry who with his black ships forcibly opened up Japan for world trade in 1853, and to the American Occupiers who came to democratize Japan after the Second World War. When Ghosn had announced 'his' plan – as the NRP is mostly seen – he was named the cost-cutter and Nissan-killer, but when Nissan started to revive Ghosn became known as the Nissan-saviour (Ghosn & Riès, 2005). His popularity appeared a very valuable asset for Ghosn because the restructuring the French-Japanese revival team proposed was to affect the core of Nissan's organizational character.

The two NRP measures that according to interviewees could never have been executed by a Japanese manager are the lay-offs that took place in Japan and the cutting of ties with suppliers. According to Ghosn, Nissan needed someone from outside the company because only an outsider could challenge anything within the company without being blamed for having contributed to the problems of the company (Stevens, 2001). Taking this argument one step further, Japanese interviewees often argued that the visible responsibility for the cuts undertaken by Nissan was given to a foreigner because this made accepting them easier for those who were to suffer; a Japanese manager from Nissan might have been held partly responsible for the critical situation Nissan found itself in. Interviewees however also complained that without the interference of Renault, the restructuring of Nissan would never have been undertaken as rigorously as it was, and referred to the changes at Nissan as *Runōka*, or the "Renaultification" of Nissan.

Slimming down the Supply Chain

In a drastic attempt to return economic vitality to its supply chain, Nissan requested rigorous price cuts – often amounting to 30 per cent – of all its suppliers. However, like the evaluation of close supplying ties in the media, Nissan's assessment of supplying relationships was heavily influenced by a *post facto* interpretation of financial performance that overshadowed the evaluation of operational systems.[4] This was eventually recognized by the Nissan management, and the New Group Enforcement process, supported by MC-AFL (Administration for Affiliated Companies) was set up in 2003 to rectify the over-zealous cutting of ties that had been undertaken.

The *keiretsu*-dissolving part of the NRP has suffered from much misunderstanding. While the relational side of *keiretsu* supplying (cross shareholding, dispatching of executives, social ties between Nissan and suppliers' executives) was targeted for drastic restructuring, there were attempts to maintain the functional side (early cooperation in product development, inter-firm cooperation) of close relations with suppliers (Heller, 2003). As in most relationships however, it is not easy to one-sidedly pick certain aspects of the relationship and maintain them, while disbanding others. Nissan learned this the hard way and found that its suppliers had become wary of the seemingly never-ending cost reduction requirements. Purchasing managers at Nissan for example complained that suppliers are unwilling now to cooperate in a similar vein as before the NRP (Stevens, n.d.).

The restructuring of Nissan's vertical supplying *keiretsu* – widely accredited for its contribution to Nissan's excellent manufacturing system and technological strength – was one of the aspects that received most attention in the international press. As was mentioned above, the evaluation in the media of the effectiveness of close supplying ties however often represented a *post facto* interpretation of financial results at Nissan. In general, during the 1980s the 'clustered control' supply chain structure described above was lauded internationally as one of the main contributors to the remarkable success of Japanese automobile producers (for example, Cusumano & Takeishi, 1990; Smitka, 1991; Nishiguchi, 1994; Dyer & Chu, 1997), and several European and American carmakers attempted to replicate Japanese supplying ties. However, the downturn of the 1990s changed this positive outlook and embedded ties were now seen as an impediment to the economic strength of carmakers (for example, Gargiulo & Benassi, 2000; De Bruin & De Bruin, 2001; Itoh, 2001; Sugiyama, 2002).

One answer to the increasingly demanding requests of carmakers has been the surge in international cooperation between large suppliers, as well as between suppliers from different *keiretsu*. This process could be seen as a second phase of clustering; similar to the above-mentioned clustering *within* the supplying structures of Japanese carmakers that happened during the 1960s. Like the developments described by Nishiguchi (1994), the recent surge in cooperation between suppliers across company borders and across international borders leads to increased specialization and the concomitant increased bargaining power of suppliers vis-à-vis carmakers. An example of this is the 1999 alliance between Nissan supplier Unisia Jecs and Renault supplier Valeo, forged in response to the NRP. This tie-up gave birth to a successful and strong supplier with global reach, which is not dependent on one or a few large customers.

Technology Transfer in Strategic Learning Alliances

Mutual Learning

Technology transfer often invokes the image of the transfer of skills and knowledge from an advanced partner to a developing partner. In the East Asian automobile manufacturing industry, the predominant flow of skills is that of productive capabilities from Japan to other East Asian countries where local carmakers mostly do not possess the same level of productive and managerial skills as the Japanese. In the case of the alliance between Nissan-Renault however, technology transfer takes place between *equal partners* with *different* but *complementary skills*. As in the case of technology transfer from Japan to East Asia, the partners in the Nissan-Renault alliance come from different historical, cultural and economic backgrounds, but in the relationship between them there is not a clearly identifiable partner that only teaches or a partner that only learns. Both partners are simultaneously teaching and learning from each other. The driving force of the investments done by both partners is building best practice through mutual learning. Having mutual learning at multiple hierarchical levels at the base ensures that these alliances differ substantially from old-style mergers and they are therefore classified as a new type of capability-enhancing strategic learning alliance (Fujimoto, 2004).

The novelty of the pattern emerging in the Renault-Nissan alliance lies in that

> it features a two-way, long-term orientation to inter-partner learning that is characterized by ongoing close interaction between partners at upper managerial and other hierarchical levels, [a form of alliance identified as] a high-commitment horizontal alliance ... [that] seeks to maximize over the long-term the mutual accumulation of superior organizational capabilities (Heller & Fujimoto, 2004: 36).

Phases of Foreign Influence

While Japan's automobile manufacturers throughout the 1970s and until the early 1990s were known for their unresponsiveness to foreign automotive companies that were looking for a foothold in the Japanese market or a Japanese partner that could introduce them to the much admired Japanese production skills, international alliances are not a new phenomenon in the Japanese automobile industry. In order to recover from the technological standstill the Second World War had created, MITI in 1952 financially supported domestic automobile manufacturers to form alliances with European carmakers in order to learn from them (Johnson, 1998). MITI envisioned arrangements whereby Japanese companies assembled cars from imported knockdown sets for three or four years in order to improve their technology, and gradually become able to manufacture cars in Japan using components made in Japan (Cusumano, 1989). For foreign carmakers, hindered by the restrictions on the import of complete cars and the prohibition of foreign investment, these tie-ups were the best – and arguably only – way to enter the Japanese market. This promotion by the government of tie-ups with foreign carmakers and the assistance with exports enabled Japanese automobile manufacturers to prepare gradually for international competition.

Benefits of International Alliances

As mentioned above, the lower profitability that burdened Nissan during the 1990s does not automatically imply that Nissan's globally lauded manufacturing performance in productivity, manufacturing quality, production lead times, and product development lead times had become inferior to that of its western rivals. On the contrary, Nissan's manufacturing skills are considered to have been consistently world-class (Fujimoto, 2001). While Japanese automobile manufacturers in general exhibited low profitability performance during the 1990s, they retained their advantages in many areas. Nissan's main problem however was turning its manufacturing performance into profit performance.

A potentially successful, but also risky solution for this imbalance in capabilities is allying with a partner that possesses capabilities in areas where you miss them. And because of their strong manufacturing capabilities, Japanese carmakers have been attractive targets for international tie-ups. In the Nissan-Renault alliance, Renault offered Nissan badly needed financial support and management skills, whereas Nissan contributed to Renault's manufacturing capabilities. The alliance between Ford and its Japanese partner Mazda is a similar example of a western partner offering strategic and administrative skills and a Japanese partner contributing productive and operational capabilities to the alliance. In both alliances two-way technology transfer takes place between equal partners of different backgrounds, with different but complementary capabilities. Dussauge *et al.* (2000) argue that inter-firm partnerships in which partners contribute different capabilities lead to greater levels of learning and capability acquisition between partners than do partnerships to which partners contribute similar capabilities, because complementary skills offer more opportunities for learning. In their view, 'for cultural and organizational reasons, international alliances create more potential for capturing valuable knowledge through collaboration than domestic alliances' (Dussauge *et al.*, 2000: 112).

Like in most cases of technology transfer, mutual influences gradually develop into new models of industrial organization; in this case the mutual learning alliance. Technology transfer in these mutual learning alliances could be defined as the *passing and sharing of complementary skills and knowledge between equal partners from different historical, cultural and economic backgrounds.*

The advantage, or arguably necessity, of becoming partners with a firm that has compatible capabilities, rather then trying to acquire the sought-after skills through the market, is that the knowledge companies are looking for is mostly organizationally embedded and therefore not easily diffused across the boundaries of a firm (Kogut, 1988). A learning alliance can solve this transfer problem because both partners benefit from the relationship, and interaction is mostly planned to be frequent and long term.

International alliance patterns have been extensively studied and compared, and many advantages of this organizational form have been documented, while even more numerous were the potential problems that have been identified (Kogut, 1988; Hamel, 1991; Dussauge *et al.*, 2000). Generally, these problems all concerned the dissatisfaction of expectations, varying from learning less than expected or learning less than your partner, to being placed at an outright disadvantage or even being abused by your partner. According to Hamel,

> bargaining power at any point in time within an alliance is, *ceteris paribus*, a function of who needs whom the most [and] this, in turn, is a function of the perceived strategic importance of the alliance to each partner and the attractiveness to each partner of alternatives to collaboration (1991: 100).

Therefore, as long as Nissan and Renault continue to complement each other as they have been doing during the past years, fundamental changes in the status quo of ties between them are not expected.

Implications and Conclusions

While Japanese carmakers share the same domestic setting and certain organizational characteristics – like early governmental protection and efficient vertical supplying structures – it is clear from the diverging paths of Nissan and Toyota that there is not one model for Japanese automobile manufacturers. The evidence in this contribution suggests that the financial support Nissan received from the government throughout most of its history and the early independence of Toyota from this support, as well as Nissan's reliance on technology acquired from outside and Toyota's reliance on internal strengths, both contributed to the relative failure of Nissan and Toyota's success in catching the waves of globalization.

Whereas the literature is dominated by accounts of defensive mergers and acquisitions, the Nissan-Renault alliance has been successful because the two companies worked on harnessing the complementary strengths of each other – technological and manufacturing capabilities of the former and financial and managerial capabilities of the latter – to produce a potent partnership. The question however is whether this successful example can be replicated. Every alliance is unique and predicting outcomes of other alliances is difficult. One unprecedented aspect of the Nissan-Renault alliance for example is that never before did a much smaller company have such far-reaching managerial impact on a large manufacturer in the automobile industry. The Nissan-Renault alliance should therefore be closely followed as an illuminating example of foreign influence on the Japanese economy. The theoretical implications of this case are that the success of the Nissan-Renault merger shows that the motives and relative strengths of potential partners are crucial in strategy building as firms seek partners as an alternative route to achieve their goals.

Notes

1 The alliance is officially known as the Renault-Nissan alliance, but is commonly referred to as the Nissan-Renault alliance in Japan. This paper takes Japan as its vantage point and uses the latter title.

2 Approximately 30 semi-structured interviews were conducted between September 2001 and March 2006 with, amongst others, Nissan employees (including chief executive officer (CEO) Carlos Ghosn), Nissan Union members, Japanese government officials, representatives of local chambers of commerce, and academics in related fields. About 25 site visits were undertaken to Nissan production facilities and Nissan supplier companies. For the case studies a qualitative in-depth approach was chosen (Van Maanen, 1979; Granovetter & Swedberg, 1992).

3 It should be remarked here that while at the Nissan headquarters there may have been a lack of cross-functional and cross-sectional interaction, at Nissan's technical centres this was not the case. Fujimoto for example argues that at Nissan's product development centre in Atsugi, cross-sectional and cross-functional teams existed long before the NRP (Fujimoto, 2004).

4 I am indebted to Takahiro Fujimoto for pointing this out.

References

Cusumano, M. A. (1989) *The Japanese Automobile Manufacturing Industry: Technology and Management at Nissan and Toyota* (Cambridge, MA: Harvard University Press).

Cusumano, M. & Takeishi, A. (1990) Supplier management and performance at Japanese, Japanese-transplant, and U.S. auto plants. MIT Sloan School of Management Working Paper 3159–90.

De Bruin, A. & De Bruin, J. (2001) An interdisciplinary extension to understanding the 1990s Japanese economic slowdown. Auckland Working Paper Series No. 01.08, Department of Commerce, Massey University.

Dussauge, P., Garrette, B. & Mitchell, W. (2000) Learning from competing partners: outcomes and durations of scale and link alliances in Europe, North America and Asia, *Strategic Management Journal*, 21, pp. 99–126.

Dyer, J. H. & Chu, W. (1997) The determinants of inter-firm trust in supplier-automaker relationships in the U.S., Japan, and Korea. Draft MIT International Motor Vehicle Program, mimeo.

Dyer, J. H. & Nobeoka, K. (2000) Creating and managing a high-performance knowledge-sharing network: the Toyota case, *Strategic Management Journal*, 21, pp. 345–367.

Fujimoto, T. (2001) Why Product Architectures Matter, *Look Japan*, 47(542), pp. 12–16.

Fujimoto, T. (2004) *Nihon no Monotsukuri Tetsugaku* (Japan's Manufacturing Philosophy) (Tokyo: Nikkei Business Press).

Gargiulo, M. & Benassi, M. (2000) Trapped in your own net? Network cohesion, structural holes, and the adaptation of social capital, *Organization Science*, 11, pp. 183–196.

Ghosn, C. & Riès, P. (2005) *Shift: Inside Nissan's Historic Revival* (New York: Random House).

Granovetter, M. & Swedberg, R. (Eds) (1992) *The Sociology of Economic Life* (Boulder, CO: Westview Press).

Hamel, G. (1991) Competition for competence and inter-partner learning within international strategic alliances, *Strategic Management Journal*, 12, pp. 83–103.

Heller, D. A. (2003) An inquiry into the role of interfirm relationships in recent organizational change initiatives in Japanese Automobile Firms, *Shinshu University Economic Review*, 49, pp. 45–48.

Heller, D. A. & Fujimoto, T. (2004) Inter-firm learning in high-commitment horizontal alliances: findings from two cases in the world auto industry, *Annals of Business Administrative Science*, 3(3), pp. 35–52.

Itoh, R. (2001) *Goon ga Idomu Nanatsu no Byou: Nissan no kigyou kaikaku* (Seven Illnesses that Ghosn Challenges: Corporate Reform of Nissan) (Tokyo: Nikkei Business Publications).

Johnson, C. (1998) *MITI and the Japanese Miracle: The Growth of Industrial Policy, 1925–1975* (Stanford, CA: Stanford University Press).

Kogut, B. (1988) Joint ventures: theoretical and empirical perspectives, *Strategic Management Journal*, 9, pp. 319–332.

Lincoln, J. R. & Gerlach, M. L. (2004) *Japan's Network Economy: Structure, Persistence, and Change* (New York: Cambridge University Press).

Nishiguchi, T. (1994) *Strategic Industrial Sourcing: The Japanese Advantage* (Oxford: Oxford University Press).

Nissan Motors (2006) Renault-Nissan Alliance 2006 Booklet.

Noguchi, Y. (1996) *1940 Nen-taisei: Saraba 'senji keizai'* [The 1940 Regime: Good bye to the 'War-Time Economy'] (Tokyo: Tōyō Keizai Shimpōsha).

Smitka, M. J. (1991) Competitive ties: subcontracting in the Japanese automotive industry (New York: Columbia University Press).

Stevens, M. (2001) Interview with Carlos Ghosn, 26 November.

Stevens, M. (n.d.) Interview with RNPO manager.

Sugiyama, Y. (2002) Transforming knowledge into strategic action: an explorative study on the process of Nissan's recovery (draft). Paper presented at European Group for Organizational Studies (EGOS) 18th Colloquium, 4–6 July, Barcelona.

Takeishi, A. (2003) *Bungyou to Kyousou: Kyousou Yuui no Autosooshingu Manejimento* (The Division of Labour and Competition) (Tokyo: Yuhikaku).

Van Maanen, J. (1979) Reclaiming qualitative methods for organizational research: a preface, *Administrative Science Quarterly*, 24, pp. 520–526.

Van Wolferen, K. G. (1989) *The Enigma of Japanese Power* (New York: Alfred A. Knopf).

'Detroit of the East'? Industrial Upgrading, Japanese Car Producers and the Development of the Automotive Industry in Thailand

ROGIER BUSSER

Introduction

In early 2001 the then Thai Prime Minister Thaksin Shinawatra came forward with the suggestion to develop Thailand into 'the Detroit of the East' (*Bangkok Post*, 2002). This idea did not occur unexpectedly but can be understood against the background of a long history of governmental involvement in the Thai automobile industry. In the 1960s the automobile industry was one of the first industrial sectors in Thailand to receive a specific industrial policy. In fact it was an industrial sector born out of trade protection. Soon after the speech by Thaksin, 'The Detroit of the East' slogan was adopted by numerous Thai governmental, semi-governmental offices and by many in the industry and the press. Investments in the Thai automobile sector by American and European producers added to the hopes that Thailand could develop into a major car-producing nation.

An important difference between Thailand and Detroit is the fact that American companies dominate the automobile industry in Detroit while Thailand has no car company with its own brand name.[1] Instead Japanese companies dominate the automobile industry in Thailand. Foreign domination has been the case since the start of the industry in the 1960s but over time the Japanese domination has become much stronger. Notwithstanding foreign domination, successive Thai governments have actively been engaged in the development of the industry. An important reason for promoting the automobile industry in Thailand, as is the case in many developing countries, is the fact that the industry harbours a broad range of technologies. It is reasoned that once a country houses these technologies, that country will have a relative strong point of departure for developing its industrial base further.

Until the mid-1990s government policy on the automobile sector in Thailand focused on local content, which was based on the assumption that setting high ratios of local content would stimulate domestic economic activities in the processing of raw materials and intermediate inputs, which was considered as critical to support upgrading in the automotive industry in Thailand. It was also viewed as important to forge linkages between foreign direct investors and local firms to help indigenization and assist the development process (Rasiah, 2003).

However, such a rationale of the Thai government disregards the question of nationality of the enterprises producing the final products, parts, components and other inputs. There are no Thai companies making Thai cars under Thai brand names. In Thailand, the production of parts and components is also dominated by Japanese firms. On the other hand it might be noted that an increasing number of technologies in use in the automobile industry can these days also be found in Thailand. This raises the question of whether nationality of producers matters or not. Michael Porter, who was invited to Thailand, to advise the Thaksin government on the issue of how to raise competitiveness, proposed the establishment of a Thai car brand (Porter, 2003). Porter also touched upon the need for industrial upgrading of the automobile industry in Thailand. Industrial upgrading refers to continuous improvement in which the industry level moves from low-tech to high-tech, in both production processes as well as products requiring a movement in innovation from simple activities to more sophisticated design and R&D (Chia, 2006).

The Thai government has long realized the weaknesses of local enterprises and the difficulties of forging links between local suppliers and Japanese carmakers. Policy makers in Thailand have also been unhappy with the Japanese domination of the industry.[2] However, Thai entrepreneurs with vested interests enjoying strong ties with the political elite, have continued to obstruct policy changes. Thai investors could for a long time make easy profits in the joint ventures with Japanese investors. Only because of changes in the political landscape in Thailand since the mid-1990s have policy changes for the automobile industry become possible. The Thai government has recognized the importance of competition in the industry and hence has begun to invite American and European carmakers to compete with the dominant Japanese firms.

While automobile production has expanded and suppliers have upgraded, however, this essay seeks to argue, using both secondary information and primary data,[3] that much of these developments have been confined to foreign firms. In other words the rest of the study attempts to provide evidence of little technology transfer from foreign to local automotive firms in Thailand. The new technologies that are in use in Thailand to assist and sustain the growth in output by carmakers can almost exclusively be found within Japanese enterprises producing in Thailand.

This contribution is divided into five sections. The first section offers a theoretical framework and discusses some methodological considerations. The second section gives an overview of the development of the Thai automobile industry and the role of state policies. The third section addresses some recent changes in the Japanese automobile industry at home while the fourth section analyses the Japanese role in the Thai automobile since 1997. The fifth section gives the results of a survey among three Japanese car producers in Thailand and 15 suppliers. The same 18 companies were visited ten years earlier in 1995. Primary information gathered in 1995–2005 is used to argue that industrial upgrading in the Thai automobile sector has taken place but little of it has occurred in local firms.

Theoretical Framework

The majority of theories on foreign direct investment (FDI) attempt to explain the behaviour of multinational enterprises (MNEs). Few theories on FDI take a host country perspective. The major objective of this study is to analyse how FDI in the Japanese dominated Thai automobile industry affects industrial upgrading. Therefore, this essay applies a theoretical framework that offers tools to assess the influence of Japanese automobile MNEs on Thai industrial development.

Theories on industrial upgrading have so far only had limited success in establishing a clear correlation between levels of FDI and development of a host industry. Theoretical advancements have been made in the field of measuring industrial upgrading by technology or productivity spillovers. Research that deals with technology spillovers from MNEs to local firms and the local economy has shown that spillover effects may positively influence local firms in several ways: intra-industry, inter-industry, vertically and horizontally (see Liu, 2000; Bosco, 2001; Blomstrom & Kokko, 2003; Chia, 2006).

However, most empirical studies on spillovers and productivity increases in host economies use cross-section data on average industry characteristics. This approach has been criticized because a positive simple correlation between industry productivity and the presence of multinationals is in principle just as likely to mean that multinationals are attracted to high-productivity industries as it is to mean that multinationals raise host-country productivity (Hanson, 2001).

Moreover, much of the empirical research underpinning theories on spillover effects is based on research on FDI by MNEs from one developed country into another developed country. Studies focusing on the correlation between FDI and spillovers in developing countries are less conclusive. Therefore Lall & Narula (2004) ask for a qualitative approach towards spillovers from MNEs rather than just using a quantitative framework. This contribution takes such a qualitative approach.

The methodology applied in this study to measure technology spillovers distinguishes five levels of technological capabilities:

(1) the capability to obtain operational technology;
(2) the capability to maintain new machinery and equipment;
(3) the capability to do repairs and small adjustments;

(4) the capability to design new products;
(5) the capability to produce production technology.

This methodology forms the basis of the questionnaires and interviews of which the results are discussed in section five.

The Thai Automobile Industry

The automobile industry in Thailand was founded in the 1960s and was born out of trade protection just as the automobile sectors in most other Association of South East Asian Nations (ASEAN) countries. Japanese-Thai joint ventures, European-Thai joint ventures and US-Thai joint ventures, assembled Japanese, European and American brands in Thailand. The foreign investors linked up with large Thai conglomerates for marketing, to forge linkages with the Thai political elite and to seek protection. Also in the parts industry, local capital played an important role. Few foreign parts producers were willing to invest in Thailand leaving a rather big role for local enterprises, or in some cases foreign-Thai joint ventures.

The policy for the automobile sector was part of a broader import substitution industrial policy pursued by Thailand and many other developing nations in Asia and Latin America. Tariffs on imported cars were set at high rates so as to stimulate domestic production. Japanese assemblers invested in setting up assembling plants while American and European companies lost interest in the relative small Thai market. Most of the non-Japanese companies withdrew from the market in the late 1960s or did not upgrade their plants and lost market share. The second objective of the Thai government in promoting foreign direct investment in general and FDI in the automobile sector in particular was to stimulate technology transfer. But this goal was not structurally pursued and often made secondary to other goals (Thammavit, 2004).

During the 1970s numerous small policy changes occurred but the effective protection rate for important substitution enterprises remained almost unchanged. Political patronage remained strong and successive military governments made decisions to satisfy those entrepreneurs who supported the military governments (Doner, 1987). Most of the policy changes were made to stimulate local content because Thailand experienced severe balance of trade problems. A positive side effect of stimulating local content was further enhancement of technology transfer. During the late 1970s local content was set at higher levels both for passenger cars, pick-up models, buses and trucks. At the same time the imports of Completely Built Up cars (CBUs) was banned. Import duties on Complete Knock Downs (CKDs) were raised to 80 per cent. The ban on the imports of CBUs implied more protection for local assembly. This stimulated local companies to increase investment in parts production. Other measures taken during the 1970s concerned restricting new entrants thereby protecting the interests of the companies that were already producing behind the tariff walls.

In the 1980s the Thai government presented many different and at times contradictary policies for the automobile sector. This highly inconsistent set of policies harmed the industry. The policies alienated foreign investors, both car manufacturers and parts producers, and by 1987 the Thai automobile industry was in a deplorable state. Only with the improvements in the Thai economy in 1987 and 1988 did the sector recover somewhat. Since then, the automobile sector has also started to liberalize but with the increase in Japanese investment, Japanese influence in policy making has also started to grow. At times this influence has hampered liberalization and obstructed further opening up of the market (Kamaruding, 2003).

Generally speaking, Thailand has been an obedient follower of shifts in thinking among economists in the World Bank and other American dominated international organizations advising on economic development (Paitoon & Ukrist, 2005). However, since the late 1980s it has been Japanese industrial organization, Japanese labour relations and Japanese style public-private cooperation that have become well known in Thailand. Also because of the strenuous efforts of Japanese agents Japanese industrial organization has more than before been adopted in Thailand (JETRO, 2004).

During the early 1990s Thailand's automobile policy was liberalized further. In 1991 a new tariff structure for both passenger cars and commercial cars set lower tariffs and market prices started to drop, thus stimulating domestic demand and boosting production. Meanwhile, the Thai Board of Investment, attempting to upgrade the activities of local suppliers, embarked upon an ambitious programme BUILD (BOI Unit for Industrial Linkage Development). This programme was successful in terms of the growth in the number of transactions between suppliers and assembling companies (JETRO, 2003).

The outbreak of the financial crisis in 1997 triggered an overall economic crisis in Thailand and the domestic demand for both passenger cars and commercial vehicles plunged. Production and sales declined to about one-third of pre-crisis levels. In part the crisis within the automobile industry was solved by exporting more then before. This in itself was only possible because the assembling companies in Thailand were almost all Japanse at the time of the crisis. These companies were willing or forced and at the same time also able to increase exports from their Thai factories and divide the pain over a larger number of their domestic and foreign plants. The same happened with Japanese parts suppliers in Thailand (JETRO, 2004). These enterprises could also export more through either their Japanese customers in Thailand or through the *keiretsu* or industrial group that they belonged to.

After the announcement of the Detroit of the East plan in 2001, the Thai government attempted to stimulate private-public cooperation for the automobile sector further. In fact, the establishment of the Thai Automobile Institute very much resembles the cooperative way in which the Japanese automobile industry is organized (Thai Automotive Institute, 2002). We may also explain the Thai policy shift from leaving it to the market during the immediate post-Asian crisis period (1998–99) to a cooperative policy between government and private sector, as a choice to follow a Japanese developmental model.[4]

Changes in the Japanese Automobile Sector

Japan, being the major investor and producer in the Thai automobile sector is changing rapidly. Both the economy as a whole, but also the automobile sector in

Japan is changing swiftly. These changes within Japan and the internationalization of the Japanese automobile industry affect the development of the Thai automobile industry in many respects. Therefore this section outlines a number of important recent changes within the Japanese automobile industry.

Since the early 1990s the Japanese economy has not been doing well. Low growth rates are succeeded by years with negative growth rates only to recover to low growth rates again. The Japanese economy has shown this pattern of going from one recession to another. Only very recently there seem to be some indications that Japan is on the right track again. Exports of the transportation sector do play an important role in this process. Over the last ten years Japan has gone through a process of adjustment. Well-known institutions of the Japanese economy like cross shareholding, *keiretsu* and bank centred corporate governance have lost, at least some, ground. It goes without saying that also the automobile industry in Japan was affected by the many years of low or negative growth: domestic demand was sluggish for a long period and foreign markets became of ever more importance to realize growth for car producing companies.

The Japanese automobile sector has also gone through a series of organizational changes, partly triggered by external changes. All Japanese automobile assemblers have since the early 1990s gone through large scale restructuring operations, often resulting in more concentration within the industry. Also at the level of suppliers many important changes have taken place. Probably the most important change being that suppliers sharply increased their levels of value added. Another important catalyst for change within the Japanese automobile industry has come from the internationalization of the sector. Foreign companies have come to Japan and Japanese producers have increased overseas production sharply. Both developments have led to an increase in global procurement by Japanese carmakers. Data from the Japan Automobile Manufacturers Association (JAMA) clearly indicates that the average number of customers for suppliers (being assembling companies) is on the increase. At the same time, the number of suppliers used by assembling firms is also on the increase (JAMA, 2005). This illustrates the fact that fixed, long-term relations within the industry are declining.

But internationalization has also reinforced the cooperation between Japanese carmakers and a group of strong Japanese supporting companies that supply these car manufacturers at overseas locations. First tier suppliers are more then before engaged in decisions about future foreign operations of their major customers because Japanese car manufacturers need Japanese suppliers of parts and components more then before at overseas locations. This argument goes in particular for production in Asian countries where operations of Japanese car manufacturers are no longer limited to serving local markets. Instead, export has become more important for certain types of vehicles. At the same time Japanese car manufacturers at overseas locations do not exclusively make use of the suppliers that they work with in Japan but they make increasingly use of other Japanese suppliers as well. In general Japanese car manufacturers abroad prefer Japanese suppliers to local suppliers or suppliers of a third nationality.[5]

It is impossible to make generalizations about the internationalization processes of Japanese car manufacturers. On the one hand, Toyota and Honda are more or less the only remaining fully Japanese owned car manufacturers and the two companies are very successful, both in growth and financially. These two enterprises have clear internationalization strategies – both global strategies and regional strategies. For Nissan and Mitsubishi the situation is rather different. Nissan is now fully engaged in executing the worldwide coordination of activities that will further shape the Renault-Nissan alliance. This concerns both cooperation at the manufacturers' level but also affects the integration of purchasing operations. To this end a joint company Renault Nissan Purchasing Organisation was established in 2001. The aim is to have 70 per cent common procurement by 2008. Mitsubishi Motors was until recently part of the Daimler-Chrysler-Mitsubishi group and was integrating its operations with Daimler-Chrysler. The overall restructuring of Mitsubishi's supply network was one of the consequences of the cooperation with the German-American company. Recently, the Daimler-Chrysler-Mitsubishi group has disintegrated and this will definitely have implications for the global strategy of Mitsubishi Motors Cooperation.

Japanese Domination

Automobile Assembling Companies in Thailand

Thailand counted 21 automotive assembling companies in 2006, 16 producing cars and five producing motorcycles (Thai Automotive Industry Association, 2007). Of these 21 companies four are located in Bangkok while 10 are located in Samutprakarn, a province next to Bangkok. The more recently established factories are located in Rayong (4), Chachoengsao (1), Chonburi (1), Aydhaya (1) and Pathumthani (1). These are all located somewhat further from Bangkok but closer to the industrial port of Laem Chabang. In this port almost all imported inputs for the production processes arrive and most exports of parts, components and Completely Built Up cars (CBUs) leave Thailand from this place. Toyota and Honda both have two assembling plants in Thailand, Suzuki, Hino, while Mitsubishi, Isuzu, Nissan, Yamaha, and Kawasaki each have one. Figure 1 shows the market share of Japanese car producers in Thailand. Together Japanese brands have 91 per cent of the market, leaving just 9 per cent to non-Japanese brands. The domestic car sales in 2003 were

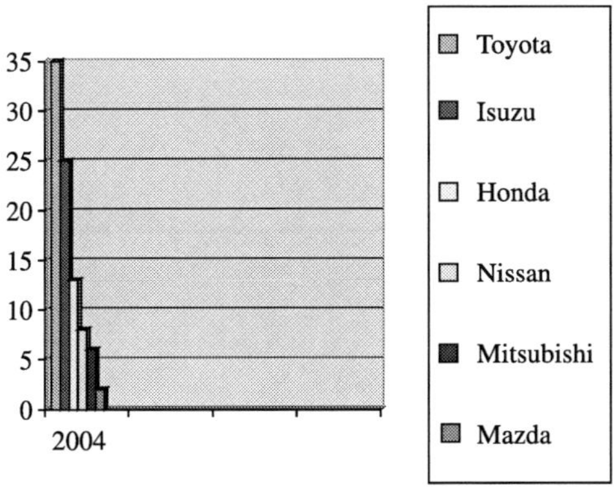

Figure 1. Market share of Japanese brands in Thailand, 2004. *Source:* Toyota Motors Thailand (2005).

533,176 cars (Toyota Motors Thailand, 2005). Due to both the taxation structure and the market demand, one-ton pick models constitute a very important part of the Thai automobile market. Toyota, Isuzu, Mazda and Mitsubishi are major players in this market while Honda concentrates on the production and sales of passenger cars.

The domestic automobile market is expected to grow further in the next five years. The growing demand will both be for one-ton pick-up trucks and for passenger cars. All Japanese producers have invested or have announced investment plans to meet the growing domestic demand, while Toyota, Isuzu and Mitsubishi already have made Thailand into their primary production base for one ton pick-up models. Toyota was the first company that relocated its production base of pick-up trucks from Japan to Thailand making an investment of over one billion US dollars. With this investment Toyota will produce almost 200,000 pick-up cars per year by 2006. The financially troubled Mitsubishi Motors Company is expanding production of pick-up trucks in Thailand rapidly from the current 90,000 to 180,000 in 2007. This schedule is based on an investment plan of almost 250 million US dollars. Isuzu Motors has just like Toyota relocated its production of pick-up models to Thailand. For this reason Isuzu closed down factories in the USA and in Japan. Honda is not producing pick-up models but is in Thailand focusing on the production of small-sized and fuel efficient models. Honda is exporting some of its models and is since early 2003 the first company exporting CBUs from Thailand to Japan (*Bangkok Post*, 2005a). Mazda and Ford have fully integrated their production in Thailand into an enterprise named Auto Alliance. Also this company aims at a larger share of the domestic market for one ton pick-up cars and produces Sports Utility Vehicles (SUVs). Auto Alliance is investing approximately 500 million US dollars to upgrade its production facilities.

Japanese companies do not only dominate production but are also the dominant exporters of CBUs. Figure 2 shows that almost 90 per cent of total exports are produced by Japanese companies.

It is low labour cost in particular that allows Japanese manufacturers in Thailand to maintain cost competitive assembly plants. Automation in most plants is at low levels and this is reflected in the fact that assembly plants in Thailand produce fewer cars per employee then the international benchmark (11 versus 45 per year).

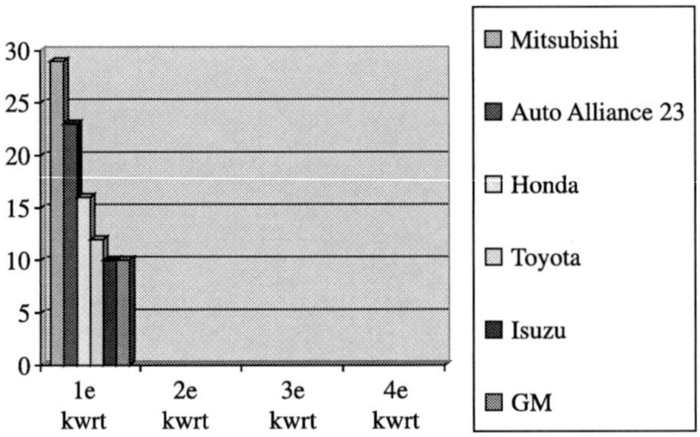

Figure 2. Number of cars exported from Thailand in 2003. *Source:* Mitsubishi Motors Corporation (Thailand) 2004.

Suppliers

There are over 2,000 automotive suppliers in Thailand, the majority being Thai companies (Thailand Automotive Institute, 2005). Among these 2,000 suppliers 709 are registered by the Thailand Automotive Institute as principal producers. 525 of these producers are located in Bangkok (232) and in four provinces close to Bangkok. In the neighbouring provinces (Samut Prakarn 158 producers, Pathumthani 39) in Chonburi 55 producers and Rayong 41. Among these 709 principal suppliers, 287 firms have a majority of foreign ownership. The list of 709 principal suppliers made by the Thai Automotive Institute does not provide information on the capitalization and nationality of the companies. However a comparison of this list with data from the Japanese Chamber of Commerce in Bangkok learned that about 90 per cent of these 287 companies are Japanese enterprises. Another 68 firms have a Thai majority but foreign investors hold an important minority of shares. Here again a comparison with data from the Japanse Chamber of Commerce in Bangkok states that the minority stake is often made by Japanese companies (80 per cent). The other 354 firms are fully Thai owned companies. Many of these Thai companies work with technical licenses from Japanese companies. Most of the 709 principal suppliers are located close to the factories of their main customers. This goes in particular for the suppliers to Toyota in Thailand. For Honda, a company with a less exclusive supplying network, the suppliers are often further away from the assembly lines (JETRO, 2005a).

The much debated negotiations about a Japanese-Thai Free Trade Agreement clearly illustrates both the weakness of the Thai supplying and supporting industries in the automobile industry and the high tariff rates (10 to 40 per cent) that are still imposed by the Thai government to protect certain Thai industrial groups. Apart from the problem about rules of origin, the hottest debated issue in the trade negotiations was the lowering of tariffs for automobile parts and components. The Japanese negotiators, strongly representing the interests of the Japanese automobile sector, pushed very hard for phasing out tariffs on automotive parts. In the tentatively agreed Free Trade Agreement, tariffs on automobile parts will be phased out by 2011 and this was felt as a victory for the Japanese negotiators who in return proposed to extend some more access to Thai agricultural products on the Japanese market. Non–Japanese car manufacturers criticized the preliminary trade agreement for discriminating against non-Japanese automotive producers (*Bangkok Post*, 2005b).

Empirical Analysis

In January, June and July 2005 three major Japanese car manufacturers (Toyota, Isuzu and Mitsubishi) and 15 supplying companies in Thailand were visited. All three of the car manufacturers produce both pick-up models and passenger cars. Next, interviews were held with 15 suppliers of these three assemblers. Ten of these suppliers were Japanese enterprises (some with a minority holding by Thais) and five were Thai suppliers. The same 18 companies were visited in 1995 and in Table 1 certain aspects of the operations of these companies at two points of time were measured (1995 and 2005).

Table 1. Breakdown of automotive suppliers interviewed, Thailand, 2005

	Japanese		Thai	
15 suppliers	10	(10)	5	(5)
First tier supplier	9	(8)	4	(5)
Technical agreements	10	(8)	5	(5)
Average number of customers	5	(3)	4	(3)
Production of body parts	1	(1)	4	(4)
Production of engine parts	9	(9)	1	(1)
Maintenance machinery	10	(8)	5	(2)
Repairs	10	(6)	5	(1)
Designing of new products	2*	(2)	0	(1)
Production of new technology	1**	(1)	0	(1)

Note: Figures between parentheses refer to 1995 figures;
* Eight Japanese suppliers answered that designing of new products took place in Japan;
** Nine Japanese suppliers answered that production of technology was conducted in Japan.
Source: Author's interviews.

The interviews were conducted with the aim of measuring industrial upgrading. Questions were asked about the following five capabilities:

1. obtaining operational technology;
2. maintenance of new machinery and equipment;
3. repairing and making small adjustments to (foreign) machines and equipment;
4. designing new products and;
5. production of technology (Hayashi, 1990).

These questions were put both to the three car manufacturers and to the 15 supplying firms.

This section is divided into an analysis of a) the final assemblers' companies, b) the suppliers, and c) the implications for the relations between the assemblers and suppliers.

Final Assemblers

It was learned from the interviews with the three assemblers that all three assembling enterprises purchased over 80 per cent of the value of the parts and components used in pick-up models in Thailand. However, all three companies also indicated that most of the locally purchased parts and components were produced by Japanese enterprises in Thailand. Among the three companies Toyota had the highest score with over 90 per cent delivered by Japanese enterprises in Thailand. Even more striking is the fact that these percentages are at higher levels than they were 10 years ago (Busser, 2002). Thus, it can be concluded that the increase in scale economies for the production of one-ton pick-up cars has stimulated more Japanese suppliers to set up production facilities in Thailand and serve Japanese customers from the factories in Thailand. It was discovered from the interviews that this development, together with the financial problems during the Asian crisis, has pushed many Thai suppliers back from first suppliers to second tier suppliers. Other Thai companies were driven out of the market. Although we cannot simply conclude from this development alone that technology transfer from Japanese enterprises to Thai enterprises does not take place, the interviewed Japanese purchasing managers often indicated that the capabilities of Thai parts producing enterprises did not develop fast enough. Therefore when Japanese car manufacturers shifted from producing for the Thai domestic market to export markets, they had to look for parts producers that could deliver stable quality on time. When too few local suppliers could fulfil this role, a new group of Japanese suppliers started production in Thailand after 1998. However, Japanese purchasing managers indicated that both in Japanese enterprises in Thailand and in Thai companies, the capabilities of local (production) engineers and technicians graduating from local educational institutions was still insufficient.

Suppliers

Table 1 shows the 15 supplying enterprises visited and interviewed for this study. Of the 15 suppliers, 10 were owned by Japanese investors and five were Thai owned enterprises. Both the Japanese suppliers and the Thai suppliers held technical agreements with Japanese companies. For the Japanese suppliers this often serves as a way to transfer profits back to Japan or in some cases the Japanese suppliers in Thailand pay fees to Japanese providers of technology that do not have investments in Thailand. All five Thai suppliers who had technical agreements with Japanese enterprises explained that their major Japanese customers expected them to draw such agreements. Without buying the Japanese technology, the Thai companies could not have been suppliers to Japanese customers. Thus for obtaining production technologies all five Thai suppliers relied on Japanese enterprises.

As for maintenance of machinery there proved to be substantial differences as compared to the situation in 1995. In 1995 only two of the Thai enterprises were able to maintain the machinery by themselves but in 2005 all companies were able to do so. The ability to repair machinery and make small adjustments to (foreign) machines and equipment shows a similar tendency. In 1995 only one of the five Thai enterprises was able to make repairs; in 2005 all companies had acquired this ability.

The designing of new products is rarely done by Japanese suppliers in Thailand. For Thai suppliers this is even more rare. The only Thai company that was designing new products in 1995 had ceased doing this because its major Japanese customer had pressured the company to produce only according to the drawings and specifications set by the Japanese customer.

Production of new technology did not take place in any of the Thai suppliers. In one of the Japanese suppliers the production of new technology was already long established. It concerns a Japanese maker of engine parts. The next subsection looks into the changes in supply relations among the interviewed enterprises.

Changes in Supply Relations and the Role of Keiretsu

Japanese car manufacturers became well known for the organization of their supply networks. Economists using transaction cost models indicated the advantages of 'Japanese-style' supplying relations (Dyer, 1996). However, since the reorganization of the Japanese automobile industry in the 1990s many car manufacturers were forced to rationalize their supply networks. In some cases this was because of pressure of new foreign partners or foreign partners were used as an excuse to rationalize supplying networks. For example, Nissan undertook a major reorganization of their supplier's organization in Japan after Renault had invested considerably in Nissan. Toyota was in much better shape and needed much less reorganization of its supplier's organization. Mitsubishi on the other hand had to give up its supplier's organization after the cooperation with Daimler-Chrysler was established. Mitsubishi is now – just like Isuzu – a car manufacturer without its own supplier's organization.

Japanese car manufacturers in Thailand prefer to work with Japanese suppliers that are located in Thailand or in other ASEAN countries. Toyota holds a very strong and extensive network of Japanese enterprises that also supply to Toyota in Japan. But differently from the situation in Japan, these Toyota suppliers in Thailand supply to almost all Japanese makers, including Mitsubishi and Isuzu.

Production *keiretsu* (in Japanese, *sangyo keiretsu*) are different from suppliers' organizations in the sense that in most production *keiretsu* the customer holds a financial stake in the supplying enterprise. This pattern can be observed at the top level, in which a car manufacturer holds a financial share in a primary supplier but can also be found at the level at which a primary supplier holds a capital share in a secondary supplier. It goes without saying that most enterprises that belong to the production *keiretsu* of, for example, Toyota also belong to the suppliers' organization of Toyota. However, not all companies belonging to the suppliers' organization do necessarily belong to the production *keiretsu*.

In the cases of Toyota, Isuzu and Mitsubishi production *Keiretsu* still play some role in Thailand. In all three cases the Japanese companies have Thai suppliers for certain components that work with technology licences supplied by Japanese enterprises that do not have production facilities in Thailand but that do belong to the *keiretsu* organization in Japan. In these cases Toyota and Mitsubishi indicated in the interviews that the Thai supplier in these cases is often indirectly subsidized because the Japanese enterprise that extends the technology agreement does this on very friendly terms. The companies set payments for royalties at lower levels then market prices.

European suppliers in Thailand are not competitive with Japanese or Thai suppliers. Almost all European suppliers stick, for different reasons, to European standards and this makes their products relatively expensive. Many Japanese suppliers both produce at Japanese standards and at local standards, making their products more varied both in terms of quality and price.

All three Japanese car manufacturers ranked their Japanese suppliers above their Thai suppliers. According to the purchasing managers at Toyota, Isuzu and Mitsubishi, Thai suppliers have difficulties in delivering on time and more importantly have difficulties in delivering at stable quality. All three Japanese car manufacturers had projects running to improve the quality of their Thai suppliers. These projects were often time-consuming and expensive but were deemed as necessary because there is no possibility to switch to other suppliers in Thailand due to the fact that there are no other suppliers. This explains the stance of the Japanese negotiators in the bilateral Free Trade Talks between Japan and Thailand for lowering tariffs on automotive parts and components.

When the Japanese car manufacturers were asked about the technological development of their suppliers they were rather negative. Toyota, Isuzu and Mitsubishi had all helped their Thai suppliers in obtaining operational technology. Maintenance of new machinery and equipment was not perceived as a problem by the major Japanese customers of the Thai suppliers. Also the ability to do small repairs and make small adjustments of (foreign) machines and equipment was seen as developing in a positive way. Designing of new products and production of technology did not take place in the Thai companies under consideration in this research, according to the purchasing managers of the three car manufacturers. The results of these interviews are similar to the answers given by the representatives from the supplying companies.

Japanese manufacturers were much more positive about their Japanese suppliers in Thailand. These were on average delivering according to specifications and on time. In the case of Japanese suppliers in Thailand, designing of new products and production of technology did not take place in Thailand but was done in Japan,.

Conclusions and Implications

The output of the automotive sector in Thailand has grown fast over the last five years. Production of cars has increased from 411,721 in 2000 to 928,081 in 2004 and to 1.1 million cars in 2005. This ranks Thailand as number 13 on the list of car producing countries. Exports of CBUs have tripled from 50,000 in 1999 to almost 250,000 in 2004, to 440,000 in 2005 (JETRO, 2005b). Also production and export of parts and components has grown quickly over the last five years. In value the export of CBUs reached US$5 billion in 2005 while the value of the export of parts and components was almost half this amount, US$2.3 billion (see Tables 2 and 3).

Japanese companies in Thailand make up a very large percentage of both total production and of exports. Toyota, Honda and Isuzu are the major exporters of CBUs. Also the strong growth of exports of parts reflects the investments made by Japanese suppliers since the crisis of 1997. Of all parts and components bought by Toyota in Thailand, Japanese affiliated companies supply 90 per cent. Figures for Mitsubishi and Isuzu are in the range of 70 per cent to 80 per cent. Moreover, Toyota, Mitsubishi and Isuzu have decided to make Thailand into their major production base for pick-up models. All three have made considerable investments and have invested in the development of supply networks of both Japanese and local suppliers in Thailand.

Technology transfer from Japanese companies to Thai companies is limited. The interviews with Japanese company representatives show that Japanese car assemblers are not satisfied with the technological capabilities of the Thai suppliers, and hence have attracted large numbers of Japanese suppliers to Thailand. However, the influx of Japanese suppliers has weakened the position of Thai enterprises in the supplying networks. The lack of upgrading has resulted in

Table 2. Automobile production, Thailand, 1990–2006 (unit/vehicle)

Year	Total production	Passenger car	Pick-up & double cap	Other
1993	419,861	144,449	245,903	29,509
1994	434,001	109,830	287,284	36,887
1995	525,680	127,658	346,992	51,630
1996	559,428	138,632	369,913	50,883
1997	360,303	112,041	223,243	25,046
1998	158,130	32,008	121,963	4,159
1999	327,233	72,716	244,223	10,294
2000	411,721	97,129	299,435	15,157
2001	459,418	156,066	281,747	11,605
2002	584,951	169,321	376,782	38,848
2003	750,512	251,684	465,060	33,768
2004	928,081	299,400	589,240	39,841
2005	1,125,316	277,603	762,025	85,688
2006	1,176,840	298,678	804,503	73,659

Source: Compiled by author, based on material from The Thai Automotive Industry Association (2007).

many Thai suppliers being downgraded from first tier supplier to second tier suppliers. The push by Japanese investors for lower tariffs might weaken further the position of Thai primary and secondary suppliers.

Although the primary research reported in this paper showed upgrading activities and indicated that more enterprises are able to maintain machinery and undertake minor repairs, none of them participated in designing of new products over the period 1995–2005. The reliance on Japanese suppliers has reduced the demand for Thai suppliers to upgrade into such innovative activities. This has restricted the capacity of suppliers in Thailand to upgrade into R&D activities because designing of new products is still, in most cases, only, conducted in Japan.

Hence, the conclusion is that it is too early for Thailand to be classified as the 'Detroit of the East'. Japanese firms are dominating the Thai automobile industry in both manufacturing of CBUs and in parts production. An important cause for the low level of technological upgrading within Thai enterprises is the extreme dependency on strategies of individual Japanese companies and also the dependency on Japanese governmental agencies. Both the Thai government and Thai enterprises have little means to influence the strategies and operations of Japanese firms in Thailand, which has been illustrated recently by the negotiations for a Japanese-Thai Free Trade Agreement, in which the influential Japanese automobile lobby was able to persuade the Japanese negotiators to bargain strongly for a lowering of tariffs on parts and components.

To limit the deleterious consequences of overdependence on Japanese firms, Thai suppliers should make technological upgrading their first priority, which – given the lumpy nature of investment in automotives – would inevitably require strong support from the Thai government and their industry association. The experience of automobile production in Thailand also provides broader implications for other developing economies – that strong government support is still critical to stimulate significant levels of upgrading in the industry.

Table 3. Automobile and automotive parts exports, Thailand, 1996–2006 (millions)

Year	Total amount	CBU	CBU	Engine amount	Spare part amount	Jig & Die unit	Jig & Die amount	O. E. M. Body part	O. E. M. components	Others amount
1996	6,295.55	14,020	4,253.36	801.98	215.44		43.66	373.62	602.16	5.33
1997	20,722.84	42,218	16,226.99	2,023.89	505.28	17	56.34	1,037.60	845.16	27.58
1998	34,110.33	67,857	28,125.55	1,536.77	722.79	6,013	63.70	1,347.27	2,288.36	25.89
1999	60,105.53	125,702	50,187.21	3,731.81	883.42	177	141.35	1,424.40	3,678.86	58.48
2000	83,245.46	152,835	63,349.15	7,106.22	1,245.65		119.96	1,556.45	9,531.17	336.86
2001	107,110.16	175,299	83,894.70	7,481.38	1,758.56	5	141.19	1,989.49	11,748.57	96.71
2002	107,729.72	181,471	82,474.66	6,087.28	1,796.41	18	145.26	2,879.77	14,196.28	150.06
2003	123,161.39	235,122	102,208.06	5,290.96	2,182.00	2	171.53	4,220.41	23,499.89	588.54
2004	202,079.90	332,053	149,232.80	4,316.05	2,909.43		797.48	5,384.80	36,488.59	920.21
2005	294,243.90	440,705	203,025.36	7,900.79	4,100.74		683.42	6,462.11	70,328.58	1,742.90
2006	222,653.33	348,645	155,470.74	5,907.08	3,338.86	94	485.91	4,412.75	52,488.95	549.04

Source: Compiled by author, based on material from The Thai Automotive Industry Association (2007).

Notes

[1] Japanese automobile producers have chosen not to locate their production facilities in or near Detroit but have opted for factories in the southern states of the USA. Later, Korean automobile companies followed this successful example.

[2] Personnel communication. Interview with official of the Thai Ministry of Industry, July 2005.

[3] The case study in section five is based on interviews and questionnaire responses from three Japanese car manufacturers and 15 suppliers in Thailand and enlightens further on this point. The car manufacturers are Toyota Motors Thailand, Mitsubishi Motor Thailand, and Isuzu Motors. Among the 15 suppliers are Ampas Industry, Jibuhin, NHK, Nippondenso Thailand, Summit Auto Seats Industry, Thai Koito, Thai Radiator and Thai Stanley. The other enterprises preferred to cooperate anonymously in this research project.

[4] For further explanation of the Japanese developmental model see Johnson (1995); Woo-Cumings (1999); and Wong (2004).

[5] Personnel communication. Interview with engineer at Isuzu, Thailand, June 2005.

References

Bangkok Post (2002) Automobiles, *Bangkok Post Year-End Economic Review*, 15 February.

Bangkok Post (2005a) Increase in automotive exports, 21 July, p. 48.

Bangkok Post (2005b) Germans worry about impact of free-trade deal with Japan, 2 August, p. 42.

Blomstrom, M. & Kokko, A. (2003) Human capital and inward FDI. Centre for Economic Policy Research, London, Working Paper 167.

Bosco, M. G. (2001) Does FDI contribute to technological spillovers and growth? A panel data analysis of Hungarian firms, *Transnational Corporations*, 10(1), pp. 43–68.

Busser, R. (2002) Technology transfer through Japanese investment in the automotive and electronics industry in Thailand, in: J. Th. Lindblad (Ed.) *Asian Growth and Foreign Capital, Case Studies from Eastern Asia* (Amsterdam: Aksant).

Chia, T. P. (2006) *Transplanted or Endogenized? FDI and Industrial Upgrading in Developing Countries: Case Study of Indonesia* (Maastricht: Shaker Publishing).

Doner, R. (1987) Domestic coalitions and Japanese auto firms in Southeast Asia: a comparative bargaining study, Ph.D. thesis, University of California, Berkeley.

Dyer, J. (1996) Does governance matter? Keiretsu alliances and asset specificity as sources of Japanese competitive advantage, *Organizational Science*, 7(6), pp. 649–667.

Hanson, G. (2001) Should countries promote foreign direct investment? G-24 Discussion Paper No. 9, United Nations Conference for Trade and Development, New York and Geneva.

Hayashi, T. (1990) *The Japanese Experience in Technology: From Transfer to Self-Reliance* (Tokyo: United Nations University Press).

JAMA (Japan Automobile Manufacturers Association) (2005) *The Motor Industry of Japan* (Tokyo: JAMA).

JETRO (Japan External Trade Relations Organization) (2003) *ASEAN Kakoku no Hattensenryaku to Bushinesu Kankyo no Henka* (*Development strategies of the ASEAN countries and changes in business environment*), (Tokyo: JETRO Overseas Research Department, in Japanese).

JETRO (2004) *Towards the Strengthening of Economic Ties between Thailand and Japan* (Bangkok: JETRO Office Bangkok).

JETRO (2005a) *2004 Survey of Overseas Research Department, Japanese Affiliated Manufacturers in Asia* (Tokyo: JETRO).

JETRO (2005b) *The Current Japanese Economy and Business Relations between Japan and Thailand* (Bangkok: JETRO).

Johnson, C. (1995) *Japan: Who Governs? The Rise of the Developmental State* (New York & London: W.W. Norton & Company).

Kamaruding, A. (2003) *Building Technological Capabilities of Local Auto Parts Firms under Contrasting industrial Policies: A Comparative Study of Malaysia and Thailand 1960-2000* (Lund: Lund University Press).

Lall, S. & Narula, R. (2004) Foreign direct Investment and its role in economic development: do we need a new agenda?, *European Journal of Development Research*, 16(3), pp. 447–464.

Liu, X. (2000) Productivity Spillovers from Foreign Direct Investment, *Journal of International Business Studies*, 31(3), pp. 407–425.
Mitsubishi Motors Corporation (2004) Year report 2003 (Bangkok: Mitsubishi Motors Corporation (Thailand)).
Paitoon, W. & Ukrist, P. (2005) Role of state towards industrialization in Thailand. Paper presented at the International Symposium on Practices of Economic Growth in China, Indonesia, Malaysia, the Philippines and Thailand, Chulalongkorn University, 27–29 January.
Porter, M. (2003) Thailand competitiveness: creating the foundations for higher productivity. Presentation in Bangkok, May.
Rasiah, R., Ofreneo, R., Wood, E. & Carvalho, R. (Eds) (2003) Transnational corporations, learning and innovation, Trade policy brief, 2(1), pp. 1–12.
Thai Automotive Industry Association (2007) Statistical data (Bangkok: Thai Automotive Industry Association).
Thai Automotive Institute (2002) *Master Plan for Thai Automotive Industry 2002–2006* (Bangkok: Thai Automotive Institute).
Thai Automotive Institute (2005) *Thailand Automotive Industry Directory* (Bangkok: Thai Automotive Institute).
Thammavit, T. (2004) Thai Policies for the Automobile Sector, in: R. Busser & Y. Sadoi (Eds) *Production Networks in Asia and Europe, Skill Formation and Technology transfer in the Automobile Sector* (London and New York: Routledge).
Toyota Motors Thailand (2005) Year Report 2004 (Bangkok: Toyota Thailand).
Wong, J. (2004) The Adaptive Developmental State in East Asia, *Journal of East Asian Studies*, 4, pp. 345–362.
Woo-Cumings, M. (1999) *The Developmental State* (Ithaca, NY: Cornell University Press).

The Development of Automotive Parts Suppliers in Korea and Malaysia: A Global Value Chain Perspective

PETER WAD

Introduction

The objectives of South Korea's (henceforth Korea) and Malaysia's national automobile policies included the establishment of domestic vehicle manufacturers as well as automobile supplier industries emphasizing the importance of localization of parts production in order to create economic growth, investments, jobs and technological development. In this sense, both the Korean and Malaysian automobile (henceforth auto) industries were born global because they were established as peripheral sectors of the international automobile industry conditioned by domestic post-colonial, protectionist, import-substituting industrialization policies on the one hand and by the emerging internationalization of western and Japanese vehicle manufacturers on the other hand.

The reluctance of foreign auto firms and technology providers to increase local production of auto components contributed to the shift of the auto industrial policy of developing countries from an industry relocation perspective to a national ownership perspective, assuming that the vehicle manufacturers determined the growth, development and location of the automakers' original equipment suppliers.

Hence, if the government wanted to expand and upgrade the domestic auto parts supplier industry the vehicle manufacturers had to be nationally owned. In practice, Korea embarked on a national auto industry policy in 1974 and Malaysia in 1983, following the establishment of automobile assembling of foreign makes and models in 1962 and in 1967 respectively.

Although this kind of 'industrial nationalism' was very much in line with the early historical evolution of the automobile industries in the USA, Europe and Japan, it did not necessarily fit into the contemporary historical situation at the time of initiation. Recent research questions whether it is possible or beneficial for society to sustain nationally embedded auto manufacturing industries of manufacturers and suppliers in developing countries in the early twenty-first century (Corswant & Fredriksson, 2002; Humphrey & Memedovic, 2003; Maxton & Wormald, 2004). Among changes impeding the rise of successful national auto manufacturers and suppliers in developing countries (the South) are the following:

- The global auto industry has been consolidating into fewer globally or at least regionally based auto corporations and alliances, centred around General Motors (GM), Toyota, Ford, Volkswagen, Daimler-Chrysler, and Renault-Nissan respectively.
- Economies of scale are even more important in the auto component industry than in the vehicle manufacturing industry.
- Economies of scope and speed demand huge investments in basic technologies together with product and process development.
- Automakers increasingly outsource modules and components production (and even assembling), and auto suppliers are taking over more key and complex functions while increasing their share of value adding relative to vehicle makers.
- Specialization and standardization in accordance with product focus and key competences unfold on a regional and global basis among vehicle manufacturers and their core component suppliers based on the principles of follow design and follow sourcing, that is 'using the same design as far as possible across different markets' and 'using one supplier for a particular part or system across all the markets where it is required' respectively (Humphrey & Salerno, 2000: 149–150).

The crisis or collapse and foreign acquisitions of national auto manufacturers in Korea and Malaysia in the wake of the East Asian financial crisis 1997–98 may be taken as an indicator of the dominance of the global value chain and the rule of the leading multinational automakers. However, the dire straits of the US giants, GM and Ford, and the insolvency and reorganization of Delphi, the leading auto supplier of GM, underline that financial problems are not reserved for indigenous automakers in developing countries. In fact, one important change counts in favour of the emergence of sustainable auto manufacturing in at least some Asian areas, and this is the growth of auto demand and auto manufacturing capacity in the fast industrializing countries (China, India) and regions (Association of South East Asian Nations or ASEAN) in Asia while overall demand is stagnating and production capacity is decreasing in mature markets of the North (USA, Western Europe, Japan).

The core assumption is, then, that the rise of global auto suppliers in close collaboration with the global automakers makes it of strategic importance for the survival of domestic auto industries in developing countries that global auto suppliers are part of these industries. Choosing Korean and Malaysian auto industries as the focal industries due to their 'auto industry nationalism' the contribution aims to address two interlocking problem areas pinpointed in two questions:

(1) Whether, how and why world class auto suppliers are operating in Korea and Malaysia?
(2) Whether, how and why the national automobile policies in Korea and Malaysia have furthered the evolution of world class auto suppliers among indigenous auto firms?

The first question regards the influence exerted by the leading firms of the global auto industry on the existence of globally competitive auto suppliers in the Korean and Malaysian industries, while the second question concerns the impact of national auto policies and institutions on the emergence of an international competitive domestic and indigenous auto supplier industry and firms.

The contribution falls into five parts including the Introduction. The second section critically examines and revises the theory of Global Value Chains in order to adapt it for the present purpose and questions posed. The third section describes the top layer of the global auto supplier industry and discloses whether Korean and Malaysian auto suppliers are among the global top 50 firms. The fourth section investigates the activities undertaken by the global top suppliers in Korea and Malaysia and whether, how and why Korean and Malaysian auto suppliers are being integrated and upgraded within the global value chain or not. The fifth section concludes the contribution.

Theory and Methodology

A global value chain (GVC) perspective is applied for the analysis of the local and global automobile industries. Few comprehensive and systematic empirical studies have been undertaken of the global auto component industry and its leading multinational companies (MNCs) until now (see Veloso, 2000; Veloso & Kumar, 2002). These firms represent some kind of a 'black box' of the otherwise extensively researched global auto industry undertaken for example by the International Motor Vehicle Program (IMVP) of the Massachusetts Institute of Technology and the French based GERPISA programme (Permanent Group for the Study of the Automobile Industry and its Employees) or the studies of auto industries in developing countries (Humphrey & Memedovic 2003), or we could say at least a 'grey' box if we include the rather expensive and unfortunately often publicly inaccessible consultancy reports on leading auto suppliers in the global market (for example, those by Just-auto).

This knowledge gap may be a consequence of the conception of the auto industry as a rather vertically integrated industry at the corporate level where the vehicle makers pulled the strings, but this power structure contrasts with the rising importance of the auto supplier MNCs in the global auto manufacturing system and the local domestic auto industries. Outlining the position of auto supplier MNCs in the regional and domestic value chains of Korean and Malaysian auto industries, hence, provides an X-ray picture of the access and position of domestic auto firms to the world market, advanced technologies and value adding functions of the global auto industry.

The comparative analysis of the Korean and Malaysian auto supplier industries and the MNC component suppliers is based on secondary data, illuminated by the author's own experiences and primary data generated during field studies on vehicle makers and component supplier firms in Korea and Malaysia in 1999 and Malaysia again in 2004. The author undertook field research of industrial relations issues in the auto industries of Korea and Malaysia in 2001–03. Secondary data includes automotive consultancy reports and books, consultancy electronics news, press releases, company websites, research publications and so forth, while primary data includes interviews with company executives and factory visits. Acknowledging the scarcity of research in the field and the lack of comparative material on global and local Korean and Malaysian auto suppliers this investigation is explorative and the conclusions are tentative.

The Global Value Chain of Automotive Manufacturing

Gerry Gereffi formulated the 'global commodity chain' (GCC) framework (Gereffi, 1994, 1995, 1999; Bair, 2005), and the comprehensive GCC approach comprised in fact five elements around the turn of the century:

(1) the value-adding input-output mechanisms of the commodity chain;
(2) the governance structure;
(3) the geographical dispersion of activities;
(4) the upgrading of firms and industries; and
(5) the institutional context of chain activities.

Focusing on governance, Gereffi distinguished between two types of global commodity chains (GCC). The first is the 'buyer-driven' GCC, in which large retailers or product designers and branders govern the supply chain through their market, design and brand control and without taking on manufacturing operations and foreign direct investments because these activities are outsourced to product and parts producers in East and South East Asia especially; the typical industry is in the labour-intensive, low-skilled, low-capital and low-technology sectors, for example, the garments industry. The second is the 'producer-driven' GCC, in which vehicle manufacturers with proprietary ownership of technology, design and brands govern the upstream supply chain and the downstream distribution and sales chain; the typical industry is capital-intensive, high-tech, mixed-skilled, for example, the automotive industry. The difference between the two types of GCCs are pinpointed in the divergent use of the original equipment manufacturing (OEM) concept, which in the producer driven GCC is taken to be the chain leading producers (the OEMs), while the OEMs in buyer-driven GCCs mean firms undertaking full-package manufacturing (also termed the OEM model).

In the view of Gereffi the potential upgrading of developing countries' firms and industries were more prominent in buyer-driven GCCs than in producer-driven GCCs due to the more decentralized production system and the space for organizational learning. In reality, East Asian garment firms and industries went through an upgrading process from original equipment manufacturing (full-package or OEM model) to original brand manufacturing (OBM), or more fully described by original equipment assembling (OEA) to OEM and further on to original design manufacturing (ODM) and finally to OBM. The electronics industry has been considered a producer-driven GCC, but Sturgeon (2002) argued that a new modular production network emerged in the US electronics industry whereby manufacturing was undertaken by huge turnkey suppliers while the former producers switched into product development and marketing and bought the end product from the turnkey (or OEM) manufacturers, hence turning the GCC into a buyer-driven GCC.

At present the argument is that the trend of global value chains are moving from producer-driven to buyer-driven global value chains (Ponte & Gibbon, 2005). However, considering the global auto industry the point is that the auto GCC is changing from a producer-driven GCC toward a component supplier GCC or at least toward a producer-supplier driven GCC. This trend contrasts the evolution in the electronics industry as outlined by Sturgeon (2002) and demonstrates that producer-driven GCCs can evolve in different if not opposite directions of chain governance.

The GCC thinking has been criticized in several ways. First, the term 'commodity' carries notions of raw materials although most studies have focused on manufacturing activities (Bair, 2005), at least until the early 2000s where systematic research on Sub-Saharan Africa in the global economy was undertaken in a GVC perspective (Gibbon & Ponte, 2005). Second, the conceptual simplicity of the GCC governance analysis contrasted empirical evidence which demonstrated a variety of governance patterns, forms of coordination and inter-firm networking (Gibbon, 2001; Fold, 2002; Humphrey & Schmitz, 2004). By implication, researchers decided to switch to the *value chain* perspective, designed for business analysis by Michael Porter and others, and turn it into a *global value chain* (GVC) framework focusing on inter-firm and intra-firm aspects of GVCs (Bair, 2005).

Aiming for a more differentiated and coherent theory of GVC governance Gereffi *et al.* (2005) joined hands and distinguished between five types of governance labelled hierarchical, captive, relational, modular, and market governance, and varying from high power asymmetry (hierarchy) to low power asymmetry (market). This differentiated typology enabled a better analysis of the multiple forms of coordination and networking which took place not least within the global auto industry where the automaker-supplier relationship changed from a vehicle maker having thousands of direct (tier-1) suppliers towards a hierarchy of suppliers (tier-1, tier-2, tier-3 suppliers, and so forth) where the automaker only dealt with their first tier suppliers, which again steered the second tier suppliers, and so on. Such a structure paved the way for closer collaboration between automakers and auto suppliers (relational governance) and/or the emergence of modular production and governance whereby different and fewer first tier suppliers provide composites of components (modules) to the automaker which assembled them into the final product (here, modular manufacturing is not understood as delivering turnkey products). Lower tier suppliers were contracted either on market terms or tightly bound to higher up suppliers (captive governance). By implication, the shift from relatively integrated auto manufacturing (hierarchy) toward different forms of outsourcing and offshoring could be better grasped by the more complex typology of the GVC perspective.

However, did the new governance typology make the old dual typology redundant? Ponte & Gibbon (2005) rejected this conclusion pointing out that the five GVC types of governance described aspects of linkage coordination and not the overall governance of the whole chain. One GVC could and probably would include several forms of governance, epitomized by the stratification of suppliers within the globalizing auto industry. Moreover, Ponte & Gibbon (2005) identified a new mechanism of overall GVC governance: the emergence of quality standards with accompanying certification processes and agencies. This trend is also seen in the global auto industry where the more general standards of ISO 9000 have been surpassed by more sector specific standards (for example, GS 9000) before they were merged into the new TS 16949 standard as the present state of the art (Nadvi & Wältring, 2004; Wad, 2006a). Standard setting as a pre-qualification mechanism of inclusion and exclusion of the auto GVC is the prerogative of the chain leaders.

Even a complex typology does not make a theory, and in order to explain the variety and changing forms of governance, Gereffi *et al.* (2005) suggested that three aspects of the generic business transaction could determine the outcome in terms of specific forms of governance: the complexity of transactions, the codification of the information enabling the transaction, and the capability of the suppliers undertaking the production of the items. Using binary values (high, low) of each factor eight configurations are possible, but Gereffi *et al.* excluded three configurations which were considered to be unrealistic: the two configurations of low complexity and low codification were theoretically impossible because low complexity would enable high codification, and the configuration of low complexity, high codification and low supplier capability would be eliminated in practice due to competition from higher capable suppliers.

Yet, what explains the changing forms of governance over time? Gereffi *et al.* (2005) suggest for example that innovation of new technologies are enduring and customers will increase their demands on suppliers for more complex items, or that customers may codify and standardize transactions and hence increase codification and reduce complexity. In this sense the particular global value chain will be in a dynamic and instable flux between processes of simplification and increasing codification and supplier capability on the one hand, and processes of increasing complexity, decreasing codification and supplier capability on the other hand.

What enables upgrading, which is understood as improvement of the production process and/or products, or the move to higher value adding functions (activities) within a GVC, or transition to GVC at a higher value adding level? Based on a governance typology which excluded modular governance Humphrey & Schmitz (2004) argued that different types of GVC governance framed the opportunities for upgrading in different ways. Captive governance provided for process and product upgrading but impeded functional and chain upgrading, while relational governance opened up for functional upgrading, and market based governance was neutral regarding upgrading opportunities.

In sum, the comprehensive GVC approach can be summarized in the following matrix assuming that causation or influence moves from left to right between the three main columns (see Table 1).

For an analysis of GVCs in the global auto industry with a focus on the emergence of global auto suppliers and their position in domestic auto industries in developing countries, even the expanded GVC approach is a bit deficient. First and foremost, the GVC theory is based on a hidden assumption that automakers are characterized by high capability (relative to suppliers), and this is not necessarily the case in developing countries and probably not the case in countries when the governments become committed to auto industry nationalism and start building up a national auto industry like what happened in Korea and Malaysia. Adding the dimension of automaker capability (with binary values) makes the approach more relevant for the present purpose but also more complex by way of generating another eight configurations. For example, it is a big question as to whether a new national automaker like Malaysian Proton has ever achieved the capability to undertake and codify complex export transactions which are extremely important for the viability of the national auto project. Proton's original technology provider, Mitsubishi Motor, and its affiliates of Japanese auto suppliers were not eager to assist Proton in this endeavour. Moreover, Proton did not have the capability to upgrade their new Malaysian auto suppliers while it was trying to cope with its own problems and initiate a learning process. In line with this argumentation it is suggested that the typology includes governance types in which both the producer and the supplier have low capability ('producer deficient' governance), where the maker has low capability and the supplier possess high capability, for example in collaboration between new auto OEMs and global auto suppliers (for example, Proton and Japanese Denso or German Bosch). Two configurations are included in the matrix, depending on the values of transaction complexity and codification: supplier-efficient governance and supplier-driven governance (see Table 2).

Second, the GVC approach suffers from institutional amnesia or at least a downgrading of institutional explanations. This is natural given the emphasis on

Table 1. Types of governance of global value chains by complexity of transactions

Determinants of governance				
Complexity of transactions	Codification of transactions	Capability of suppliers	Governance type	Upgrading of suppliers
Low	High	High	Market	Independent of chain
High	High	High	Modular	Open ended
High	Low	High	Relational	Open ended
High	High	Low	Captive	Product, process
High	Low	Low	Hierarchy	n/a

Source: Humphrey & Schmitz (2004); Gereffi *et al.* (2005: 87, Table 1), adding upgrading to 2005 table.

Table 2. Types of governance of global value chains by capability of producers

	Determinants of governance				
Capability of producer	Complexity of transactions	Codification of transactions	Capability of suppliers	Governance type	Upgrading of suppliers
High	Low	High	High	Market	Independent of chain
High	High	High	High	Modular	Open ended
High	High	Low	High	Relational	Open ended
High	High	High	Low	Captive	Product, process
High	High	Low	Low	Hierarchy	n/a
High	Low	High	Low	Vendor	Product, process
Low	Low	Low	Low	Producer deficient	Stalled at low level
Low	Low	Low	High	Supplier efficient	Upgrading of producer and sub-suppliers
Low	High	Low	High	Supplier driven	Upgrading of producer and sub-suppliers
Institutional context and conditions					

Source: Inspired by Humphrey & Schmitz (2004); Gereffi *et al.* (2005: 87, Table 1), adding one extra explanatory factor and a conditioning factor composed of social institutions. This allows for logical possibilities considered theoretically impossible according to Gereffi *et al.* Several new configurations are not addressed although they are not excluded as impossible per se.

global commodity flows and value chains, but turning the blind eye to the influence of state agencies and other organizational actors and networks makes explanation an uphill struggle. For example, the exclusion of the configuration of low complexity, high codification and low supplier capability assumption could be said to be falsified by reality, based on the fact that in the early phase of national auto manufacturing domestic suppliers may be newly recruited and possess low capabilities. But as it happened in Malaysia with the National Automobile Project, indigenous vendors were protected and supported by the state as part of its positive affirmative strategy targeting the Malay majority for economic and functional 'upgrading' relative to the on average less poverty-stricken ethnic Chinese and Indian minorities. Hence, this configuration does exist and could be termed 'vendor' governance due to the establishment of vendor support programmes in the auto manufacturing sector (see Table 2).

The revised GVC matrix is not all-inclusive. For example it does only address vertical inter-firm relations and not horizontal relations in terms of competition and collaboration, and this limitation is a drawback for auto GVC analysis in so far as alliances between competitors among automakers and suppliers respectively are widespread and important.

Automotive Suppliers in the Northern TRIAD

The changing landscape of auto manufacturing in the post-Second World War period discloses the existence of three patterns of vehicle maker-supplier relationships although these patterns evolve from a producer-driven and largely vertically integrated structure of auto manufacturing.

The three huge US automakers established *vertically integrated production* systems with hierarchical governance. Henry Ford made the blueprint for an extreme centralization of the national value chain of production, owning businesses for everything from iron mines, steel works and glass production to component manufacturing and assembling of vehicles, while GM developed the divisional corporate structure, including auto component divisions and specialized GM subsidiaries (Maxton & Wormald, 2004: 144). The vertical integration came under fire during the 1980s and 1990s, with Chrysler being the first to emulate the Japanese *keiretsu* supply system of networking firms in the 1980s, and GM and Ford abandoning vertical integration, incorporating and divesting their component divisions in the 1990s (Delphi and Visteon respectively). However, the two auto supplier MNCs ended up in dire straits with huge deficits renegotiating their de-investment contracts with their former parent companies. Estimates on the changes of the North American auto supplier industry say that the group of North American suppliers decreased from 30,000 in 1990 to 10,000 in 2000 and is predicted to fall as low as 4,000 in 2010 (Automotive Team, 2004, note 27). The Automotive Team argues that in principle the new 'Big Three' (with DaimlerChrysler, DC)

> are utilizing the same supply model, which Henry Ford developed in 1913. The thrust of this system is a set of independent suppliers bidding on short-term contracts (market governance). The cost orientation of the assemblers drives down the profit margins of the suppliers (2004: unpaged).

Although independent suppliers were marginal to the model for a long time, the Automotive Team add that this business model is now considered broken by many experts due to its negative impact on the North American supplier industry. GM and Ford are also believed to be trying to change their supplier relationship in a more 'Japanese' direction aiming for more collaborative and long-term relationships, combined with European practices like supplier organized part systems. The present turbulence with the 'Chapter 11' bankruptcy protection of Delphi testifies to the crisis of the US automotive industry and the continued strong linkages between the two global corporations.

The Japanese auto industry was very small after the Second World War and evolved into a *vertical keiretsu pattern of networking*, in which automakers and their key suppliers exchanged technicians and loans within a framework of long-term relationships and asymmetrical cross-shareholding. This was the case for the two biggest corporations, Toyota and Nissan, but not for Honda, which did not comply very much with the keiretsu-pattern. Japanese auto suppliers primarily served the only vehicle maker within the keiretsu business group. Denso evolved as the core supplier of Toyota and later on diversified its customer base. In the GVC governance typology, the Japanese governance pattern seems to be a mix of relational and captured transaction patterns between automakers and suppliers.

Europe's auto industry developed a third position between the US vertical integration and the Japanese network integration. The region's auto industries evolved as national industries with a few auto manufacturers and thousands of independent suppliers, of which some possessed their own technologies or were given design and development responsibilities. Due to the small markets many relative independent suppliers transformed into *international specialist suppliers* with a diversified customer portfolio and their own proprietary technology. In GVC terms, the Europeans had been positioned between the marked and the relational governance pattern, and in the 1990s they were pioneering the *modular* type of vehicle maker-supplier types of coordinated transactions.

Summing up, in each national auto market the auto industry was an oligopoly with a few more or less vertically integrated auto production systems, and only Europe saw the development of rather independent international auto suppliers. Yet, the increasing internationalization triggered tremendous changes, not least among the US vehicle makers and their sourcing system, but also among European automakers and finally backfiring on the Japanese auto supplier industry. The trends toward *lean* auto manufacturing and increased *outsourcing and relocating offshore* were compelling.

The new trends and structures are manifested in a few facts (Maxton & Wormald, 2004: 144–153, if no other sources are mentioned). First, the vehicle assemblers' share of the total vehicle value decreased from 75 per cent in 1955 and 50 per cent in 1975 down to 25 per cent in 1995, with suppliers making 25 per cent, 50 per cent and 75 per cent respectively. Couch (n.d., but probably 2004) estimates that the outsourced content of vehicles is around 80 per cent and the suppliers make 70 per cent of the design, while Corswant & Fredriksson (2002) doubts that vehicle makers will outsource more than 60 per cent.

Second, the auto supplier system is dominated by first tier suppliers generating 38 per cent of value added, second tier suppliers making 26 per cent and third tier suppliers having 11 per cent in 1995.

Third, the stratification of the auto supply chain is changing further with new specialization among first tier suppliers, comprising system integrators (including module suppliers), global standardized-systems manufacturers (for components or systems), component specialists (including subassemblies) and raw material suppliers (Veloso & Kumar, 2002: 13). System integrators and global standardisers are also termed half-tier suppliers, while specialized component suppliers are more like the first tier suppliers of the supplier hierarchy.

Fourth, the internationalization of auto MNC vehicle makers has been accompanied by an internationalization of especially first tier suppliers (for example, through follow design and follow sourcing), but the automakers as well as auto suppliers are still fairly regionalized in their market orientation, with the North American market being dominated by North American component companies and secondly by European suppliers, while in Europe European suppliers are selling most but North American suppliers are strongly present, and the Asian market is controlled more or less by Asian suppliers (based on the top 100 auto suppliers worldwide).

Fifth, company-wise, North American component suppliers sell primarily in North America and far less in Europe and Asia, European firms deliver more parts in Europe than in North America and far more in North America than in Asia, while Asian suppliers primarily supply Asia and deliver more items in North America than in Europe.

Sixth, among European suppliers German firms dominate with more than twice the sales (2002) of French firms, which again sell three times as much as the British suppliers.

A listing of the top 10 global OEM suppliers indicates the gradual decline of US suppliers and the global rise of non-US suppliers in a period where the world top 10 auto suppliers increased their total sales with more than 50 per cent (see Table 3 below; this is in US dollars which have however declined against the euro in these years). In this listing European suppliers (German Bosch, French Faurecia), Japanese Aisin Seiko and Canadian Magna International have climbed the ladder. Denso has stayed high as number four in all three selected years, probably related to the strong and steady performance of Toyota. The global top 10 listing has two Toyota affiliated companies (Denso and Aisin Seiki). Johnson Controls is the only US supplier, which rose during the early 2000s.

The national origin of auto manufacturing in North America, Europe and Asian still affects the landscape of international auto manufacturing, emerging into regional based assembler-supplier structures with their national champions: GM and Delphi and Ford and Visteon in the USA; the Toyota and Denso in Japan; and the more independent structures between DaimlerChrysler/BMW/VW and Bosch/Siemens/ZF in Germany; the PSA Peugeot Citroën/Renault and Valeo/ Faurecia in France; and the defaulted British auto industry with Austin/Morris/ Rover and Lucas/GKN (Lucas has been swallowed by US TRW); Magneti Marelli is part of the FIAT group.

The de-integration process triggered by the competitiveness of Japanese automakers and increasing the pressure on especially the US auto industry paved the way for increased supplier stratification in line with the Japanese inspired tier-structure, most noticeable in the incorporation and disinvestment of Delphi from GM and Visteon from Ford. A very competitive European supplier industry emerged with MNCs like Bosch, Valeo and GKN, and German firms in particular pursued the strategy of modularization pioneered by VW in Brazil. The US and Japanese vehicle makers are slowly following this new sourcing strategy, which aims to further reduce the number of top suppliers of systems and modules (half-tier suppliers), transfer more responsibility (and costs) regarding design, development and supply chain management, and reintegrate very fragmented component supply chains (Shimokawa, 2002: 27).

However, the quest for modularization is questioned among Japanese vehicle and parts firms and also among auto consultants (Mercer *et al.*, 2004: 3; Wad, 2006a) and the profitability of the various supplier positions and strategies are unclear. Veloso & Kumar (2002: 17, Figure 11) estimate for 1993–98 that the worst performers are firms with unclear strategies (Magneti Marelli, Phoenix and Donnelly). No reliable figures can be established for system integrators, but firms

Table 3. The top 10 OEM global suppliers, ranked after global OEM sales 2000–04

Rank (after sales)	2000		2002		2004	
	Company	Sales US$ billion	Company	Sales US$ billion	Company	Sales US$ billion
1	Delphi	26.5	Delphi	25.5	Bosch @)	34.4
2	Visteon	18.6	Bosch	19.1	Delphi	28.7
3	Bosch	17.8	Visteon	16.9	Johnson Controls	26.6
4	Denso	16.4	Denso	15.3	Denso ¤)	26.2
5	Lear	14.1	Lear	14.4	Magna Int'l	20.7
6	Johnson Controls	12.7	Johnson Controls	13.7	Visteon	18.7
7	TRW Automotive	10.2	Magna Int'l	12.2	Aisin Seiki ¤)	17.1
8	Magna Int'l	10.1	Aisin Seiki	10.7	Lear	17.0
9	Dana	9.5	Faurecia	10.0	Faurecia @)	14.6
10	Valeo	7.0	TRW Automotive	9.9	TRW Automotive	12.0
Top 10')		142.8		147.7		216.0
Top 100		350.6		353.385		n.a.

Source: Automotive Team (2004), annex Table 8, 2000–02.
Notes: Top 10 sales in 2000 miscalculated or misstated in source. @) Only Bosch's automotive sales (1 euro = 1.36 to the $ at the end of 2004). ¤) 1$ = 107 yen. Tyre manufacturers are excluded.

moving in that direction (JCI, Lear) under-perform, while Magna International is doing very well, maybe because it is in fact not heading for a system integrator status, but staying as a global standardiser-system supplier. In this category 16 per cent average ROE (Return on Equity) 1993–98 is the average, which includes firms like Denso, Aisin Seiki, Dana, Faurecia, Valeo and Dana. Delphi and Visteon are probably to be classified as standardisers. Component specialists are doing best on average ROE (31 per cent) and counts firms like GKN, Brembo, Gentex and Kiekert. No firms are identified as moving from unclear strategy to component specialist positions, while Swedish Autoliv is earning well (15 per cent) shifting from component specialist to standardiser. Continental moving from unclear strategy to standardiser is increasing earnings 20 per cent per year in 1993–98.

The squeeze by the vehicle makers of their half-tier/first tier suppliers makes its way to the bottom line, and this pressure for cost reduction is passed on to the lower tiers of suppliers. Yet, contrary to GVC theory holding that the governing firms can in- and outsource activities depending on their value adding and profit, component specialization (combined with economies of scale) may not be that bad for short/mid-term profitability. The available information is contradictive and suppliers have to muddle through and learn fast while market conditions and governance structures are changing at national, regional and global levels.

Finally, a comparision of the global top 50 auto suppliers with the 80 major suppliers in East Asia discloses that no Korean and Malaysian suppliers are among the global top 50 (Hiroaki, 2003: 35, 37; Just-auto.com, 2005). Contrary to this bleak picture more than 60 per cent of the top 50 global auto suppliers (32 firms) had manufacturing facilities in East Asia, comprising major Japanese, American and European suppliers in the region. Considering the rapid growth of auto manufacturing in East Asia some Asian auto suppliers may still be in a process of upgrading for world status.

Global Value Chain Locations

The sheer size and consolidation of the Korean automobile market and industry made Korea interesting for global suppliers, while the same could not be said about Malaysia. Both countries followed a policy of progressive de-linking with foreign auto firms aiming for a domestic and later national owned auto industry driving overall industrial and technological catching-up. Although the national projects began as joint ventures and relied on foreign technology transfer special vendor programmes were set up in support of indigenous auto supplier development.

The international perspective changed, anyway. In Korea the auto industry had a huge amount of success in exporting followed by outward foreign direct investment (FDI) during the 1990s, after having tried and failed in North America in the late 1980s. A national policy of economic globalization gained priority during the mid-1990s until the financial crisis in 1997, which again opened up for inward FDI and foreign acquisition of several auto firms, makers as well as suppliers. In Malaysia, the national auto policy did not generate an export success, and national protectionism ruled until the end of the era of Mahathir-led governments (1981–2003), for example, exempting the Malaysian auto assembling industry from ASEAN Free Trade Agreement (AFTA) intra-trade liberalization beyond 2000. New licences were given and new so-called 'National Projects' were initiated even after the crisis by the Mahathir-government concomitant with the denationalization of the second National Project, Perodua, in which Daihatsu/Toyota acquired equity control of the manufacturing part of the company. For the time being Proton is also negotiating with foreign automakers to take a stake in the ailing but nationally owned automaker after MMC left a few years ago. Proton's market share has declined from 51 per cent in 2001 to 33 per cent in 2005 (Kubo 2006, calculated from tables on pp. 2, 5) without rising exports compensating for the loss of domestic market share.

Foreign auto suppliers and in particular Japanese and US suppliers were dragged into Korea from the very start, while European were latecomers. Among the major 40 Japanese auto suppliers with East Asian operations in 2003, 12 Japanese firms were undertaking production in Korea and 13 in Malaysia, but out of these firms three had their own operations in Korea and two in Malaysia (Hiroaki, 2003: 34; see also Table 3 & Table 11 which relate Hiroaki data to data on the top 50 and top 20 global auto suppliers). Denso had joint ventures (JVs) in both countries, but only subsidiaries in Korea, while it had six JVs in China, four JVs and two subsidiaries in India and three subsidiaries and two JVs in Thailand. Aisin Seiki had no operations in Korea, nor in Malaysia, but it was strongly represented in China and had two JV firms in Thailand. The third global Japanese auto supplier, Yazaki, was not present in Korea and Malaysia, too, but it was also very active in China (four subsidiaries and two JVs), Indonesia (five firms of which four were subsidiaries), and the Philippines (four firms, of which three were JVs). Only Denso was present in all East Asian countries with auto industries, including Australia. None of the 40 major western auto suppliers could match Denso in this respect.

North American (mostly US) firms had 40–50 JVs in the mid-1990s, which had been founded in the late 1980s with GM and Ford participating in one out of four JVs. Since then, US auto suppliers have dropped JV FDI in Korea, and only returned after Delphi and Visteon had been de-merged from GM and Ford respectively. Delphi became the largest (foreign) auto supplier in Korea in 1999. Delphi had 22 bases in East Asia in 2003, of which Korea counted seven JVs, only surpassed by China with eight JVs and two subsidiaries. In Malaysia, Delphi had one JV. Johnson Controls (JCI) was only present in Malaysia and not in Korea, but concentrates its investments in China and India. Magna International favoured China with six companies and had two JVs in Korea and one JV in Malaysia, followed by investment (subsidiary) in India. Visteon had 17 operations in the region, with the same focus on China (six JVs) and Korea (five JVs), then also some companies in India and Thailand, but none in Malaysia. Lear was heavily engaged in China (six JVs), had one JV in Korea, and none in Malaysia. TRW is very present in East Asia with 13 companies, of which four are in India, three in China, two in Korea and two in Malaysia, while Thailand counted two TRW companies.

European suppliers were not involved at the very beginning of the Korean auto industry. German equity investments were found in 33 companies of which six took place during and after the crisis, and eight were wholly-owned subsidiaries and six were majority owned by German firms. Bosch was the first German supplier in Korea in 1984 as a joint venture partner in Doo Woo Precision (O'Brien, 1998: 63–64, Table 6.7). Bosch's first majority owned JV came in 1989 with Bosch Korea, and its first fully-owned subsidiary came in December 1998 (after the collapse of the Won) with KBME. In July 1998, Bosch had seven companies in Korea and was the most visible German and European corporation in Korea, and Bosch sustained that position in 2003 with three JVs and four subsidiaries. Bosch had altogether 24 investment locations (subsidiary of joint venture firms) in East Asia this year, with the highest number in Korea, sharply followed by China (with five JVs and one subsidiary), Thailand (four JVs), India (three JVs) and Malaysia (one subsidiary and one JV). Faurecia was present primarily in China (five JVs), with one subsidiary in India and one JV in Korea, but no investment in Malaysia, although the former owner of Proton, DRB-Hicom, collaborated with PSA Citroën in the mid-1990s. Other active European firms in East Asia are Hella (12 operations excluding Australia), including three JVs in Korea; Swedish Autoliv has 15 bases and a presence in Korea and Malaysia; and former Danish Roulunds Fabriker had 9 bases in East Asia in all, of which China had three JVs, Thailand two, India one subsidiary and one JV, and finally Korea and Malaysia had one JV each.

The foreign acquisition of indigenous auto suppliers happened primarily in Korea, where the larger, first tier suppliers were badly hit by the collapse of the Korean auto market and the defaulting of most of the vehicle makers: Kia Motor before the outbreak of the financial crisis, and Samsung Motor and Daewoo Motor Co. after the crisis erupted. The automobile market did not face the same collapse in Malaysia, where the government intervened to protect the national and later on also the non-national auto producers, which again spilled over into the auto suppliers industry. In fact, *Sime Darby's* tyre division was the only larger indigenous auto supplier to be partly acquired by a global auto supplier, the German tyre manufacturer, Continental, establishing the JV Continental Sime Tyre (CST).

Global auto suppliers targeted key Korean auto suppliers in trouble, and several were acquired. In 2000, *Mando Machinery*, the largest indigenous auto supplier, had sold off three out of five plants to foreign firms and was negotiating on the de-investment of the last two; Halla Climate Control Corp. had been acquired (70 per cent) of Visteon, which also achieved majority control of another Korean firm. Delphi bought Korea Door Systems and other firms and achieved management control over Daesung Electronics, before the US firm merged its activities in Korea Delphi in 1999 to become the largest domestic auto supplier that year (KARI, 2000: 119).

By the end of 2001, foreign firms had captured ownership control or management rights in nearly 20 per cent of Korean auto suppliers (204 out of 1,104) (KARI, 2002: viii). The only surviving independent Korean auto assembler, HMC, was forced to adapt to the financial problems and the more open and competitive Korean auto market. HMC has embarked on modularization, and it incorporated its auto component division (Hyundai Mobis) in 2000, and Hyundai Mobis is perceived as an affiliate of the Hyundai Group. Hence, it may be a semi-independent company of HMC/Kia. Hyundai Mobis, originally established as a container manufacturer in 1977 switching to auto part production in the 1990s, employed 3,800 employees at the end of 2002 with capital of 426 billion Won, and had sales in 2004 of 6,436 billion Won (around US$6.4 billion) (see Hyundai Mobis, 2004). These figures make Hyundai Mobis a large player in the Korean auto supplier industry and even an important player at the regional and global level. The management of Hyundai Mobis has it as a goal to be a global top 10 company in 2010, but as of now it has not reached the ranks of the global top 20 or top 50, although the company is expanding and internationalizing through foreign direct investment into China and the USA, and is planning FDI in India and the Slovac Republic.

In East Asia, the ASEAN region has been 'embraced' by Japanese production networks (Hatch & Yamamura, 1996), and the auto industry is no exception at the beginning of the twentieth-first century (Wad, 2006b). However, both US and European companies are also present, and they focus very much on China, Korea and India. While Japanese firms are also scrambling for China and India, they are also keen about business in Thailand and Indonesia. Malaysia has been less integrated into the regional and global value chain of the automotive industry. Yet, out of the 'big four' global suppliers in 2004, Bosch, Delphi and Denso have bases in Korea as well as Malaysia, while Johnson Controls is missing in Korea but present in Malaysia due to its recent inroads there.

While the auto supplier industries of Korea and Malaysia are becoming part of the global top auto suppliers' worldwide sourcing, the indigenous firms are relegated to lower tier positions while aiming for upgrading by way of shifting from vendor and captured governance into modular governance. The main difference between the Korean and Malaysian auto supplier industry seems to be the lack of capability of Malaysia's national auto manufacturers to undertake market upgrading into exporting and upgrading of its national supplier base (Wad, 2006a). The Malaysian government chose to form an alliance with a weak auto MNC, the MMC, instead of collaborating with its own ethnic Chinese auto supplier firms. Hence, in Malaysia a state-owned company was created to catch up with the very same Japanese automakers and suppliers that supplied the technology, while the Korean national automakers were established by private owned *chaebols*, large conglomerates with experienced management and a larger domestic market as a stepping stone for aggressive export promotion. Even large Korean auto companies failed, but the Korean auto industry survived and so did the dominant player, Hyundai Motor with its subsidiary Kia Motors and its affiliated core supplier, Hyundai Mobis. Hyundai Motor responded to the crisis by way of restructuring for modular manufacturing – Hyundai Mobis played a crucial role in this (HMWU, 2004). Hyundai Mobis seems to have the capacity and capability to go for the top layer (the top 10 group) of global auto suppliers to OEMs. Malaysian auto suppliers have also aimed for modular production (Proton has shifted toward modular manufacturing based on collaboration with world class (foreign) auto suppliers), and they may be happy to find niches in the regional aftermarket, until a new alliance with a global automaker and its core global suppliers can revitalize the Malaysian national auto sector. The non-national auto sector is already being expanded by the market share of Toyota/Daihatsu, and this even impacts on the competitiveness of Proton in the home market, resulting in declining market shares.

Conclusions and Implications

In a global value chain perspective, local auto suppliers in both Korea and Malaysia were either integrated into the national auto manufacturing corporations or governed as 'vendor' or 'captured' companies, being wholly dependent on the same national auto assembler and the customer's (and government's) technological and financial support. In the changes driven by the transformation of the global auto industry and the financial crisis 1997–98, local first tier suppliers were integrated into global auto suppliers' hierarchy through acquisition and management control. By implication, the global auto suppliers became localized especially in the Korean auto industry. Indigenous suppliers tried to turn toward modularization in order to stay competitive, and the potential for success seemed better in Korea with its huge vehicle and components production and export than in Malaysia, where suppliers were left alone and marginalized from the global value chain (with one exception). Relying on their key customer 'protected' first tier suppliers were governed by a national automaker with little capability to accomplish its enormous task of vendor upgrading (deficient producer governance) while aiming for modularized production itself. Being relegated to second or third tier position with market or 'captured' governance by upper tier suppliers may be the bleak options for Malaysian suppliers if they do not outright choose 'downgrading' and GVC exit in order to go for the regional aftermarket – an opportunity for survival in the emerging regional auto market of East Asia, that is, a market-governed regional value chain for the replacement market segment. Only Hyundai Mobis, the global auto supplier of HMC, may have a chance to reach the top tier of global auto suppliers, which are now establishing themselves in both countries. At the global auto market half tier or first tier MNC auto suppliers have acquired a key position as co-drivers of the global value chain of auto manufacturing.

References

Automotive Team (2004) U.S. *Automotive Parts Industry Assessment*, U.S. Dept. of Commerce. Available at http://www.ita.doc.gov/td/auto/staffstudies.html (accessed 5 August 2005).

Bair, J. (2005) Global capitalism and commodity chains: looking back, going forward, *Competition & Change*, 9(2), pp. 153–180.

Corswant, F. V. & Fredriksson, P. (2002) Sourcing trends in the car industry: a survey of car manufacturers' and suppliers' strategies and relations, *International Journal of Operations & Production Management*, 22(7), pp. 741–758.

Couch, E. (n.d.) Automotive parts technology developments. Available at http://www.ita.doc.td/auto/staffstudies.html (accessed 5 August 2005).

Fold, N. (2002) Lead firms and competition in 'bi-polar' commodity chains: grinders and branders in the global cocoa-chocolate industry, *Journal of Agrarian Change*, 2(2), pp. 228–247.

Gereffi, G. (1994) The organization of buyer-driven global commodity chains: how US retailers shape overseas production networks, in: G. Gereffi & M. Korzeniewicz (Eds) *Commodity Chains and Global Capitalism*, pp. 95–122 (Westport, CT: Praeger).

Gereffi, G. (1995) Global production systems and third world development, in: B. Stallings (Ed.) *Global Change, Regional Response: The New International Context of Development*, pp. 100–142 (New York: Cambridge University Press).

Gereffi, G. (1999) International trade and industrial upgrading in the apparel commodity chain, *Journal of International Economics*, 48 (1), pp. 37–70.

Gereffi, G., Humphrey, J. & Sturgeon, T. (2005) The governance of global value chains, *Review of International Political Economy*, 12(1), pp. 78–104.

Gibbon, P. (2001) Upgrading primary production: a global commodity chain approach, *World Development*, 29(2), pp. 345–363.

Gibbon, P. & Ponte, S. (2005) *Trading Down – Africa, value chains, and the global economy* (Philadelphia, PA: Temple University Press).

Hatch, W. & Yamamura, K. (1996) *Asia in Japan's Embrace: Building a Regional Production Alliance* (Cambridge: Cambridge University Press).

Hiroaki, N. (2003) Asia: global suppliers' strategies in the Asia Pacific Region, *Asian Automotive Business Review*, 14(4), pp. 34–39.

Humphrey, J. & Memedovic, O. (2003) *The Global Automotive Value Chain: What Prospects for Upgrading by Developing Countries* (Vienna: UNIDO).

Humphrey, J. & Salerno, M. S. (2000) Globalisation and assembler-supplier relations: Brazil and India, in: J. Humphrey *et al.* (Eds) *Global Strategies and Local Realities: The Auto Industry in Emerging Markets*, pp. 149–175 (London: Macmillan & GERPISA).

Humphrey, J. & Schmitz, H. (2004) Chain governance and upgrading: taking stock, in: H. Schmitz (Ed.) *Local Enterprises in the Global Economy. Issues in Governance and Upgrading*, pp. 349–381 (Cheltenham: Edward Elgar).

HMWU (Hyundai Motors Workers union) (2004) Restructuring of Hyundai Motor Company and the union's response, in: D. Chang & E. Shepherd (Eds) *Automobile Workers and Industry in Globalising Asia*, pp. 105–120 (Hong Kong: AMRC & CEC).

Hyundai Mobis (2004) Non-consolidated financial statements, December 31, 2004 and 2003. Available at http://www.mobis.co.kr:1100/eng/datafiles/auditor_report/2004_annual.pdf (accessed 1 August 2005).

Just-auto.com (2005) Available at http://www.just-auto.com (accessed 15 June 2005).

KARI (Korea Automotive Research Institute) (2000) *Korea Automotive Industry Annual Report* (Seoul: KARI).

KARI (2002) *Korea Automotive Industry Annual Report* (Seoul: KARI).

Kubo, T. (2006) Asia: from assembly to production, asia stepping into the stage of mass production, *Asian Automotive Business Review*, 17(4), pp. 2–5.

Maxton, G. P. & Wormald, J. (2004) *Time for a Model Change: Re-engineering the Global Automotive Industry* (Cambridge: Cambridge University Press).

Mercer *et al.* (2004) The right restructuring for the US automotive suppliers, *The McKinsey Quarterly*, available at http://www.mckinseyquarterly.com, October (accessed 11 August 2005).

Nadvi, K. & Wältring, F. (2004) Making sense of global standards, in: H. Schmitz (Ed.) *Local Enterprises in the Global Economy. Issues in Governance and Upgrading*, pp. 53–94 (Cheltenham: Edward Elgar).

O'Brien, P. (1998) *Korea's Automotive Future* (London: *Financial Times*).

Ponte, S. & Gibbon, P. (2005) Quality standards, conventions and the governance of global value chains, *Economy and Society*, 34(1), pp. 1–31.

Shimokawa, K. (2002) Reorganization of the global automotive industry and structural change of the automobile component industry. International Motor Vehicle Program paper, available at http://dspace.mit.edu/handle/1721.1/1417.

Sturgeon, T. (2002) Modular production networks: a new American model of industrial organization, *Industrial and Corporate Change*, 11(3), pp. 451–496.

Veloso, F. (2000) The automotive supply chain organization: global trends and perspectives. Working Paper (Cambridge: MIT).

Veloso, F. & Kumar, R. (2002) The automotive supply chain: global trends and Asian perspectives. *ERD Working Paper Series* No. 3 (Asian Development Bank: Manila).

Wad, P. (2006a) The automotive supplier industry between localizing and globalizing forces in Malaysia, India, and South Africa, in: M-W. Hansen & H. Schaumburg-Müller (Eds) *Transnational Corporations and Local Firms in Developing Countries – Linkages and Upgrading*, pp. 221–249 (Frederiksberg: Copenhagen Business School Press).

Wad, P. (2006b) The ASEAN automobile industry: between the devil and the deep blue sea? Paper for presentation at the International Conference on Learning, Innovation and Competitiveness: Achieving social welfare through sustainable manufacturing in Southeast Asia, Faculty of Economics & Administration, University of Malaya, Malaysia, with support from Friedrich Ebert Stifting, 14–15 June 2006.

Arrested Development: Multinationals, TRIMs and the Philippines' Automotive Industry

RENE E. OFRENEO

Introduction

The Philippine economy is a disaster in Asia. Afflicted by a never-ending cycle of mild recoveries and deep recessions since the 1960s, the economy has failed to expand at a rate sufficient to meet the job and income needs of a rapidly-growing population (85 million as of 2005). As a result, the country has become more and more dependent on the foreign exchange remittances of over 5 million overseas Filipino workers (OFWs) and three million immigrants in various parts of the globe (Ofreneo & Samonte, 2002). Massive poverty, unemployment and backwardness engendered by a poorly-performing economy are at the root of one of Asia's long-running insurgencies, the separatist movement in southern Philippines and the growth of lawless industries – illegal drug, kidnapping, gun-for-hire, prostitution, gambling, organ 'donations' (sales of body parts) and smuggling.

There is a plethora of political and economic explanations for the Philippine economic failure. This contribution focuses on one explanation – the absence of a determined programme of deepening and broadening the industrial structure, such as China and the Asian newly industrialized countries (NICs) have apparently done. The absence of such a programme explains the haphazard and incoherent way by which the Philippines adopted a policy shift in its industrialization drive, from the import-substituting industrial (ISI) strategy of the 1950s-1960s to the promotion of EOI in the 1980s-1990s. The glaring absence of a determined programme of industrial deepening and the haphazardness and incoherence in industrial development are best illustrated in the performance of the Philippine automotive assembly industry and its sister car parts industry under the government's programme promoting the 'progressive' utilization of locally-manufactured automotive parts or contents.

This contribution gives an historical account of the failure of the 'localization' programme, from its inception in the 1970s up to its official phasing out in 2003 under the WTO's TRIMS. The study ends with a broad outline of the emerging car production-market landscape in Asia and what are the prospects for the Philippine car assembly and car parts industries.

Data for this study is based on interviews with key industry informants (industry leaders, human resource managers and union leaders), government industry reports/circulars and secondary studies. The contribution also benefited from several academic and research exchanges on the subject of automotive industrial development in Asia.[1]

Post-war Growth

Before and after the Second World War, the Philippines imported completely-built-up units (CBUs) of cars and other motor vehicles, mainly from the United States. But starting in 1951, the CBU imports were banned. In 1952, the CBUs were even classified from 'non-essential consumers goods' (NEC category) to 'unclassified or banned consumer goods' (UI category), meaning products with the lowest priority in the entitlement for dollar rations (Magallanes & Batalla, 1991).

The CBU import ban was in line with the general prohibition on the importation of finished products under the import-substituting industrialization (ISI) programme put in place in 1949–52. In these difficult years, the Philippine Republic, which acquired its independence in 1946 (after the Second World War), had to address two difficult survival challenges: one, the threat of a full-blown Communist rebellion, whose armed contingents were knocking at the doors of Manila in 1949, and two, the imminent collapse of the economy due to the weak agro-industrial recovery in the post-war period aggravated by the unchecked outflow of foreign exchange (Ofreneo, 1993). At the roots of the economic crisis was the resumption of the 'free trade' arrangement between a resurgent United States of America and a war-impoverished Philippines. Thus, to stabilize the economy and check the foreign exchange bleeding, the beleaguered government had to institute a series of measures ('controls') regulating imports and foreign exchange transactions, measures which eventually fuelled the growth of ISI industries such as the car assembly industry.

The CBU ban paved the way for the development of a car assembly industry, a truck assembly industry and a motorcycle assembly industry, all of which engaged in the assembly of imported CKDs and SKDs from the United States.

The new assembly plants were classified as 'new and necessary industries', which were given their share of dollar allocations. In turn, the assemblers used their foreign exchange allocations for CKD/SKD imports. A Filipino company, Fabar Inc., was the first to go into assembly business by venturing into the assembly of Austin and Studebaker cars. Later, the American pre-war car exporters – General Motors, Chrysler and Ford – established their respective assembly plants. A number of enterprising Filipino industrialists also set up their own assembly plants. By 1960, there were 12 assemblers. By 1968, the number was 29 (Magallanes & Batalla, 1991). The majority were Filipino companies importing CKD/SKD packs from the United States, Europe and Japan. This number did not include yet the backyard makers of the 'Philippine jeepney', a popular, colourful and rugged public utility vehicle plying the streets of Manila and other cities.

Although the import and foreign exchange controls were abolished in the early 1960s due to a policy conditionality from the International Monetary Fund (IMF), the ban on CBUs virtually remained in place through the high tariffs erected by the Diosdado Macapagal Administration (Ofreneo, 1993).

Rise and Fall of the Progressive Car Manufacturing Programme (PCMP)

The idea of producing vehicles with more local contents and less CKD/SDK imports came from the Central Bank. As a result of the recurrence of the balance-of-payments (BOP) crisis in 1968–70, the Central Bank decided to restrict the allocation of foreign exchange reserves to CKD/SKD importers. However, some Filipino vehicle assemblers, after a decade of acquiring skills in assembly work, also openly expressed their ambitions to develop a 'Filipino car'. One of them, Domingo M. Guevarra, an assembler of Volkswagen cars, tried to produce a prototype of a Filipino car he dubbed as *Sakbayan* or *Sasakyang Katutubong Bayan,* which means 'original national vehicle'. Guevarra also conceived of a similar product in the truck category, a *Trakbayan* or 'truck of the nation' (Jabson, 2003).

In 1971, the newly created Board of Investments (BOI) elaborated on the concept of developing a Filipino car through the PCMP. The programme called for a ban on CBU imports and extended CKD/SKD import privileges only to those able to meet the government's set targets on the progressive increases in the local content of assembled cars and those able to generate foreign exchange earnings through the export of locally-made car parts or other 'creditable' exports by the carmakers. Officially, the aims of the programme were to develop a viable automotive component sector, promote small and medium enterprises engaged in automotive parts manufacturing and generate foreign exchange earnings through exports of automotive components to other Asian countries (Magallanes & Batalla, 1991; Aldaba, 2000).

The programme took off in 1973, the first year of the martial-law government. Aside from the PCMP, the government also launched a Progressive Truck

Manufacturing Programme (PTMP) and a Progressive Motorcycle Manufacturing Programme (PMMP). The original target of the PCMP was an increase in the domestic content from 15 per cent in the first year, 25 per cent in the second year and 35 per cent in the third year, and progressively increasing thereafter. Aside from saving foreign exchange in terms of increased parts manufacture, the programme also sought to build up exports based on a regional automotive complementation programme in the context of the newly-organized regional grouping called the Association of South East Nations (ASEAN).

To ensure the PCMP's success, the government limited the number of participants to only five joint venture (JV) assemblers involving two American and three Japanese carmakers. The five JVs were Delta Motor Corporation (Toyota), Ford Philippines Incorporated, Canlubang Automotive Resources Corporation/PAMCOR (Mitsubishi), Franciso/Yutivo/General Motors Philippines and DMG, Incorporated/Nissan Motors Philippines.

The entry of the Japanese carmakers, in joint venture with Filipino companies, was made possible by the investment liberalization programme under the martial-law government (Ofreneo, 1993). At this time, the Japanese carmakers, after making successful beachheads in the global market, were starting to globalize their production by setting up offshore assembly plants in Asia and elsewhere.

Because the PCMP participants were the only ones allowed to import CKDs, the non-PCMP assemblers either closed down or tried to survive by merging with the PCMP participants or by doing subcontracting work for them. The CKD imports were allowed on the condition that these imports were partly paid through the foreign exchange earnings generated by exports made by PCMP participants. Since PCMP participants were not in the business of assembling cars for export, they set up related car part production businesses such as the manufacture or assembly of transmissions, diesel engines and other critical automotive parts exported to other Asian countries, usually subsidiary assemblers too of the transnational carmakers (Magallanes & Batalla, 1991; Aldaba, 2000).

Achievements of the PCMP

The PCMP took off auspiciously in 1974, with foreign investors initially sinking US$84.3 million (PAMCOR, 1995). A number of car parts makers mushroomed, with the PCMP participants themselves investing in parts production.

PAMCOR, through its affiliate Asian Transmission Corporation (ATC), set up an engine transmission manufacturing plant. The engine transmissions and related transmission components such as rough forgings and castings were marketed to the local PAMCOR's assembly plant and to Mitsubishi Japan and other Mitsubishi subsidiaries in Asia. Delta Motors established an automotive engine plant producing engine assemblies fitted with Delta-manufactured engine packs, cylinder heads and bearing caps as well as clutch housings for other PCMP participants. DMG invested in press-forming facilities to produce varied engine parts and stamped and pressed steel body components for its 'Sakbayan' passenger cars. Partial machining of the Volkswagen engine was also undertaken. Ford incorporated Ford Ensite Limited, a car body stamping company based at the Bataan Export Processing Zone. The plant manufactured Cortina sheet metal body stampings and sub-assemblies for export to Ford's affiliates in the Asia-Pacific region, with Ford Australia as the lead market. General Motors ventured into the manufacture of engine transmissions, which were exported to Australia, New Zealand and other Asian countries (Magallanes & Batalla, 1991).

Independent Filipino car parts makers, with licences or in joint ventures with the big carmakers, concentrated on less sophisticated car parts such as mufflers, floor carpet, horn, silencer, and so on. The local parts generated by PCMP included engine support, accelerator, clutch pedal assembly, fan belts, axle boot, headlights, coil/leaf springs, glass, seat assemblies, seat frames and adjusters, harness, wheel, tyre, battery, pipe and tube, rubber hoses, radiator, door trim, brake drum/disc, fuel tank, air conditioner, car stereos, speakers, rubber bumpers, shock absorbers, trunk trim, shelf trim and weatherstrip (Magallanes & Batalla, 1991).

There were 32 car parts makers in 1974; by the end of the 1970s, there were more than 200. In the 1980s, there were over 250 car parts makers registered with the Board of Investments; however, there were also unregistered backyard or small car parts producers doing contracting work for the bigger parts makers. All the PCMP, PTMP and PMMP participants claimed that they were able to attain a 40 per cent local content – the minimum requirement – in the second half of the 1970s (Magallanes & Batalla, 1991).

In the case of the motorcycle assembly, the PMMP participants proudly claimed to have attained over 50 per cent local content (Pineda, 1994), which is understandable given the lower technological make-up of motorcycle production. The localization success was also partly fuelled by the growth of the domestic market for motorcycles, especially for the three-wheeled ones (or 'tricycles') which are extremely popular as public conveyances in many towns and side streets of metropolitan Manila. The PMMP participants included Norkis, a licensee of Yamaha and a 100 per cent Filipino firm. The others are joint ventures with Kawasaki, Honda and Suzuki, all Japanese motorcycle makers. Table 1 shows the localization progress in the motorcycle assembly.

As to the PTMP, the government has been sparing in reporting progress, ostensibly due to the limited assembly work in the bigger vehicles such as bus and

Table 1. PMMP local content and sales, 1973–80

Year	Local content (%) Prescribed	Local content (%) Attained	Sales (No. of units)
1973	10	21	19,796
1974	20	22	29,075
1975	30	33	29,456
1976	40	45	31,028
1977	50	46	42,188
1978	50	52	51,769
1979	50	54	49.059
1980	50	55	44,774

Source: Pineda (1994).

truck, most of which were imported in CBU forms. However, there has been substantial localization success in the production of commercial vehicles called the Asian utility vehicles (AUVs), which are ideal as family vehicles or all-around vehicles for small enterprises.

The Collapse of the PCMP

Despite its success in the 1970s, the PCMP collapsed in the first half of the 1980s due to the shrinking domestic market. The global oil shock in 1979–80 depressed the vehicle market. It got further depressed as a result of the economic recession in 1980–86 precipitated by the crisis of political succession under the Marcos regime and the explosion of the debt crisis in 1983–85 (Ofreneo, 1993).

In 1983–85, the debt crisis became a letter-of-credit crisis, meaning importers had to deal with the outside world on a cash basis. This greatly affected the operations of the CKD importers and local parts assemblers, who also had to deal with a fast-shrinking domestic market. This was the period when three of the five PCMP participants dropped out. Ford and GM closed down their Philippine operations and justified this as part of their global streamlining programme. Delta Motors, assembler of Toyota cars, had to mothball its facilities because of massive indebtedness triggered by the peso devaluation and depressed market (Magallanes & Batalla, 1991).

During the crisis years of the 1980s, the government was virtually unable to monitor and enforce the local content programme for the original PCMP, PTMP and PMMP participants. However, one of the participants, Domingo M. Guevarra, also blamed the Marcos administration for the failure of the PCMP, specifically the government's inconsistent support for the programme. For example, two companies who could not get in under the PCMP, Renault and Mercedes Benz, were allowed to bring in CBU units without setting up a manufacturing facility. Worse, some CBUs were even allowed to enter the Philippine market tax-free. In the end, DMG, the company of Guevarra, was taken over by one of the cronies of President Marcos. According to Guevarra, all the original PCMP participants lost money (Jabson, 2003).

CDP and the SAP Liberalization Programme

In 1987, the Aquino administration revived the localization programme by re-baptizing the PCMP as the Car Development Program (CDP). The CDP essentially had the same implementation elements – a ban on CBUs, local content targets and foreign exchange earnings through exports. CDP covered passenger cars with engine displacement of up to 2,800 cubic centimetres. The CDP participants were limited to three – PAMCOR, Nissan Philippines and Toyota Motors Philippines, a Toyota JV which took over the idle facilities of the bankrupt Delta Motors. Local contents were set as follows: 32.26 per cent for 1998; 36.58 per cent for 1989 and 40 per cent by 1990. The CDP participants were also asked to generate 50 per cent of their foreign exchange requirements through their own exports, with the automotive parts exports accounting for the entire 50 per cent by 1993. Further, the CDP participants were required to invest in the development of at least one major automotive component that would account for at least 9 per cent of the net local content (Economic Research Department-PDCP Bank, January 1997).

At about the same time, the Commercial Vehicle Development Program (CVDP) was launched to replace the PTMP. Like the CDP, the CVDP increased the 1990 local content targets – ranging from 13.7 per cent to 54.8 per cent for various categories of vehicles. The CVDP were also required to earn at least 25 per cent of their foreign exchange requirements through exports. In the motorcycle assembly, the PMMP was replaced by the Motorcycle Development Program (MDP). The local content target for MDP producers was 55 per cent by 1990 (Pineda, 1994). As in the 1970s, this was easily exceeded by the MDP participants, given the lighter nature of the industry.

Entry Liberalization

In 1990, the CDP was amended to include the assembly of smaller cars called 'people's car', with an initial price ceiling of Php 175,000. New car assemblers joined the 'people's car program' such as Honda Motors, Columbian Autocar (to assemble Kia), Transfarm (Norkis Gurkel), Italcar Pilipinas (Fiat) and Asian Carmakers (Daihatsu). Participation in the people's car programme meant eligibility for inclusion in the CDP proper, at the higher engine category, after a while. Thus, by 1990, there were officially 8 car assemblers and 26 commercial vehicle assemblers (Aldaba, 2000; PDCP, 1997).

In 1992, another amendment in the CDP was made, this time to allow the assembly of high-end passenger cars with engine displacement greater than 2800 cc. This amendment allowed the entry of Volvo International of Sweden and Daimler Benz of Germany. Finally in 1994, the CDP was again amended, to allow the entry of new assemblers under the ASEAN Industrial Joint Venture (AIJV) Scheme. A joint venture with Proton of Malaysia was set up in this regard. This never took off. But officially, the number of the CDP participants reached 11 by 1994, from the original 3 in 1987.

The reality, however, is that the CDP was rendered meaningless in 1991, with the passage of the Foreign Investments Act which allows 100 per cent foreign investment in pioneer and non-pioneer, export-oriented or not, activities so long as they do not fall under the 'short negative list'. Investment liberalization was part of the government's compliance with SAP (see discussion below).

Tariffs Going Down, Imports Going Up

In the meantime, as part of the general Philippine commitment to SAP, tariffs for cars had been going down. The high tariff rates and the import restrictions on numerous agro-industrial items were the targets of the SAP-inspired economic liberalization programme concluded by the Marcos technocrats with the World Bank and the International Monetary Fund (IMF) in 1979–80. SAP called for the liberalization of the trade regime (via tariff reduction and elimination of import restrictions), privatization of government-owned-or-controlled corporations (GOCCs), the deregulation of certain economic sectors (financial, agriculture, and so on) and the liberalization of the investment regime.

Thus, under SAP, automotive tariffs started declining in 1981, with car tariffs going down to 70 per cent. In 1982, these were slashed to 50 per cent; these eventually went down to 40 per cent in 1993. However, the tariff rates for CKD imports went down even faster. They averaged 30 per cent in the 1980s, dropped to 20 per cent in 1993–94 and further to 10 per cent in 1995 before reaching 3 per cent in 1996–97. These CBU and CKD tariffs were the lowest among the ASEAN car producers. These tariff reductions, which were applied more aggressively on the car parts and components, means that the local assembly of cars was protected but the local part and component producers were not. Table 2 shows the tariff rates for motor vehicles and parts as of 2001. Table 3 shows how low Philippine tariffs are vis-à-vis its ASEAN neighbours.

In February 1996, the government issued Memorandum Order No. 346 liberalizing the importation of CBUs or all types of passenger cars, commercial vehicles and motorcycles – subject, of course, to tariffs, which have been cascading down. One immediate impact of this liberalization policy was the entry of new car models and the decline in car prices, to the delight of consumers. Nevertheless, the established car assemblers were able to overcome the more competitive economic environment through a higher volume of production, as the economy was bullish in 1995–96. Thus, even if the system of protection under the original PCMP/CDP was being dismantled, the registered car assemblers did not register any strong opposition to the liberalization/deregulation programme because their individual markets were growing. Moreover, the assemblers helped themselves by also importing CBUs of various models and sourcing cheaper and quality CKD packages produced by their sister companies in other countries (Aldaba, 2000; PDCP, 1997).

Table 2. MFN tariff rates for motor vehicles and parts, Philippines (2001)

Imported items	Motor vehicles	Duty (%)
CKD	Passenger car	10
	Commercial vehicles:	
	Buses	3
	Trucks	3
	Motorcycles	3
Selected auto parts	Engine	3–10
	Body stamping	3–10
	Transmission	3–10
CBU	Passenger car	30
	Commercial vehicles	
	Buses	15–20
	Trucks	30

Source: Hernandez (2001).

Table 3. MFN Vehicle tariff rates of ASEAN Countries (2002) (%)

Products	Malaysia	Thailand	Indonesia	Philippines
CKD				
Cars	42–80	33	35–50	10
CV	Nil	20–33	0–25	3
CBU				
Cars	140–300	80	45–80	30
CV	30–50	40–60	40–45	20–30

Source: DTI Motor Vehicle Product Team (2003).

The Crisis in the Automotive Industry since 1997

In 1997–98, however, the industry was back in crisis. The Asian financial contagion drastically affected the market (see Table 4). Thousands of workers were laid off with the closure of a number of parts manufacturers and the downsizing operations by all car assemblers, including the closure of the facilities of Korean car assemblers.

After the Asian financial crisis, the low capacity utilization among the assemblers and car parts producers persisted and is continuing up to the present, with Toyota, the best-performing car assembler-distributor operating at 60 per cent or so. There are several reasons for this persistent crisis in domestic assembly.

Firstly, there is a flood of imported brand-new vehicles and parts. With the declining tariffs and the general perception that imported vehicles and automotive parts are better in quality than locally-produced ones, the imported brand-new vehicles and CKD packages have been displacing the local ones in the market. In response to complaints from the assemblers, the government raised the tariffs for CKD packages to 7 per cent in 1998 and to 10 per cent in 1999. These rates were still comparatively low compared to other Asian producers (see Table 3) and did not dampen the importation urge.

Secondly, the government imposed new 'excise taxes' in 2003–04 which do not distinguish between the locally-assembled and the imported. This was partly a response to the pressure of the IMF for a shift from taxation based on engine displacement to taxation based on values. Thus, all vehicles, locally-assembled and imported, are now uniformly taxed based on value. The problem is that in terms of value, those at the low-end bantam category have been given a very low 2

Table 4. Total domestic vehicle sales, Philippines, 1995–99

Year	Passenger cars	Commercial vehicles
1995	65,808	53,392
1996	79,673	58,815
1997	69,070	51,418
1998	32,134	35,769
1999	25,130	39,505

Source: Board of Investments (2003).

per cent tax based on the argument that such cars should be affordable for the rising middle class. But most of these bantam cars are not assembled in the Philippines because of the economy-of-scale limitations. Most of these cars are imported from the other Asian countries, principally Thailand.

One major victim of this automotive excise taxation 'reform' is the Philippine production of the Asian utility vehicles (AUVs), which are classified under the low-end category of commercial vehicles. The AUVs are products of earlier ASEAN industrial complementation schemes, which were developed in the 1970s and 1980s. In the 1990s, these AUVs, which enjoyed fiscal incentives, experienced a sales boom. With 8–10 seats and sporting new stylish designs, these AUVs became 'hot' items for big Filipino families, small family enterprises and operators of the new 'mega' taxis, which bring white-collar commuters to their places of work or at home along specified routes. By the second half of the 1990s, more than half of the locally-assembled vehicles were accounted for by the AUVs. Moreover, the local contents of Toyota's 'Revo', Mitsubishi's 'Adventure', Honda's 'CRV' and Isuzu's 'Crosswind' reached 50 per cent or more. Since the imposition of the new excise taxes in 2004, the market for AUVs has slowed down, with Toyota deciding to phase out its 'Revo' in favour of 'Innova' (Salvosa, 2005).

Thirdly, the domestic market has been flooded with second-hand vehicles (of all types and sizes) and 'surplus parts' (in reality second-hand parts), coming mainly from Japan, South Korea and Taiwan (Federation of Philippine Industries, 2004). These vehicles, priced at virtually give-away prices, have captured the imagination of the middle and lower classes. Records of the Land Transportation Office (LTO) indicate that there are over 200,000 'new' vehicles being registered nationwide, and yet the local assemblers are able to account for less than 100,000 in the aggregate (see Table 5). Which means almost half of the 'new' vehicles are second-hand imports. The backyard 'jeepney' assemblers account for the difference.

The local assemblers have launched a campaign against the second-hand imports and the leniency of the government in allowing the massive entry of the imports. The campaign is anchored on environmental grounds (a clean air law frowns upon the importation of second-hand vehicles), safety grounds (many imports require 'conversion' from 'right-hand' to 'left-hand' drives), employment grounds and industrialization grounds. Additionally, the Philippines appears to be the only East Asian country allowing the massive entry of second-hand vehicles.

The Subic Freeport or special economic zone is the favourite entry point for the imports. Cebu in central Philippines, San Fernando in northern Philippines and

Table 5. Newly registered vehicles, Philippines, 2000–03

	2000	2001	2002	2003
Locally-assembled	83,994	76,671	85,594	92,336
Others	88,057	97,023	113,336	103,228
Total	172,051	173,694	198,930	195,564

Source: Chamber of Automotive Manufacturers of the Philippines, Inc. (2005).

General Santos in southern Philippines are also popular dumping ground for these imports. These freeports are supposed to allow the entry of imported vehicles only for use by investors-locators, and yet the vehicles passing through these ports number in the thousands. Moreover, the imports are given very low valuation, for example a two-year-old Mitsubishi Pajero valued at US$350 in order to reduce the 10 per cent VAT (Fair Trade Alliance, 2006). This is 'technical smuggling'.

The Demise of the Local Content Programme

If the car assembly industry is delirious, the car parts industry producing for the former is comatose. Although the BOI claims that there are 250 or so registered car parts makers, the reality is that the active ones have dwindled to less than a hundred, with most of the survivors either operating below capacity or engaged in parts production on a per order basis. In contrast, Thailand has over a thousand active car parts makers today (Lees, 2004).

As to the localization project, this requires a decent burial.

As outlined above, the car parts industry developed in tandem with the assembly industry based on the CBU ban and the high-tariff regime of the 1960s. In the 1970s, the CBU ban and high tariffs were supplemented by the official local content and foreign exchange requirements under the PCMP. These performance requirements, dubbed as TRIMS under the WTO, were supposed to be phased out with the establishment of the WTO in 1995. In fact, the Philippine unilateral liberalization programme under SAP had rendered these requirements meaningless. And yet, the Philippines still applied for the extension of the TRIMS twice – in the first place, up to 2000 and, later on, up to 2003.

In seeking for the TRIMs' extension, the Philippines aligned itself with its ASEAN neighbours – Thailand, Malaysia and Indonesia, which all asked for the same extension. But in 1995–96, Thailand had already become a regional automotive hub, Malaysia's Proton programme was in place and Indonesia had just announced its 'national car' project, while the Philippines were then putting the finishing touches for its vehicle liberalization/deregulation programme that would undo much of its past efforts to build a car or truck or motorcycle with high domestic content!

Automotive Workers' Resistance Against Liberalization

Given the shrinking car market in a liberalized and globalized environment, the automotive workers themselves, mostly from the car assembly industry, started taking up the issue of tariff reduction. Since the year 2000, the Automotive Industry Workers Alliance (AIWA), with some support from the industry itself, has been agitating for a postponement of the reduced tariff rates for the car industry under the ASEAN Free Trade Agreement (AFTA) and the WTO.

AIWA is an alliance of trade unions in the car assembly industry, all of which suffered during the painful downward restructuring of the industry in 1997–98 as a result of the Asian financial crisis. A number of car assemblers either closed shop, such as Hyundai, or temporarily shut down, such as Nissan. Mitsubishi was hit by a one-month paralysing strike, after it laid off nearly a third of its workforce.

In the other car assembly plants such as Honda, strikes were only prevented because the Secretary of Labor assumed jurisdiction over their labour disputes. Many car parts makers, including the big export-oriented ones, such as UE Tech, went out of business. Overall, the car assembly industry recorded over 3,000 job losses in 1997–99, and the automotive parts industry, over 4,000 (AIWA, 2001).

Thus, with the scheduled further trade liberalization in the industry in 2001–04, the AIWA affiliates saw bleaker prospects on the horizon. Hence, their decision to forge an alliance and to force the Department of Labor and Employment to set up a Tripartite Industry Council for the Automotive Industry. Indeed in January 2003, under AFTA, tariff rates for CBUs went down to as low as 5 per cent. In January 2004, under the Philippine commitment to WTO, most-favoured-nation (MFN) tariff rates went down to 5 per cent. It is not clear to the leaders and members of AIWA how the car assembly industry and their jobs would survive under the liberalized regime of AFTA and WTO. Their anxieties are further aggravated by the failure of their principals, mainly their Japanese car employers, to disclose what are the overall plans of the Japanese carmakers under AFTA and WTO.

The anxieties of the AIWA officers and members are not misplaced. Despite the deep downsizings and massive retrenchments that hit the industry in 1997–99 as a result of the Asian financial crisis, lay-offs in the industry have continued (see Table 6). AIWA lamented: 'In the 1960s, we were second to Japan in Asia in the vehicle assembly. In the 1970s, we were overtaken by South Korea; in the 1980s, by Malaysia; and in the 1990s, by Indonesia and Thailand. Today, Viet Nam might overtake us' (AIWA, 2001).

In 2003, AIWA extended their advocacy for the protection of the car assembly industry by denouncing the new excise tax on motor vehicles. According to AIWA, the tax rationalization programme was 'irrational' because it imposes a measly 2 per cent tax on the cheapest-selling cars, most of which are imported, and radical tax increases of close to 20 per cent for the Asian utility vehicles (AUVs), which are the leading vehicles assembled locally. AIWA has also been critical of the widespread 'smuggling' of second-hand vehicles imported through the special economic zone of Subic and the porous ports of Cebu, Ilocos and South Cotobato. Even if imported legally, these second-hand vehicles are given very low valuations, for example, a 2-year-old luxury Mitsubishi Pajero declared to cost

Table 6. Lay-offs in automotive industry, Philippines, 1999–2002

	Establishment		Displaced workers	
Year	Closure	Reduction of workforce	Closure	Reduction of workforce
1999	0	15	234	224
2000	7	10	784	274
2001	4	15	492	502
2002	5	26	79	596

Note: Classification of Industry into minor industries was only implemented only in 1999. From 1990–98, classification is by major industry.
Source: Bureau of Labor and Employment Statistics (2003).

only US$350; hence, the duty and excise taxes are correspondingly low, too (Fair Trade Alliance, 2006).

The Philippines in a Changing Asian and Global Car Market

Despite the automotive liberalization/deregulation programme and the phasing out of the local content and foreign exchange requirements as a result of the TRIMS, the assembly industry and automotive parts manufacturing industry are not about to collapse or disappear, the numerous downsizing programs notwithstanding. First, there will always be a demand for vehicles in the Philippines, even if such a demand of over a hundred thousand units a year is considered among the lowest in the South East Asian region. Such a demand will always require that some assembly work on some vehicle models and production of selected parts are done locally.

Secondly and more importantly, the car industry is heavily regionalized and internationalized. Japanese carmakers will continue to maintain or even expand their investments in the Philippines as part of their regional and global operations. In fact, the Philippines, in the twenty-first century, is now an exporter of CBUs in the region! Ford Philippines started it. The Japanese carmakers are now slowly doing the same and deciding on which car models to assemble for export and which to import. However, the volume of CBU exports is much less compared to the CBU imports.

In this context, it is important to understand the changing car production programme of the Japanese, American and other global carmakers in Asia.

The Changing Asian Strategies of Japanese and Other Carmakers

In the 1970s and 1980s, when the Japanese began relocating car assembly and parts production facilities offshore, the idea was to avoid the prohibitive cost of labour in Japan's miracle economy and develop the car markets in the emerging markets of Asia, the Philippines included. In particular, in the 1980s, following the revaluation of the yen as a result of the Plaza Accord of 1985, some US$15 billion of Japanese foreign direct investment (FDI) were ploughed into South East Asia (Bello, 2004). Unfortunately for the Philippines, Japanese transnationals (TNCs) found Thailand a more attractive investment destination, with its booming market and better infrastructures. Thailand became the South East Asian car hub of Japan, a platform for the assembly and export of popular Japanese car brands such as Toyota Alti or Mitsubishi Lancer to other Asian countries and North America.

However, Japan took care that they set up assembly plants in the different South East Asian countries, given the high tariffs and various forms of protection that these countries had erected. The Japanese carmakers also brought in, either wholly or in joint venture, facilities for the production of automotive parts, with different Asian countries specializing in certain parts. It is in this context that the Philippines became a major production base for Mitsubishi and Toyota transmissions.

Lately, there have been strategic adjustments in the Asian car programmes of the Japanese and the newly returned American and European carmakers. With tariffs in the ASEAN down to 5 per cent, the region, with over 500 million inhabitants, has become attractive as a single market for CBUs assembled in one country. Thus, some Japanese carmakers are consolidating the production of popular brands in Thailand, while allocating one or two exportable brands to each of the ASEAN countries based on capacities and market demands.

The process is aided by the decision in 1996 by the ASEAN to have an ASEAN Industrial Cooperation (AICO) scheme, which grants preferential tariffs of 0–5 per cent for companies with subsidiaries in two or more ASEAN countries. The purpose of AICO is a giveaway to carmakers and car parts producers – to promote a regional division of labour for the production of parts and final products within the region. Accordingly, an AICO product must have at least 40 per cent ASEAN local content. To date, most of the AICO participants are Japanese carmakers. In the Philippine list of AICO companies, only 5 out of 31 registered in 1999–2002 are non-auto-related (DTI Motor Vehicle Product Team, 2003).

However, with the AFTA programme now in place, the global carmakers have greater incentives to form their own regional divisions of labour in the ASEAN region and assign what models and what parts to produce in each country. They do not even have to register under the AICO programme, as any importer-exporter within the ASEAN region, with 40 per cent ASEAN local content, can do business within the region. Thus, Ford, which returned to the Philippines in 1997, is now using the country as a production platform to export Ford Focus, Mazda Tribute and Mazda 3 to other ASEAN countries. However, it is also investing in other ASEAN countries in the assembly of certain models and the production of parts. The only problem is that overall, the Philippines, with one of the lowest car sales in the region, can neither be a car hub nor a producer of the most popular exportable Japanese cars.

The Rise of Global Parts Producers and the Crisis of Domestic-Oriented Car Parts Makers

And yet, the Philippines is a major producer and even a production hub for select car parts such as wire harness and transmission. Why is this so?

Apparently, this has happened because of the decision of the Japanese carmakers to transform the Philippines as a global production platform for select automotive parts. Thus, despite the general underdevelopment of the car parts industry and the dwindling number of car parts makers, the Philippines now hosts huge factories producing car parts that are exported not only in Asia but globally. For example, Yazaki Torres in Laguna and EDI in Cavite have thousands of workers producing wire harness destined for different carmakers worldwide. According to former DTI Secretary Cesar Purisima (2004), the Philippines accounts for not less than 20 per cent of the world's wiring harness output. The Philippines has also become the 'transmission capital' of Toyota (through its subsidiary, Toyota Parts) and Mitsubishi (through ATC).

There are also Philippine-based exporters of gearboxes, tyres (Yokohama), filters, silencers, aluminium wheels, plastic grills and rubber hoses (DTI Motor Vehicle Product Team, 2003; Phil-Ged, c1995). The only exception is a 100 percent Filipino firm, Ramcar, which is able to penetrate the world market with its world-class car batteries. Table 7 shows the rising figures for exports of automotive parts and components coming from the Philippines.

However, these parts exporters are few and limited to a few components of the industry. Most have developed not necessarily in response to the requirements of the progressive car/truck/motorcycle manufacturing programme of the country but more in relation to the global and regional strategies of the transnational car manufacturers (Ishikazaki, 1996). As pointed out, many of the original car parts makers have disappeared from the market. In the context of the changing Asian car market and car production strategies of the Japanese and other car markets, this is bound to happen and continue, given the limitations of the local assembly industry.

Conclusions and Implications

For the foreseeable future, the dream of Filipino industrialists in the 1960s to develop a Filipino car or to produce a car with as much as 80 per cent local content will remain a dream. The reasons are obvious. The progressive car manufacturing programme was not carried out in a consistent and sustained manner. First, there was no clear programme at the beginning. There were many ad hoc adjustments along the way. Second, from five car assemblers, the number grew to 20. With a stagnant economy (ironically with a large potential market given the size of the Philippine population) and with too many players, most of the assemblers have a production capacity of only around 10,000 units per assembly plant per year, while actual production has been much less.

As to the increased localization of car content, the plan was never carried out in a serious, consistent and sustained manner. There was hardly any monitoring. There were no clear incentives for local parts manufacturers outside the fiscal ones, such as research and development (R & D) assistance or negotiations with the car assemblers on technical assistance and industry linkages. Moreover, the

Table 7. Exports of automotive parts, Philippines, 1991–2000

Year	Value of exports* (US$ million)
1991	228
1992	362
1993	444
1994	689
1995	755
1996	822
1997	934
1998	866
1999	842
2000	1011

Note: *Does not include yet exports of ABS, car stereos and other automotive electronic products, which are usually counted under electronics exports.
Source: DTI Motor Vehicle Product Team (2003).

tariffs for CKD parts were lowered in the mid-1990s at a rate much faster than the CBUs. This rendered the local content requirement policy, which the newly created WTO prohibits through the TRIMs, meaningless.

The successful parts manufacturers, few as they are in number, are the selected in-house manufacturers of Japanese transnational carmakers (based on their global and regional plans) and the global parts exporters, which are not necessarily tied to the local car assembly industry, such as the wire harness producers.

Above all, the car industry has not developed because, like in the rest of the country, there is no clear industrial vision and strategic plan for the industry. In the first place, how can a Philippine car industry develop by merely depending on the investment plans of transnational carmakers, who, naturally, have their own global and regional plans? This brings us back to the other weaknesses of the country's industrial development programme. Unlike the Asian NICs, the Philippines has failed to develop its own export and domestic champions and has become dependent on international subcontracting. In electronics, it has failed to scale the value chain, to graduate from assembly work to original equipment manufacture (OEM) to product application and so on, just what South Korea has done and what China is apparently doing now. The Philippines was an assembler 30 years ago; today, it is still doing assembly work. Thus, the enclave nature of the export sector has remained, and so are the limited linkages with the domestic economy.

For the Philippines to acquire or develop the full technology or more value-adding segments of a production process, it must work for it, with local industry and government working together. This is the main finding of the ADB's special report on competitiveness (ADB, 2003). The issue is not whether FDI should be allowed to operate in some industrial enclaves. The issue is how to transform low-skill, low-technology and cheap-labour-based export enclaves into high-skill, high-technology and professional-labour-based areas with better linkages with the economy to trigger, in the words of ADB, 'a sequence of beneficial changes throughout the economy' (2003: 233).

Another challenge is how to encourage local enterprises to learn from FDI and acquire the skills, know-how and market for their own products. The ADB Report cited the case of Samsung, which started as a joint venture assembler for Sanyo. Samsung began learning from the Japanese on how to manage an electronics business, then it acquired the capacity to produce standardized goods, and later it graduated into OEM and eventually into making its own innovative products by blending technology from the United States with those of Japan and doing its own experimentation. The ADB Report also talks of similar learning efforts on the part of the Korean carmakers.

The local content requirements are one of the traditional instruments used by developing countries in speeding up and deepening the industrialization process. Handled properly, they can help promote industrial linkages and, therefore, the growth of new local suppliers and subcontractors. They help shorten the learning process in the mastery of a production process through the transfer of technology and skills (Lall, 1995). This is what Malaysia and Indonesia had been trying to accomplish (with some measure of success in the case of the former) in the development of their national car projects in the 1990s.

As to the trade balancing requirements, it is only natural for developing countries short of foreign exchange to seek a win-win solution on investments requiring heavy use of foreign exchange, that is, for the investors themselves to earn the foreign exchange their projects would need.

The Way Forward

In the meantime, what can the Philippines do, if it wants to achieve a higher level of assembly work and more employment in the automotive industry? Because of WTO's TRIMS, the local contents programme and the trade balancing requirements can no longer be part of the industrial development arsenal of the Philippines. Because of the AFTA-led regional integration and the limitations in its actual and potential markets, the Philippines does not figure prominently in the production radar of the global carmakers; it is generally assigned a peripheral production and marketing role. Because of the realities of liberalization/globalization and the mistakes of the past, there is no Filipino car company in the horizon that is likely to emerge and compete with the existing global carmakers head to head in the liberalized Philippine market and in the bigger ASEAN and global markets. So what can be done?

Given the above limitations, the following three things can still be done, meagre and unpredictable though the results may be:

Address the under-utilization of existing capacity

The existing assembly plants of Toyota, Honda, Mitsubishi, Isuzu and other carmakers are grossly under-utilized, some as low as 40 per cent or thereabouts. On the other hand, these 'surviving' assemblers are not prepared to abandon these assembly plants in favour of the import-and-distribute business mode, which the Korean and other carmakers seem to have adopted. One effective way of increasing the capacity utilization of these plants is to reduce the smuggling of used vehicles, which outnumber the locally assembled and the brand-new legitimate CBUs imports. What is needed is the political will of the government enforcers to stop the smuggling of these second-hand vehicles, for after all, these are bulky imports, which cannot be hidden from the naked eyes of the customs officials.

Aside from their campaign against smuggling, the AIWA unions have also been negotiating with the Japanese carmakers to assign more car models and more automotive parts to be produced in the Philippines, including those for export to the ASEAN region. This is a step in the right direction. Of course, Japanese management is using the demand for more models/parts (or work to be done) by asking the unions, in turn, to help Philippine-based assemblers become more productive and competitive ASEAN- and Asia-wide. A win-win or mutually-beneficial solution to this is not impossible to forge.

Still another approach is the 'Malaysian solution', that is, requiring all government offices and public utility operators to buy only locally-assembled vehicles.

Consolidate the role of the Philippines as a regional hub for auto parts and components

The country has shown its capacity to produce world-class automotive parts and components such as wire harness, transmission, tyre, battery, and so on – so long as the economy of scale is there. If the Philippines cannot be a regional hub for the production of cars and commercial vehicles, it can be a hub for the production of more automotive parts and components. What is needed here is increased strategizing by the government and the private sector on how the Philippines can be marketed in the production of global parts and components and how some Philippine producers such as Yazaki-Torres can graduate into higher value-adding parts production.

Restrategize the production of AUVs. Of all the vehicles assembled locally, the Philippines has registered greatest success in the production of the Asian utility vehicles (AUVs). The market for AUVs in the 1990s boomed because of the demand of family-based and small enterprises, large Filipino families and operators of 'mega' taxis for 8–10 seaters. The Filipino automotive engineers, technicians and designers have also managed to improve the marketability of the AUVs and increased the local content to over 50 per cent, as the Isuzu management pointed out in its opposition to the excise tax hearings in the Senate in 2003. What has dampened the demand for AUVs in recent years is the illogical imposition of higher excise taxes on AUVs (and lower excise taxes on imported bantam cars, which are mostly imported) and the unchecked entry of smuggled used vehicles, most of which are 8–10 seaters. The solution to the latter is political will and the decisive exercise of the power of the State in curbing illegal activities. As to the excise taxes, it is abundantly clear, there is a need to rethink an excise tax system, which tends to penalize the local assemblers and reward the importers. Once these twin problems are addressed, the government and the local assembly industry can discuss how the AUV industry can be restrengthened and how the regional and global markets for Philippine-made AUVs can be developed.

In conclusion, in a liberalized Philippine economy and globalizing world economy, the national leaders should be able to come up with new and innovative measures to win in the national and global markets. They must strategize industrial development in the context of the realities of globalization as well as lessons from other countries, including the country's own mistakes.

Note

[1] The author contributed/participated in the following auto/technology forums: the UNU-Intech Exchange on Transnational Corporations, Learning and Innovation organized by Dr Rajah Rasiah of UNU, 2002–03 (see Rasiah, R. (ed.) (2003) *Transnational Corporations Learning and Innovation: Implications of the TRIMs Agreement* (Maastricht: UNU Institute for New Technologies)); the UNCTAD Conference on Investment, Technology and Related Financial Issues, held in Geneva, Switzerland, 6–12 March 2006; and the FairTrade-SOLAIR Forum on Roadmapping for the Auto Industry of the Philippines, held at UP SOLAIR, 29 March 2007. The author conducted interviews with the following people: Beth Lee, President, Chamber of Automotive Manufacturers of the Philippines, Inc. (CAMPI); Homer Maranan, Executive Director, CAMPI; Frank Mero, President, Automotive

Industry Workers Alliance (AIWA); and with officials of the Bureau of International Trade Relations, Department of Trade and Industry (DTI), and Motor Vehicle Products Division, Board of Investments, Department of Trade and Industry. In addition, the author used the vertical files of CAMPI, AIWA and DTI containing bits and pieces of information on the automobile industry.

References

AIWA (2001) *Appeal in re: Tariff Taxes on CKD/CBU and Importation Policies Relative to the Automotive Industry*. Amended Position Paper.

Aldaba, R. (2000) *Increasing Globalization and AFTA in 2003: What Are the Prospects for the Philippine Automotive Industry?*, DP Series 2000-42 (Makati City: Philippine Institute for Development Studies).

Asian Development Bank (2003) Competitiveness in Developing Asia, in: *Asian Development Outlook 2003*, pp. 203–272 (New York: Oxford University Press).

Bello, W., Docena, H., De Guzman, M. & Malig, M. (2004) *The Political Economy of Permanent Crisis in the Philippines* (Quezon City: UP Department of Sociology and Focus on the Global South).

Board of Investments (2003) *The Philippine Motor Vehicle Development Program* (Makati City: BOI-DTI).

Bureau of Labor and Employment Statistics (2003) *2003 Yearbook of Labor Statistics* (Manila: BLES, DOLE).

Chamber of Automotive Manufacturers of the Philippines, Inc. (2005). *Brief on Used Motor Vehicle Imports* (Mandaluyong City: CAMPI).

Doane, D. (2005) *Technology 'Laddering', Blending and Clustering: Lessons and Experiences from Several Asian Countries* (Quezon City: Fair Trade Alliance).

DTI Motor Vehicle Product Team (2001) Development Plan: Philippine Motor Vehicle Industry (Makati City: DTI).

Economic Research Department-PDPC Bank (1997) The automotive industry. *Industry Digest*, 21(1, January) (Makati City: PDCP Bank).

Fair Trade Alliance (2006) *Nationalist Development Agenda: A Road Map for Economic Revival, Growth and Sustainability* (Quezon City: Fair Trade Alliance).

Federation of Philippine Industries (2004) Is the Philippines an emerging junkyard? in: *Tambuli*, 1 (7, 31 August) (Makati City: FPI).

Hernandez, E. (2001) *Philippine Automotive Industry* (Makati City: Board of Investments). Hernandez was Executive Director for Industry, BOI-DTI.

Industry Development Council (1998) *Industrial Development Plan of the Philippines, I and II*, June (Makati City: Department of Trade and Industry).

Ishizaki, Y. (1996) New phase in Asia strategies of Japanese-affiliated automobile and parts manufacturers, *Pacific Business and Industries*, 1 (31), pp. 17–23 (Tokyo: Sakura Institute of Research).

Jabson, A. K. (2003) Don Domingo M. Guevara: in staunch of defense of Filipino products, *BusinessWorld* (6 January), p. 17.

Lall, S. (1995) Industrial strategy and policies on foreign direct investment in East Asia, *Transnational Corporations*, 4(3).

Lees, G. (2004) Thai Ambitions, in: *Asia Inc.*, pp. 24–25 (Singapore: Asia, Inc.).

Lim, J. & Montes, M. (1997) *The Structure of Employment and Structural Adjustment in the Philippines* (Geneva: ILO).

Magallanes, N. & Batalla, E. (1991) A note on the Philippine automotive industry. Research File of the Philippine Automotive Federation, Inc. (Mandaluyong City: Philippine Automotive Federation, Inc.).

Ofreneo, R. (1993) Labor and the Philippine economy, Doctoral dissertation, College of Social Sciences and Philosophy, University of the Philippines.

Ofreneo, R. & Samonte, I. (2002) Empowering Filipino migrant workers: policy issues and challenges. Research Report submitted to the ILO Manila Office, Makati, January.

PAMCOR (1995) *The Automotive Industry of the Philippines: A Situationer* (Cainta, Rizal: Mitsubishi Motors).

PDCP (1997) The Automotive Industry, Part 1 and Part 2, in: *Industry Digest* (Makati City: PDCP Bank).

Phil-Ged (n.d., c1995) *Philippine Automotive Parts and Accessories* (Makati City: Philippine-German Export Development Project).

Pineda, V. S. (1994) *Motorcycle and Parts Industry: Impact of Trade Policies on Performance, Competitiveness and Structure* (Makati City: Philippine Institute for Development Studies).

Rasiah, R. (Ed.) (2003) *Transnational Corporations, Learning and Innovation: Implications of the TRIMs Agreement* (Maastricht: UNU Institute for New Technologies).

Rasiah, R. & Hofmann, N. (Eds) (1998) *Workers on the Brink: Unions, Exclusion and Crisis in Southeast Asia* (Singapore: Friedrich Ebert Stiftung).

Salvosa, F. (15 Feburary 2005) Toyota phases out Revo line to give way to Innova, in: *BusinessWorld* (Quezon City: BusinessWorld Publishing).

Wad, P. *et al.* (2004) *Automobile Workers and Industry in Globalising Asia* (Hong Kong: Asia Monitor Resource Centre).

World Bank (1993) *The East Asian Miracle: Growth and Public Policy* (New York: Oxford University Press).

Foreign Ownership, Technological Intensities and Economic Performance of Automotive Parts Firms in India

RAJAH RASIAH & ASHISH KUMAR

Introduction

Although the literature using methodologies different from anecdotal and production function approaches to understand technology is growing, little work exists on their application in comparing technological intensities between foreign and local firms. This contribution seeks to build on the technological capability methodology developed by Lall (1992), and Bell & Pavitt (1995) and later expanded by Figueiredo (2002) and Ariffin & Bell (1999) to examine differences in technological intensities between foreign and local firms in India, and to explain their statistical determinants. In addition to providing implications for the technological capability methodology, this exercise is aimed at attracting further work comparing technological intensities between foreign and local firms.

India is an interesting economy to examine the potential learning effects foreign firms offer at host-sites. Despite the extremely low levels of foreign direct investment (FDI) in gross capital formation (GCF), the Indian economy offers a good example to test its impact on an economy endowed with large human resources (including human capital) and a long history of industrialization.

The Indian economy has also undergone considerable liberalization since 1991 and recorded rapid growth over the last three years. The selection of the automotive parts industry is also expected to provide valuable insights given the emergence of India as one of the few sites in the developing world predicted by analysts to retain some aspects of automobile assembly and automotive parts manufacturing following global restructuring.

Previous studies on the impact of British colonialism on the transformation of pre-capitalist formations to capitalist relations in India can be traced to Marx (1853), who argued how the disruptive processes of integration actually created the conditions for capitalist accumulation. A rich historical account of the diffusion of British technology into India's textile and garment industry was provided by Kumar & Desai (1983). Subsequent works by Kathuria (2000, 2001, 2002), Kumar (1994, 2002)and Lall (1984) addressed several issues related to the participation of FDI in the Indian economy. Using panel data and the stochastic production frontier approach on 487 firms belonging to 24 three-digit manufacturing industries for the period 1989–90 to 1996–97, Kathuria (2002) showed that after liberalization, the productivity of Indian industry, especially the foreign owned firms, has improved. Kumar (2002), *inter alia*, examined the crowding out question on foreign investment in India, including spillover effects using the production function approach – the statistical analysis producing higher and stronger productivity involving foreign than local firms. Lall (1984) showed evidence of multinational corporations (MNCs) limiting their R&D activities to adaptation and assimilation in India.

This contribution examines differences in labour productivity, export-intensity and technological intensities between foreign and local firms, and their statistical relationships, in automotive firms in India. The rest of the contribution is organized as follows. The second section presents the methodology and data used in the contribution. The third section compares export and technological capabilities recorded by foreign and local automotive parts, electronics and garment firms. The fourth section evaluates the determinants of export incidence and technological capabilities. The fifth section presents the conclusions.

Literature Review

The literature on foreign direct investment posits that MNCs located in developing economies with investment in assets across two or more countries enjoy superior technology – tangible and intangible – and market access over local firms especially from developing economies (see Hymer, 1960; Dunning, 1974). The superior technological and market capabilities of foreign firms has been viewed to offer developing economies strong spillover opportunities. However, the evidence is mixed. On the one hand, Blomström & Persson (1983), Blomström & Wolff (1994) and Blomström & Sjoholm (1999) produced evidence of positive spillovers from the presence of foreign firms. On the other hand, Haddad & Harrison (1993) produce evidence that show a lack of spillovers from foreign presence. However, as is typical with most applied work there exist little foolproof methods of tracing spillovers. As Lall & Streeten (1977) have argued, spillovers depend on several factors external to firms.

Part of the problem associated with the above contradictory findings is a result of weaknesses in the methodologies used. The first, based on case studies, lacks representation and because of the specificity of issues studied it often prevents a sufficiently exhaustive comparative assessment (for example, Allen & Donnitorne, 1957; Hughes & You, 1969; Lall, 1979). The second, based on the production frontier is undermined by at least three conceptual problems (for example, Blomström & Wolff, 1994; Aitken *et al.*, 1997; Blomström & Kokko, 1998; Aitken & Harrison, 1999; Blomström & Sjoholm, 1999). Firstly, the residue in the production function used to measure total factor productivity, as Romer (1994), Nelson (1994) and Vaitsos (2003) have argued, does not capture technology or technical change. Secondly, spillover is a dynamic concept that refers to effects captured by economic agents (including workers) external to the firms studied and hence generally do not appear in pecuniary measures. Thirdly, spillovers enjoy differences in intensity – including positive and negative elements – that are impossible to estimate exhaustively. One is neither able to estimate to any reasonable extent the intensity nor the effect of externalities using such approaches (see Rasiah, 1995, 2004a).

Like all industrial organization measures of concentration – which only refer to the potential rather than actual market power – technological intensities only denote the potential, that is, the extent of learning-diffusion that is potentially possible in a locality. Although the capacity to absorb new knowledge is easier when the gap between the leader and learner is narrow, there is neither a rigorous argument nor empirical evidence that convincingly substantiates this point. As Hirschman (1958, 1970)has argued, the bigger the gap the larger will be the potential for learning and catch-up. Marx (1853) had established the basis for rapid technological transformation when he argued over the positive role of colonialism when discussing how pre-capitalist modes of production give way to capitalist production. Despite the destruction and dislocation that accompanied capitalist integration colonial transition did quicken technical change in India (see Kumar & Desai, 1983). Unlike colonialism where the objectives of the regime in power targeted policies primarily for accumulation within the borders of the colonial grandmasters, post-colonial governments have enjoyed relative autonomy to engender technical change to generate domestic accumulation (see Warren, 1973, 1980).

In addition, studies using the technological gap either narrowly estimate differences in the pecuniary value of machinery and equipment of firms or simply use capital expenditure differences between firms. Differences in the stock of knowledge – embodied in humans, machinery and equipment and relationships – cannot be estimated this way. Besides, policy makers should be concerned about the learning potential rather than what is easiest to achieve. Also, efforts to draw absolute rather than potential policy instruments from mere differences in technological levels do not take cognizance of structural interdependence between industries and complementarities (see Kaldor, 1979).

Hence, this contribution seeks to use an alternative methodology where the focus is directly on embodied technology found in firms. By using technological intensities, the assessment can be focused simply on the potential spillovers that can arise at host-sites.[1] Although higher technological intensities need not translate into commensurate levels of absorption by local economic agents – including firms – they are a more reliable indicator to examine than spillovers when the data collected comes only from individual firms. A better method of examining spillovers will be to study the firms as a network of interconnected economic agents (for example, Rasiah, 1994, 1995). However, this methodology is too expensive and requires enormous sacrifice by researchers to construct a national database.

To examine differences in technological intensities between foreign and local firms, it is also important to establish the institutional structure within which firms operate. As Dosi (1982) and Pavitt (1984) have argued, taxonomies and trajectories are important when examining technological capabilities and demands in firms. Foreign firms with access to sophisticated technology from their plants at developed parent sites may show less R&D efforts at host-sites than local firms at home-sites who must develop their R&D capabilities to move up the technology ladder (Rasiah, 2004a).

However, the pattern of differences would vary taxonomically between human resources (HR) practices, process technology and R&D. Foreign firms are likely to show higher intensity levels than local firms in the easy to move internalized practices associated with HR, and machinery and equipment and process technology associated with it. Because of strong R&D infrastructure – especially in software engineering – in an otherwise fairly weak high tech infrastructure (including the risks arising from an underdeveloped framework of intellectual property rights), R&D intensities in foreign firms is likely to be lower than local firms in India. However, foreign firms could still enjoy higher product technologies owing to the access to know-how and brand name from their plants abroad. The large domestic market and the significant protection levels in the country is expected to allow foreign firms to use the rents to pay higher wages and attract more qualified personnel than local firms.

The discussion above leads to the examination of five hypotheses in the contribution. Firstly, HR and process technology (PT) intensities of foreign firms in automotive parts and electronics are expected to be higher than in local firms. Secondly, local firms are expected to show higher R&D intensities than foreign. The first hypothesis leads to the third and fourth hypotheses. Thirdly, overall technological intensity of local firms is expected to be higher than foreign firms. Fourthly, the low export-intensity level in the inward-oriented industry is the expected result in a statistically insignificant set of results against ownership (see Table 1). Fifthly, local firms are expected to show a stronger relationship with R&D and overall technological intensities than foreign firms.

Methodology and Data

This contribution uses a methodology that measures technological capabilities directly employing indexes normalized from related proxies. The use of indexes in examining technological capability of firms can be traced to Lall (1992), Bell & Pavitt (1995), Westphal *et al.*, (1990) and Wignaraja (2002). Wignaraja adapted the Ernst, Mytelka & Ganiatsos (1998) taxonomy of capabilities to fit a narrow range of data available to examine upgrading in firms in Mauritius.

Table 1. List of variables and their relationship with the dependent variables

		Expected relationship with dependent variables					
Variables	Acronym	VA/L	X/Y	TI	HR	PT	RD
Labour productivity	VA/L						
Export intensity	X/Y	Unclear		Unclear	Unclear	Unclear	Unclear
Skills intensity	SI			+ ve	+ ve	+ ve	+ ve
Cutting edge HR practices	CHR						
Training mode	TM						
Training expense in payroll	TE						
HR index	HR						
Process technology expense in operating expenditure	PTE						
Equipment and machinery	EM						
Inventory and quality control Techniques	IQC						
PT index	PT						
R&D expense in sales	RDexp						
R&D personnel in workforce	RDemp						
RD index	RD						
Technological intensity	TI	+ ve	Unclear				
Wage	W	+ ve	Unclear	Unclear	Unclear	Unclear	+ ve
Foreign ownership	FO	Unclear	Unclear	Unclear	Unclear	Unclear	Unclear
Size	S	Unclear	Unclear	Unclear	Unclear	Unclear	Unclear
Age	A	Unclear	Unclear	Unclear	Unclear	Unclear	Unclear

Specification of Variables

This section explains the measurement of variables used in the contribution. The acronyms used, and the expected relationships, are shown in Table 1.

Economic performance. The proxies of labour productivity and export-intensities were used to represent firm-level performance (see Table 1). Both variables have problems but they allow useful assessments.

$$\text{Labour productivity} = VA_i/L_i$$

where VA and L refer to value added and total employees respectively of firm i in 2002.

$$\text{Export intensity} = X_i/Y_i$$

where X and Y refer to exports and gross output respectively of firm i in 2002. The incidence of exporting was higher among local (65.1 per cent) than foreign firms (43.8 per cent) (see Table 2).

Firm-level technological capabilities. Firm-level dynamics include minor improvements to machinery and equipment, improved inventory control systems and training methods and R&D strategies. Since a number of characteristics and strategies have overlapping objectives and effects, it is methodologically better to integrate related proxies into a composition of indexes, which will not only help minimize double counting, but also avert multi-collinearity problems in statistical analysis. No effort was made to administer weights to the proxies used in the measurement of the technology variables owing to a lack of a priori information of the relative significance of one over the other. However, the measurements were adjusted for the number of proxies used so that the human resources practices, process technology and R&D are equally represented in the estimation of overall technological intensity.

In addition, adjusting firms' responses involving specific variables, for example, R&D – will offer a better approximation of its value than just any one proxy – for example, R&D sales as a percentage of sales, R&D staff in the workforce, process R&D, product R&D and contract R&D. Including all the proxies as separate variables can cause multi-collinearity problems. Because there are no a priori reasons to attach greater significance to any of the proxies used, the normalization procedure was not weighted. In addition, the proxies were chosen carefully to prevent the integration of endowments (for example, R&D scientists and engineers, and a share of technical human capital) acquired or poached from other

Table 2. Breakdown of automotive parts firms, India sample, 2002

	Number	X	SMEs
FO = 1	36(100.0)	33(68.8)	9(19.4)
FO = 0	48(100.0)	27(75.0)	31(35.4)
Total	84(100.0)	60(71.4)	60(71.4)

Note: X refers to firms with export experience; SMEs refer to small and medium industries.
Source: Computed from UNU-MERIT (2004).

firms, which will have direct bearing on capability. However, the indirect effects of these proxies would still remain as the hiring of key R&D scientists or engineers by one firm from another would inevitably have a bearing on its R&D capability. The following broad capabilities and related composition of proxies were used.

Human resources capability. Human resources (HR) is expected to have a positive relationship with exports and process technology. Given the little focus on R&D operations in the automotive parts industry in India, a strong relationship is not expected between HR and R&D activities.

Human resources capability (HR) was measured as:

$$\mathrm{HR_i} = 1/3[\mathrm{TM_i}, \mathrm{TE_i}, \mathrm{CHR_i}]$$

where TM, TE and CHR refer to training mode, training expense as a share of payroll and cutting edge human resources practices used. TM was measured as a multinomial logistic variable of 1 when staff are sent out to external organizations for training, 2 when external staff are used to train employees, 3 when staff with training responsibilities are on payroll, 4 when a separate training department is used, 5 when a separate training centre is used and 0 when no formal training is undertaken. CHR was measured by a score of one for each of the practices and divided by the total number of practices. The firms were asked if it was their policy to encourage team-working, small group activities to improve company performance, multi-skilling, interaction with marketing, customer service and R&D department, lifelong learning and upward mobility. The proxies were normalized using the formula below:

$$\text{Normalization Score} = (\mathrm{X_i} - \mathrm{X_{min}})/(\mathrm{X_{max}} - \mathrm{X_{min}})$$

where X_i, X_{min} and X_{max} refer to the ith, minimum and maximum values of the proxy, X.

Process technology capability. Process technology (PT) – being central to participation in export markets even in low value added operations – can be expected to show a positive relationship with exports and HR. The same can also be expected with R&D since process improvements dominate early participation in R&D activities.

Data on three proxies facilitated the computation of PT, which was calculated using the formula:

$$\mathrm{PT} = 1/3[\mathrm{EM_i}, \mathrm{TPE_i}, \mathrm{IQC_i}]$$

where EM, TPE and IQC refer to equipment and machinery, process technology expenditure in sales, and inventory and quality control systems. EM was computed as a multinomial logistic variable on the basis of being the most advanced and dated machinery and equipment used (Likert scale scores ranging from 5 to 1). IQC was measured as a multinomial logistic variable taking account of ten cutting edge process techniques used in firms (that is, Just in time, integrated materials resource planning, small group activity, total productive maintenance, computer aided design, computer aided manufacturing, teamworking, stock sharing, quality assurance and total quality management). A score of one is given to each yes answer and the total simply added arithmetically.

R&D. The learning process leads firms to eventually participate in new product development. While beginners mostly learn and absorb, more established firms typically learn and develop new products. With the exception of funding of public laboratories and universities, firms seldom participate in basic research. Hence, firm-level R&D is largely focused on process technology and product development – especially diversification of use and proliferation. Given its underdeveloped institutional and systemic facilities and the preponderance of labour-intensive assembly and processing operations, R&D is unlikely to produce statistically meaningful results involving exports and human resources. Given the R&D focus in low value added automotive parts, electronics and garments, on process technology improvements – a positive relationship can be expected with process technology.

The data collected enabled the computation of two R&D proxies, namely, R&D expenditure as a percentage of sales and R&D personnel as a share of employment. Because of the inability to differentiate R&D personnel involved between product and process technology, this proxy was measured to relate to both product and process R&D and was measured as:

$$\mathrm{RDi} = 1/2[\mathrm{Rdexp_i}, \mathrm{Rdemp_i}]$$

where RDexp and RDemp refer to percentage share of R&D expenditure as a share of sales and R&D personnel in the workforce respectively of firm i.

R&D was also differentiated on the basis of only investment shares in sales allocated for process and product R&D, and were measured as:

$$\mathrm{RDproc_i} = \text{Percentage share of R\&D expenditure in process technology/Sales}$$

$$\mathrm{RDprod_i} = \text{Percentage share of R\&D expenditure in product technology/Sales}$$

Overall technological intensity. The overall technological intensity (TI) was measured by adding the variables of HR (technology embodied in humans), PT (technology embodied in machinery and equipment and intangible processes) and RD (technology development focus embodied in products, processes and humans). TI was measured as:

$$\mathrm{TI_i} = \mathrm{HR_i} + \mathrm{PT_i} + \mathrm{RD_i}$$

The use of TI will help in the estimation of differences in overall technological intensity between foreign and local firms, and in establishing its impact on export-incidence. TI is expected to show a positive relationship with export-incidence (see Table 1).

Wages

Owing to the relatively weak position of unions in small and medium scale firms, this contribution used wages as the proxy of labour market conditions. Due to the large reserves of labour in India, however, wages may not show statistically meaningful results. Nevertheless, given the premium involving skilled workers a positive relationship can be expected between HR and wages. Since it is difficult to obtain wage figures for the workers alone, the figure was drawn by dividing the total salaries and remuneration of each company with their workforce. Average 2002 wages in 10,000 rupees was used in all the regressions and was measured as:

$$W_i = \text{Average wage} = \text{Total payroll}/(\text{number of employees}).$$

Other Critical Firm-level Variables

Three other important firm-level structural variables were included in the analysis, namely, ownership and size, and age.

Ownership. Ownership was used as a separate variable and classified using two dimensions. With the exception of RD where either a positive or negative sign is possible for reasons advanced earlier, foreign ownership is expected to either enjoy a positive or a statistically insignificant relationship with export and technological intensities if firms must have similar technologies to compete in export markets. The distribution of foreign equity shares in the sample is fairly even to enable actual shares as the proxy of ownership. Hence, foreign ownership (FO) was measured as follows:

$$FO_i = \text{foreign equity in total equity capital}.$$

The regression involving samples by ownership used FO = 1 so long as foreign equity met over 10 per cent of overall equity. This cut-off point is justified on the grounds that foreign equity may have some influence over the conduct of firms even if their ownership levels are low and also because foreign equity is generally low in India. Using this criteria foreign and local ownership accounted for 36 (42.9 per cent) and 48 (57.1 per cent) firms respectively of the sample (see Table 2).

Size. Employment was used as the proxy for defining size. As argued earlier, size may take both positive and negative signs or may not be statistically significant at all. Size is used as a continuous variable here so that:

$$S_i = \text{Number of employees in firm i}.$$

If a cut-off point of 250 and more employees is used, small and medium enterprises (SMEs) accounted for only 19.4 per cent of foreign firms and 35.4 per cent of local firms in the sample (see Table 2). The unregistered background of large numbers of SMEs obviously means that the sample is skewed towards large firms.

Age. Given that firms with longer experience are considered to enjoy greater experiential and tacit knowledge age is considered to provide a positive relationship with exports and technological capabilities. The absolute age of the firm is used as an independent variable. The statistical relationship may not be positive in the case of foreign firms using superior technology from abroad and enjoying strong access to global markets, which may have recently opened or relocated operations locally. In spite of their short experience with export markets, local Indian firms would benefit from foreign firms' longer global experience.

$$A_i = \text{years in operation.}$$

Statistical Relationships

Two types of statistical analysis were carried out in the contribution. The first used two-tail t-tests of means to examine the statistical significance of differences in labour productivity, wages, export, skills and technological intensity means between foreign and local firms. The second tested econometrically the statistical relationships that explain labour productivity, and export, skills and technological intensities in the sample. OLS regressions were used when the dependent variable was value added per worker and export intensity of output. Tobit regressions were preferred when skills and technological intensities were used because they are censored on the right and the left side of the data-sets (see Greene, 2002).[2] The models were specified as follows:

$$\mathit{OLS}: \mathrm{VA/L} = \alpha + \beta_1 \mathrm{X/Y} + \beta_2 \mathrm{TI} + \beta_3 \mathrm{S} + \beta_4 \mathrm{FO} + \beta_5 \mathrm{W} + \beta_6 \mathrm{A} + \mu \quad (1)$$

$$\mathit{Tobit}: \mathrm{X/Y} = \alpha + \beta_1 \mathrm{TI} + \beta_2 \mathrm{S} + \beta_3 \mathrm{FO} + \beta_4 \mathrm{W} + \beta_5 \mathrm{A} + \mu \quad (2)$$

$$\mathit{Tobit}: \mathrm{TI} = \alpha + \alpha + \beta_1 \mathrm{X/Y} + \beta_2 \mathrm{S} + \beta_3 \mathrm{FO} + \beta_4 \mathrm{W} + \beta_5 \mathrm{A} + \beta_6 \mathrm{SI} + \mu \quad (3)$$

$$\mathit{Tobit}: \mathrm{HR} = \alpha + \alpha + \beta_1 \mathrm{X/Y} + \beta_2 \mathrm{S} + \beta_3 \mathrm{FO} + \beta_4 \mathrm{W} + \beta_5 \mathrm{A} + \beta_6 \mathrm{SI} + \mu \quad (4)$$

$$\mathit{Tobit}: \mathrm{PT} = \alpha + \alpha + \beta_1 \mathrm{X/Y} + \beta_2 \mathrm{S} + \beta_3 \mathrm{FO} + \beta_4 \mathrm{W} + \beta_5 \mathrm{A} + \beta_6 \mathrm{SI} + \mu \quad (5)$$

$$\mathit{Tobit}: \mathrm{RD} = \alpha + \beta_1 \mathrm{X/Y} + \beta_2 \mathrm{S} + \beta_3 \mathrm{FO} + \beta_4 \mathrm{W} + \beta_5 \mathrm{A} + \beta_6 \mathrm{SI} + \mu \quad (6)$$

The equations above were repeated using foreign and local samples separately. Also, the equations were tested for collinearity problems involving the independent variables (see Appendix). SI was not used alongside TI in the models owing to strong collinearity between the two variables.

Statistical Analysis

This section compares technological capabilities of foreign and local firms, and statistical relationships involving the explanatory variables of export incidence and technological intensities while controlling for other effects.

Statistical Differences

Two-tail t statistics were used to examine the statistical significance of the labour productivity, export intensity, wages, skills intensity and technology intensity means. The exercise produced some statistically interesting results for analysis.

Table 3. Two-tailed t test of means of automotive parts firms, India sample, 2002

	FO = 1	FO = 0	t
VA/L	122.576	99.737	3.21*
X/Y (per cent)	7.261	5.510	2.43**
HR	0.688	0.580	2.11**
TE (per cent)	5.067	4.265	1.87***
PT	0.711	0.593	2.23**
PTE (per cent)	5.504	4.598	2.05**
RD	0.453	0.347	2.18**
Rdexp (per cent)	1.411	1.178	2.27**
TI	1.852	1.520	2.38**
SI (per cent)	68.824	51.024	2.02**
W	21.270	14.482	2.63*

Note: *, ** and *** refer to statistical significance of 1 per cent, 5 per cent and 10 per centrespectively. VA/L and W in 10,000 rupees over the year.
Source: Computed from UNU-MERIT (2004) using SPSS package.

Labour productivity, export intensity and wages. Interestingly the two-tailed tests produced statistically significant results for labour productivity, export intensity and wages, and the t-statistics were all positive (see Table 3). Foreign firms enjoyed higher labour productivity, export intensity and wages than local firms. Although the foreign equity share in these firms generally was less than 30 per cent, the results show either that foreign firms have acquired or merged with better performing local firms or that the firms have benefited from foreign participation in equity.

Technological intensity. The two-tailed tets also produced statistically meaningful results involving skills and technological intensities. Foreign firms enjoyed higher means than local firms in skills and technology (including its components of HR, PT and RD), and the t coefficients are all positive (see Table 3). Apart from training expense (TE) where the results were statistically only at the 10 per cent level, the remaining results were either at 5 per cent or 1 per cent. The results show either that foreign firms have acquired or merged with better-equipped local firms or that the firms have benefited from foreign participation in equity. Foreign firms may have transferred more recent equipment and cutting edge instruments from the superior foreign plants. In addition, although foreign firms enjoyed an advantage in all the categories, the margin was not very high suggesting that local firms are not far from the levels achieved by foreign firms.

Statistical Relationships

The OLS and Tobit regressions used to estimate the statistical relationships involving labour productivity and export intensity, and technological intensities respectively produced important results (see Tables 4 and 5). The regressions involving the HR and PT regressions in the foreign firms' sample in Table 5 failed the model fit statistics (X^2). The results presented in Tables 4 and 5 passed the Cook Weisberg test for heteroskedasticity.

Table 4. Labour productivity and export intensity of automotive parts firms, India sample, 2002

	VA/L			X/Y		
	All	FO = 1	FO = 0	All	FO = 1	FO = 0
X/Y	− 1.072 − 2.417)**	− 0.859 (− 0.724)	− 1.090 (− 1.165)			
TI	46.226 (4.173)*	30.569 (2.470)**	111.333 (3.205)*	5.609 (2.036)**	− 5.824 (− 0.699)	8.058 (2.781)*
W	− 0.002 (− 0.315)	0.004 (0.518)	0.005 (0.319)	− 0.084 (− 0.759)	− 0.149 (− 1.170)	0.026 (0.085)
A	− 0.254 (− 1.200)	− 0.956 (− 2.232)**	0.030 (0.105)	− 0.060 (− 1.114)	− 0.144 (− 2.202)**	0.169 (1.599)
FO	0.468 (2.263)**			− 0.027 (− 0.509)		
Size	− 0.276 (− 0.637)	− 0.340 (− 0.567)	0.167 (0.311)	0.003 (1.915)***	0.006 (1.717)***	− 0.000 (− 0.079)
Intercept	45.657 (2.429)**	87.022 (3.680)*	− 84.356 (− 1.165)	− 1.720 (− 0.359)	21.930 (1.276)	− 10.880 (− 1.883)***
R2	0.317	0.269)	0.322	0.132	0.227	0.229
Adj. R2	0.264	0.182	0.213	0.076	0.127	0.157
F	5.957*	3.089**	2.951**	2.371**	2.27***	3.19**
N	84	48	36	84	36	48

Note: *, ** and *** refer to statistical significance at 1 per cent, 5 per cent and 10 per cent respectively.
Source: Computed from UNU-MERIT (2004) using E-views package.

Table 5. TI, HR, PT and RD intensities of automotive parts firms, India sample, 2002

	HR			PT			RD			TI		
	All	FO = 1	FO = 0	All	FO = 1	FO = 0	All	FO = 1	FO = 0	All	FO = 1	FO = 0
X/Y	0.002	−0.001	−0.002	0.001	0.001	0.006	0.003	−0.001	0.003	0.007	−0.001	0.005
	(1.095)	(−0.429)	(−0.955)	(0.701)	(0.337)	(2.324)**	(1.881)***	(−0.422)	(1.017)	(2.011)**	(−0.410)	(2.230)**
SI	0.002	0.000	0.008	0.004	0.001	0.014	0.003	0.001	0.006	0.009	0.003	0.029
	(3.831)*	(0.347)	(5.585)*	(5.420)*	(2.120)**	(9.989)*	(4.749)*	(1.953)***	(3.525)*	(7.829)*	(3.026)*	(22.802)*
W	−0.000	−0.000	0.002	0.003	0.002	−0.001	0.001	−0.001	−0.002	0.000	−0.001	0.004
	(−0.272)	(−0.888)	(0.348)	(1.384)	(1.110)	(−0.138)	(0.468)	(−0.633)	(−0.284)	(1.784)***	(−0.682)	(2.485)**
A	0.000	0.000	0.003	−0.001	0.000	−0.003	0.000	−0.001	0.003	0.003	0.000	−0.001
	(0.372)	(0.079)	(1.837)***	(−1.147)	(0.193)	(−1.611)	(0.182)	(−1.310)	(1.506)	(0.972)	(−0.792)	(−0.171)
Size	0.000	−0.002	−0.000	0.000	0.000	0.000	−0.000	−0.000	−0.000	−0.001	−0.001	−0.000
	(1.058)	(−1.209)	(−0.431)	(3.220)*	(1.034)	(1.170)	(−1.263)	(−1.241)	(−1.843)***	(−0.416)	(−0.271)	(−1.865)***
FO	0.002			0.001			0.000			0.923		
	(2.175)**			(1.356)			(0.069)			(1.934)***		
Intercept	0.440	0.741	0.096	0.297	0.527	−0.046	0.186	0.462	−0.008	0.923	1.721	0.041
	(8.865)*	(9.262)*	(1.038)	(4.824)*	(6.122)*	(−0.510)	(3.320)*	(5.038)*	(−0.068)	(9.143)*	(13.388)*	(0.513)
χ^2	15.40*	6.60*	55.22*	60.19*	17.128*	137.04*	65.094*	52.52**	64.850*	96.76*	52.92**	169.00*
N	84	36	48	84	36	48	84	36	48	84	36	48

Note: *, ** and *** refer to t-ratios with statistical significance at 1 per cent, 5 per cent and 10 per cent respectively.
Source: Computed from UNU-MERIT (2004) using E-views package.

Labour productivity and export intensity. Against labour productivity foreign ownership (FO) was statistically significant (at the 5 per cent level), and its coefficient was positive confirming that foreign firms were more productive than local firms (see Table 4). TI was statistically highly significant and its coefficient positive in all the three samples. The higher coefficient in the local sample shows that local firms rely much more on host-site technological intensities to drive productivity than foreign firms. The control variable of age was only statistically significant in the foreign sample. Its negative coefficient shows that newer firms are more productive than older firms.

TI was statistically positively correlated with export intensity in the overall and local firms' samples (see Table 4). Its high statistical significance in the local sample shows that local firms strengthened their technological capabilities to compete in export markets. The lack of a similar result in the foreign sample could be the result of either more low value added goods being exported compared to those sold in domestic markets, or that foreign firms simply access significant levels of their technology from their plants abroad. Age and size (also in the overall sample) were statistically significant in the foreign sample. Larger and newer firms tend to be more export-oriented than smaller and older firms in the foreign sample.

Technological intensities. TI was statistically significant in both the overall (5 per cent level) and local firms' (10 per cent level) sample. The positive coefficient of TI suggests that technological intensity enjoys a positive relationship with exports, namely, firms with higher overall intensities are likely to export. Size was statistically significant in both samples and its coefficient positive demonstrating that larger firms enjoy higher incidence of exporting. Local firms thus face a lower export incidence in India.

FO was statistically significant (at the 10 per cent level) and its coefficient positive in the TI regression confirming the advantage foreign firms have over local firms on technology (see Table 5). Reversing the regression produced similar results as export intensity was positively correlated at the 5 per cent level with TI in the overall and local firms' samples. Local firms exporting have obviously deepened their use of technology to compete in export markets. Skills intensity was also statistically highly significant (1 per cent) and its coefficient positive demonstrating that automotive parts firms in India hire higher shares of human capital when engaged in export-manufacturing. The higher coefficient in the local firms' sample also suggests that local firms rely more on human capital to drive exports. Wages were also statistically significant and their coefficient positive in the overall and local firms' samples. Given the importance of human capital to drive exports it seems logical that local firms also pay higher wages. The insignificance of this relationship in the foreign firms' sample could be a consequence of common wage payments normally followed by foreign firms especially when located in the same place. Interestingly, size was inversely correlated in the local firms' sample demonstrating that SMEs rather than large firms enjoy higher technological intensities.

Against HR, the explanatory variable of X/Y was statistically insignificant in all three samples, demonstrating that human resources development has not been a key determinant of exports (see Table 5). Skills intensity (SI) was statistically highly significant (1 per cent) and its coefficient was positive in the overall and local firms' samples. The presence of human capital has been a major driver of HR development in local firms. The foreign firms' sample failed the model-fit test. Nevertheless, FO was statistically significant (at the 5 per cent level) and its coefficient positive in the overall sample demonstrating that foreign firms enjoy higher HR levels than local firms.

Against PT, the explanatory variable of X/Y was statistically significant in the local firms' sample only (see Table 5). PT regression involving the foreign firms' sample failed the model fit (X^2) test. The positive coefficient of X/Y in the local firms' sample shows that local firms use newer machinery and equipment, more inventory and quality control instruments and invest more on process technology than firms targeting the domestic market. Skills intensity (SI) was statistically highly significant (at the 1 per cent level) in the overall and local firms' samples. Local firms obviously hire more human capital when needed to use more sophisticated process technology.

The RD regression passed the model fit (X^2) test involving all three samples. FO was statistically insignificant in the overall sample. X/Y was statistically significant only in the overall sample and only at the 10 per cent level. Skills intensity was statistically significant (highly in the overall and local firms' samples) and the coefficient positive in all three samples. Clearly human capital is critical in both sets of firms but much more in local firms to drive R&D. This is understandable given that local firms learn and acquire technology whilst foreign firms have the added advantage of transferring their own technology from their foreign plants. Size was inversely correlated at the 10 per cent level in the local firms' sample demonstrating that smaller local firms tend to undertake more R&D activities than larger local firms.

Taken together, foreign firms generally enjoyed higher labour productivity, export intensity, skills intensity, wages and technological intensities than local firms. SI was particularly critical in driving higher technological intensities (TI and its components). Although foreign firms enjoyed higher technological means than local firms, foreign ownership was only statistically significant in the HR regression. Local firms tended to show higher technological intensity levels when competing in export markets. The same was not observed in the foreign firms' sample, which could be a consequence of similar technology used by foreign firms in both the domestic and foreign markets. The statistically significant technological and performance advantage enjoyed by foreign firms over local firms in the face of significant capabilities enjoyed by local firms offers potentially strong room for technology transfer in the automotive parts industry in India.

Conclusions and Implications

Overall, foreign firms enjoyed higher labour productivity, wages, export, skills and technological intensities than local firms in the Indian automotive parts sample. This could be a consequence of foreign firms either acquiring or merging with the better-endowed local firms, or transferring or deepening technology and the consequent positive effect on productivity and export performance. Although most of the firms classified as foreign here are still largely owned by local capital, the foreign influence may have given the fillip for positive developments especially to take advantage of competition and market opening arising from processes of liberalization taking place since 1991. India's rich human capital endowment has offered a good platform for firms – both local and foreign to appropriate benefits from rationalization synergies occurring on the global stage in the automotive industry.

The econometric exercise to establish the determinants showed a strong positive correlation between TI and labour productivity in all three samples. This link obviously supports the evolutionary argument that embodied technology is important in competitiveness as firms with higher technological intensities show higher labour productivity. The higher coefficient of TI in the local sample shows that local firms produce more technological effort at host sites than foreign firms, which is consistent with Dunning's (1974) arguments on asset specific advantages as the latter enjoys access to superior product technology from parent plants. Against XY, TI (on the basis of process technology) was only statistically significant in the local firms' sample demonstrating that local firms deepen their technologies when facing competition in export markets. Foreign ownership was only statistically significant in the HR regression, though, its coefficients were positive in all the technology regressions. Against the technology variables, apart for the HR and PT regressions where the foreign firms' sample failed the model fit test SI was statistically significant. Clearly human capital has been a critical driver of technology intensities in the automotive parts firms in India.

The generally higher performance and technological intensity levels of foreign firms over local firms offer room for technology transfer in the automotive parts industry in India. Consistent with Hirschman's (1958, 1970)arguments, the higher export-orientation of foreign firms also offers strong potential for the development of external market and domestic backward linkages for local firms. India's fairly attractive human capital endowments and large domestic market offers room for pursuing upgrading policies. Government policy should stimulate firms' participation in technological activities but this must be attached to increased exposure to global markets.

Notes

[1] Using a range of economies, Rasiah (2004a, 2004b, 2004c)showed that differences in technological intensities between foreign and local firms also varied with the level of institutional and systemic strength embedding firms.

[2] See Gujarati (1988).

References

Aitken, B. J., Hansen, G. & Harrison, A. (1997) Spillovers, foreign investment and export behavior, *Journal of International Economics*, 43, pp. 103–132.

Aitken, B. J. & Harrison, A. (1999) Do foreign firms benefit from direct foreign investment? Evidence from Venezuela, *American Economic Review*, 89(3), pp. 605–618.

Allen, G. C. & Donnithorne, A. G. (1957) *Western Enterprise in Indonesia and Malaya* (London: Allen & Unwin).

Ariffin, N. & Bell, M. (1999) Firms, politics and political economy: patterns of subsidiary-parent linkages and technological capability-building in electronics TNC subsidiaries in Malaysia, in: K. S. Jomo, G. Felker & R. Rasiah (Eds) *Industrial Technology Development in Malaysia* (London: Routledge).

Bell, M. & Pavitt, K. (1995) The Development of Technological Capabilities, in: I. U. Haque (Ed.) *Trade, Technology and International Competitiveness* (Washington, DC: World Bank).

Blalock, G. (2002) Technology from foreign direct investment: strategic transfer through supply chains. Haas School of Business, Berkeley, mimeo.

Blomström, M. & Kokko, A. (1998) Multinational corporations and spillovers, *Journal of Economic Surveys*, 12(3), pp. 247–277.

Blomström, M. & Persson, H. (1983) Foreign investment and spillover efficiency in an underdeveloped economy: evidence from Mexican manufacutring industry, *World Development*, 11(6), pp. 493–501.

Blomström, M. & Sjoholm, F. (1999) Technology Transfer and Spillovers: Does Local Participation with Multinationals Matter?, *European Economic Review*, 43, pp. 915–923.

Blomström, M. & Wolff, E. (1994) Multinational corporations and productivity convergence in Mexico, in: W. Baumo, R. Nelson & E. Wolff (Eds) *Convergence of Productivity: Cross-National Studies and Historical Evidence* (Oxford: Oxford University Press).

Dosi, G. (1982) Technological paradigms and technological trajectories, *Research policy*, 11(3), pp. 147–162.

Dunning, J. H. (1974) *Economic Analysis and the Multinational Enterprise* (London: Allen & Unwin).

Ernst, D., Ganiatsos, T. & Mytelka, L. (Eds) (1998) *Technological Capabilities and Export Success: Lessons from East Asia* (London: Routledge).

Figueiredo, P. N. (2002) Does technological learning pay off? Inter-firm differences in technological capability accumulation paths and operational performance improvement, *Research Policy*, 31, pp. 73–94.

Greene, W. H. (2002) *Econometric Analysis* (New York: Prentice Hall).

Gujarati, D. (1988) *Basic Econometrics* (New York: McGraw Hill).

Haddad, M. & Harrison, A. (1993) Are there spillovers from direct foreign investment? Evidence from panel data for Morroco, *Journal of Development Economics*, 42, pp. 51–74.

Hirschman, A. O. (1958) *The Strategy of Economic Development* (New Haven, CT: Yale University Press).

Hirschman, A. O. (1970) *Exit, Voice, and Loyalty: Responses to Decline in Firms, Organizations, and State* (Cambridge, MA: Harvard University Press).

Hughes, H. & You, P. S. (Eds) (1969) *Foreign Investment and Industrialisation in Singapore* (Canberra: Australian National University Press).

Hymer, S. (1976) International operation of national firms, doctoral thesis submitted to MIT (1960) (Cambridge: MIT Press).

Kaldor, N. (1979) Equilibrium Theory and Growth Theory, in: M.J. Boskin (Ed) *Economics of Human Welfare: Essays in Honour of Tibor Scitovsky* (New York: Academic Press), pp. 273–291.

Kathuria, V. (2000) Productivity spillovers from technology transfer to Indian manufacturing firms, *Journal of International Development*, 12(2), pp. 343–369.

Kathuria, V. (2001) Foreign firms, technology transfer and knowledge spillovers to indian manufacturing firms: a stochastic frontier analysis, *Applied Economics*, 33(5), pp. 625–642.

Kathuria, V. (2002) Liberalisation, FDI and productivity spillovers – an analysis of Indian manufacturing firms, *Oxford Economic Papers*, 54(4), pp. 688–718.

Kumar, D. & Desai, M. (1983) *Cambridge History of India* (Cambridge: Cambridge University Press).

Kumar, N. (1994) *Multinational Enterprises and Industrial Organization: The Case of India* (New Delhi: Sage).

Kumar, N. (2002) *Globalization and the Quality of Foreign Direct Investment* (New Delhi: Oxford University Press).

Lall, S. (1979) The international allocation of research activity by U.S. multinationals, *Oxford Bulletin of Economics and Statistics*, 41, pp. 313–331.

Lall, S. (1984) Determinants of R&D in an LDC: the Indian engineering industry, *Economic Letters*, 13(4), pp. 379–383.

Lall, S. (1992) Technological capabilities and industrialization, *World Development*, 20(2), pp. 165–186.

Lall, S. & Streeten, P. (1977) *Foreign Investment, Transnationals and Developing Countries* (Basingstoke: Macmillan).

Marx, K. (1853) The British rule in India, *New York Daily Tribune*, 10 June, pp. 1–3.

Nelson, R. R. (1994) What has been the matter with Neoclassical Growth Theory?, in: G. Silverberg & L. Soete (Eds) *The Economics of Growth and Technical Change* (Cheltenham: Edward Elgar).

Pavitt, K. (1984) Sectoral patterns of technical change: towards a taxonomy and a theory, *Research Policy*, 13(6), pp. 343–73.

Rasiah, R. (1994) Flexible production systems and local machine tool subcontracting: electronics transnationals in Malaysia, *Cambridge Journal of Economics*, 18(3), pp. 279–298.

Rasiah, R. (1995) *Foreign Capital and Industrialization in Malaysia* (Basingstoke: Macmillan).

Rasiah, R. (2004a) *Foreign Firms, Technological Capabilites and Economic Performance: Evidence from Africa, Asia and Latin America* (Cheltenham: Edward Elgar).

Rasiah, R. (2004b) Technological capabilities and export performance: a study of foreign and local electronics firms in Philippines, Malaysia and Thailand, *The European Journal of Development Research*, 16(3), pp. 581–616.

Rasiah, R. (2004c) Technological intensities in East and Southeast Asian electronics firms: does network strength matter?, *Oxford Development Studies*, 32(3), pp. 433–455.

Romer, P. M. (1994) The origins of endogenous growth, *Journal of Economic Perspectives*, 8(1), pp. 3–22.

UNU-Merit (2004) Survey coordinated by Rajah Rasiah, Maastricht.

Vaitsos, C. V. (2003) Growth theories revisited: enduring questions with changing answers. INTECH Discussion Paper No. 9, Maastricht, October.

Warren, B. (1973) Imperialism and capitalist industrialization, *New Left Review*, 81, pp. 3–44.

Warren, B. (1980) *Imperialism: Pioneer of Capitalism* (London: Verso).

Westphal, L. E., Kritayakirana, K., Petchsuwan, K., Sutabutr, H. & Yuthavong, Y. (1990) The development of technological capability in manufacturing: a macroscopic approach to policy research, in: R. E. Evenson & G. Ranis (Eds) *Science and Technology: Lessons for Development Policy* (London: Intermediate Technology Publications).

Wignaraja, G. (2002) Firm size, Technological Capabilities and Market-oriented policies in Mauritius, *Oxford Development Studies*, 30(3), pp. 307–315.

Appendix: Correlation Coefficient Matrix of Automotive Parts Firms, India Sample, 2002

	X/Y	TI	RD	HRD	PT	AGE	FO
X/Y	1.000	0.244	0.203	0.161	0.174	−0.104	−0.048
TI	0.244	1.000	0.612*#	0.751*#	0.828*#	0.033	0.238
RD	0.203	0.612*#	1.000	0.188	0.198	−0.036	0.125
HRD	0.161	0.751*#	0.188	1.000	0.528*	0.118	0.237
PT	0.174	0.828*#	0.198	0.528*	1.000	0.005	0.285
AGE	−0.104	0.033	−0.036	0.118	0.005	1.000	0.224
FO	−0.048	0.238	0.125	0.237	0.285	0.224	1.000

Note: * – too high correlation; # – compositional problem.
Source: Computed using E-views 5 package using data collected from UNU-MERIT (2004) Survey.

Malaysia's National Automotive Policy and the Performance of Proton's Foreign and Local Vendors

MOHAMAD ROSLI & FATIMAH KARI

Introduction

The first national automotive project was inaugurated in 1981 following the formation of the Heavy Industry Corporation of Malaysia (HICOM). The first Proton cars rolled out in 1985. In addition to the provision of preferential loans, Proton's development was also assisted by the introduction of the vendor development programme in the late 1980s by the government. Various stimulatory and protective measures were also offered to the local suppliers to save them from too much exposure to external competition. Local suppliers were also allowed to supply foreign assemblers operating in the country, while the introduction of the country's second national car, that is, Perodua in the 1990s as well as other local companies helped boost domestic demand for the further expansion of local suppliers.

Although Malaysia continues to protect its automobile industry against the conditions contained in the Trade related Investment Measures (TRIMs) agreement of the World Trade Organization (WTO), the inclusion of automotives under the common effective preferential tariffs (CEPT) under the Association of South East Asian Nations (ASEAN) Free Trade Area (AFTA) process has brought increasing pressure for the removal of localization-based tariff protection facing automotives and parts production in the country (see Rasiah, 2005). Hence, the increasing scrutiny on protection and other forms of preferential treatment has shifted the focus towards performance levels. Put simply, have local suppliers become competitive to remain in production once the umbrella shielding them is removed? One way of answering this question is to compare the performance levels of local and foreign supplier firms in the country. Recent reports show that local suppliers lack internal technological and managerial capabilities.

Hence, this study attempts to compare the performance of Proton's local and foreign automotive parts suppliers. The rest of the contribution is organized as follows. The second section discusses government policies and projects targeted at the development of Proton and its suppliers. The third section reviews the related literature on performance. The fourth section introduces the methodology used to evaluate the performance of local and foreign suppliers. The fifth section discusses the results. The sixth section finishes with the conclusions.

Government Support Programmes

The automotive industry consists of three types of manufacturing activities, namely, components, completely knocked down (CKD) pieces and completely built up (CBU) units. The decentralization of automobile assembly initially saw the outsourcing of only component assembly. Recent developments have led to the outsourcing of even CKDs so that specialized car manufacturers relying on modularized production systems simply specialize on CBUs. In this system CKD assembly is either undertaken by sister factories or simply outsourced to independent contract manufacturers. Torri (1991: 389) had identified the stages of localization a country typically undergoes in automotive production: 1) import and sale of completely-build-up (CBU) automobiles; 2) assembly of imported completely-knocked-down (CKD) parts and localization of automotive parts; 3) local production of materials for cars and components; and 4) local design of automotive bodies and other components. Using the above categorization it can be argued that Malaysia has already entered the third and fourth stages. Torri (1991: 389) also divided the localization of automotive parts into three stages, namely i) replacement automotive parts, or components; ii) original equipment manufacturer (OEM) automotive parts for automotive assembly; and (iii) major and functional automotive parts (OEM), such as engine and transmission components. This study focuses on both component assembly (for example, pistons) as well as CKD assembly (for example, air-conditioning systems). This section discusses government policy targeted at the development of Proton and supplier activities.

The National Car Project

The first national car project was realized with the establishment of Perusahaan Otomobil Nasional (PROTON) in 1983. The first national car, the Proton Saga, rolled out from the plant in Batu 3, Shah Alam, Selangor in 1985. Proton now produces a number of car models and variants, including the Iswara, Perdana, Wira, Satria, Putra, Waja and most recently, the GEN-2 and Satria Neo. The latest models, as reported, use Malaysian developed engines through collaboration between Proton and its subsidiary, Lotus (United Kingdom).

The second national car project followed with the establishment of PERODUA in 1992. Its two wholly-owned subsidiaries, Perodua Manufacturing Sdn. Bhd. and Perodua Sales Sdn. Bhd; were set up to carry out manufacturing and distribution activities respectively. Its manufacturing plant is located in Sungai Choh, Mukim Serendah, Rawang, Selangor. With the successful launch of its first car, the Perodua Kancil, in 1994, PERODUA now produces various models and variants that include small to medium passenger cars and the two multi-utility-vehicles (MUV), namely vans and jeeps.

To date, besides PROTON and PERODUA, Malaysia has two other national status carmakers,[1] namely Industri Otomotif Komersial (M) Sdn. Bhd (INOKOM) and Malaysian Truck and Bus Sdn. Bhd. (MTB). There are also ten non-national car assemblers and three composite body sports car manufacturers in the country who manufacture or assemble a wide range of makes and models (MIDA, 2004). About 80 per cent of the total automotive production (both passenger and commercial vehicles) in 2002 was contributed by the four national carmakers. Proton and Perodua together produced 47 per cent and 29 per cent respectively of the total car production in the country.

Stimulatory and Protective Measures

The development of the Malaysian automotive industry is heavily contingent upon the undivided support of the government. Various stimulatory and protective measures, such as investment incentives, a local content policy, and tariff and non-tariff barriers were implemented to stimulate the development of both local automotive and parts production. Proton in particular is a unique case in point owing to its status as the first national project.

To date, the largest shareholders in Proton are still government-controlled agencies, namely Khazanah Nasional Berhad (42.7 per cent), the Employees Provident Fund (12.6 per cent), and Petronas (9.8 per cent). Temasek Holdings Pte. Ltd, a Singapore investment arm emerged as a new shareholder with a 5 per cent holding. The equity structure of the second national car project, that is, Perodua, is still dominated by local investors with 71.6 per cent of shares, while the rest (28.4 per cent) are held by Daihatsu Motor Co. Ltd. and Mitsui & Co (Japan). However, Daihatsu and Mitsui hold 51 per cent equity in Perodua's subsidiary, namely, Perodua Auto Corp Sdn. Bhd. – which handles the two core operation units, namely Perodua Manufacturing Sdn. Bhd. and Perodua Engine Manufacturing Sdn. Bhd.

The government has also provided generous incentives under the 1986 Promotion of Investment Act. Among them, the Pioneer Status and Investment Tax Allowance are the two most lucrative tax incentives granted to firms involved in promoted activities or products that are, from time to time, determined by the Ministry of International Trade and Industry (MITI). The eligibility for incentives for the automotive industry is classified under the transport equipment, components and accessories items.[2]

High tariffs characterized the first national car project in the mid-1980s until the turn of the millennium. However, concomitant with the agreements under the ASEAN Free Trade Area (AFTA), a series of revisions on import duties has been carried out since 2004. Effective from 1 January 2004, a significant reduction in import duties on all types and variants of CBU and CKD vehicles across regions (ASEAN and non-ASEAN) was seen under the new tax structure. However, the decrease in the import duties was overwhelmed by the increase in excise duties. While the excise duties on CKD increased slightly, the charges on CBU vehicles augmented exorbitantly. More interestingly, vehicles with a capacity of less than 1,800cc have lower excise taxes imposed on them tandem with Malaysia's concentration on the production of small and medium national cars. In line with the National Automotive Policy (NAP) which was announced in March 2006, the latest tax structure has offered a slight decline in the excise duties and a further reduction of the import duties on ASEAN CBU (from 20 per cent to 15 per cent), and non-ASEAN CBU (from 50 per cent to 30 per cent). However, import duties on ASEAN CKD (0 per cent) and non-ASEAN CKD (10 per cent) have remained.[3]

Non-tariff barriers, such as licensing and import quotas (Approved Permits), are still applied on the automotive industry. The first import licensing requirement for all distributors and dealers was introduced in 1966. In 1967, manufacturing licences were issued to several firms for the assembly of passenger and commercial vehicles. Import licensing at the early stage was confined to imported CBU vehicles, but it was extended to CKD vehicles in the later period. To overcome overcapacity in the domestic automotive market, the National Automotive Policy (NAP) has recently stopped the issuance of new manufacturing licences, while at the same time it has been encouraging the assemblers to use the existing excess capacity of their assembly lines.

A 10 per cent import quota was imposed on CBU passenger cars and commercial vehicles from 1989 to 1990. Starting from 1991, the quota was reduced by 1 per cent a year to 5 per cent by 1995 (MACPMA, 1996). For commercial vehicles, the quota is equally applied between dual purpose vehicles (7–9 seater vehicles) and other types of commercial vehicles. The NAP aims to phase out Approved Permits (APs), including those for second-hand vehicles (except for personal use) by 31 December 2010. In the interim, APs will be given only to assemblers whose production of certain models is significant for the export market, but they are conditional upon the import of models complementary to their product range for the local market. This privilege will also be offered to a limited number of vehicles not assembled in Malaysia.

A local content requirement policy was also introduced to protect the national automotive industry. In this connection, the 1980 Mandatory Deletion Programme prohibits local car producers, or franchisors from importing all automotive parts and components listed as 'mandatory deleted components' for use in local automotive assembly. The local content policy was tied to tax incentives in 1992, requiring all automotive assemblers or manufacturers to meet new minimum local content targets of between 45 to 60 per cent by 1996 subject to the engine capacity of automobiles (Abdulsomad, 2003).

The mandatory deleted components comprised 13 items for motorcycles and 30 items for passenger and commercial vehicles (MIDA, n.d.). Among other unlisted items for vehicles were air filters, batteries, carpets and underlay, coil springs, exhaust systems, fuel tanks, radiators, seats, spark plugs, tyres, wiper motors, and wire harnesses (MACPMA, 1996). In 2002, the local items constituted 50 to 80 per cent in the Proton cars, 35 to 65 per cent in the Perodua cars, and 35 to 65 per cent in other vehicles (MIDA, 2004). The calculation of the reported local content is based on gross value – the percentage would be much lower if the calculation is based on net value due to the fact that most semi-processed materials (such as steel and plastic) to make parts are imported.

In the case where an assembler purposely used such imported items, the cost of the imported parts was deducted from the approved 'net selling price' of the assembled automobiles (MACPMA, 1996). Some exceptional cases to the regulation are provided only if the Joint Technical Committee on Local Content (JTCLC) chaired by the Chairman of the Malaysian Automotive Components Parts Manufacturers' Association (MACPMA) is satisfied that locally available components are not suitable for a particular car model.

Following AFTA initiatives, the government had begun phasing out local content requirements from 1 January 2002 with the initial removal of 11 items from the Mandatory Deleted Items List (MDIL). By the end of December 2003, the remaining 19 items contained in the MDIL were removed (MIDA, 2004); this move should provide more room for carmakers or assemblers to do multi-sourcing of automotive parts and components. The Promotion of Investment Act 1986, however, offers lucrative tax exemptions under the Pioneer Status and Investment Tax Allowance for the manufacture of various parts and components. All small firms which produce any types of automotive components and accessories are eligible for the Pioneer Status (MIDA, 1998).

Vendor Development Programme

The government introduced the Vendor Development Programme (VDP) to create greater linkages and integration between small and medium enterprises (SMEs), and large firms and multinational corporations (MNCs), and financial institutions. In December 1988, the first VDP was implemented by Proton through the Proton Component Scheme to develop SMEs as vendors (suppliers) of intermediate and capital goods, as well as services to PROTON. It was also in line with the export requirement under the Generalised System of Preference (GSP) of developed countries that local end products should contain at least 60 per cent local content. Some foreign firms operating in Malaysia were also appointed as new vendors to speed up the achievement of the GSP requirement (Anazawa, 1997). Perodua has undertaken a similar vendor development programme since the early 1990s (MIDA, n.d.).

There is an exclusive programme under the Proton Component Scheme that is known as the Proton Bumiputera Vendor Scheme. It is specially designed for nurturing Bumiputera[4] vendors in the auto-component industry. Many Bumiputera vendors, under the scheme, were granted financial facilities through the Proton Technical Assistance Programme for purchasing capital goods and intermediate inputs, as well as for acquiring technology. Bumiputera vendors could also participate in the Quality Improvement Programme (QIP) organized by SIRIM with potential grants provided by the Industrial Technical Assistance Fund (ITAF).

Proton has been one of the key drivers of the VDP. It was reported that the local content in Proton cars has increased steadily since the launch of VDP: from 18 per cent in 1985 to 40 per cent in 1987, 70 per cent in 1989 (Meyanathan and Ismail, 1994), and 80 per cent in 1992 (Abdul Rahman, 1994). Total vendors of Proton increased from merely 17 in 1985 to 134 in 1994 and 186 in 1999, of which 80 per cent were members of the Proton Vendor Association supplying over 3,000 automotive components (MITI, 1994). The total number of vendors registered with Proton reached 284 in 2005, of which about half are members of the Proton Vendor Association (PVA, 2005). About 50 per cent of the suppliers were SMEs and 50 per cent of these SMEs were Bumiputera-owned (Mohd Shah, 1995). The vendors produced the original equipment manufactured (OEM) parts and components, such as metal stamped and pressed parts, plastic injection moulded parts, wire harnesses, wipers, lamps, radio cassettes and air-conditioners (MIDA, unpublished).

In 2004, the total value of component parts and accessories manufactured in Malaysia reached about RM5.19 billion, but the import of automotive parts, such as engines, transmissions and automotive electronic components amounted to about RM7.2 billion during the same year.[5] The import-supply deficit involved obviously show that automotive parts and component makers in the country still have room to expand production. There were 350 component manufacturers (both local and foreign) supplying the automotive industry in 2005.[6]

Literature Review

There is a great deal of literature on performance analysis of both the individual firm as well as the industry as a whole. At the company level, performance can be defined as the ability of a firm to deliver outcomes in a priori determined dimensions in relation to a set of targets as required by its owners, stakeholders or managers in order to achieve desired profit goals and strategies (Simons, 1999). Performance measurement is usually used to track position, communicate performance, verify priorities and improve performance (Neely, 1998). It can also be used 'as strategy formulation and communication of goals, information for decision making and motivation for employees' (Schmitz & Platts, 2003: 719); and more importantly this can be applied for comparing the present position and performance of one firm to another.

Performance measurement appears in many different forms. Derived from the resource-based model, Coplin (2002) highlights three performance indicators, that is, market, sales and financial performance. Tvorik & McGivern (1997) in their study of organizational performance adopted two types of measurement, namely, economic values (return on sales and return on invested capital) and organizational indicators (return on assets and return on investments). Garrigos-Simon *et al.* (2005) in their study of Spanish hospitality firms used four performance indicators, namely profitability (return on assets, return on investment and return on sales), growth (in sales, market share increase, and wealth creation), stakeholder satisfaction, and competitive position. McNamee *et al.* (1999) in their study of Irish small business used two performance measurements: growth (in sales volume and employment) and profitability (return on assets, return on sales, profit per employee). Powers & Hahn (2002) in their study of the banking industry in New England only used one indicator, return on assets (ROA), to compare the performance of 98 banks. Abu Kasim *et al.* (1989) found that local and foreign firms operating in Malaysia preferred using financial (sales, sales growth, contribution margin, gross margin and cash flow) and non-financial indicators (quality of product, market share, throughput rate and labour productivity) to measure their firms' performance.

Several measures of determinants of a firm's performance are also used in the literature. Traditionally, industrial organization exponents argue that a firm's performance is determined by the conduct (strategies) of firms in the market, which is in turn influenced by the structure of the market (Ferguson, 1993). Market structure refers to the composition or characteristics of individual markets in the economy, such as the number and size of buyers and sellers (market concentration), the extent of product differentiation, the extent of entry and exit barriers, and the extent of firms' integration or decentralization. In other words, it reflects the environment within which firms operate in a particular market, which then influences the behaviour or action of the firms, either to work independently or collectively in determining price, as well as doing advertisements and research. This conduct will ultimately determine firms' performance, whether they are productively efficient (avoiding wasteful use of scarce resources) or allocatively efficient (producing the right goods in the right quantities) as reflected, amongst others, by their profitability. According to Rogers (2000), the structure-conduct-performance (SCP) approach asserts that the higher the level of industry or market concentration (as measured by a firm's or a group of firms' market share), the higher the profitability would be or vice versa. Bothwell *et al.* (1984) reveal that there are six factors contributing to different levels of a firm's profitability, that is, the different levels of a firm's concentration, both a firm's concentration and barriers to entry, a firm's efficiency or innovativeness, risk differentials, advertising intensity, and a firm's growth.

More specifically, there are two competing hypotheses in the SCP paradigm, namely, the traditional 'structure performance hypothesis' and 'efficient structure hypothesis' (Shapiro, 1983). The former argues that the market concentration (such as sales concentration) has a positive impact on the performance of the firm (irrespective of the degree of efficiency of the firm). In contrast, the latter holds that the performance of the firm is positively related to its efficiency. Market concentration which emerges from a competition would enable the firms with a low cost structure to increase their profits by reducing prices and expanding market shares. As such, firms that are more efficient will have better performance. This efficient structure hypothesis would be supported if the firm's market efficiency has a positive impact on its performance (regardless of the degree of concentration in the market).

Several arguments exist to explain company-level performance. Rogoff *et al.* (2004) assert that internal and external factors determine business success or performance. Internal factors are those that could be controlled by the firm itself, whilst external factors are beyond the control of a firm and are determined by the environment, such as government policy, the economy and competition (see also Rasiah, 2004: Figure 1). Wijewardena & Tibbits (1999) in their comprehensive literature review found that a firm's performance is determined by individual entrepreneurs, company-specific characteristics and external factors. Recent strategic management studies stress that company-specific factors are more important in determining a firm's performance (McGahan & Porter, 1997). Ownership structure as one of the company-specific characteristics strongly influences a firm's performance for two reasons. Firstly, differences in identity, concentration and resource endowments among different owners would determine their relative power, incentives and ability to monitor managers; and secondly, different owners with dissimilar goals would bring about different influences on a firm's performance (Douma *et al.*, 2003).

The literature on the relationship between ownership by nationality and a firm's performance is extremely limited. Kiggundu (2002) found that nationality or ethnicity did matter. He found that Chinese, East Indian, Lebanese, as well as Koreans, Japanese, Chinese and Indians who operated in Europe and North America were more successful, whilst the less successful were the African blacks, Afro-Americans and Russians. Ramachandran & Shah (1999) in their comparative study in Kenya, Tanzania, Zambia and Zimbabwe found that European and Indian-owned firms performed better than the African blacks. Among other factors which contributed to the low performance of the blacks were their low level of formal education and lack of business networks.

Companies with foreign corporate shareholdings are endowed with superior technical, organizational, financial and managerial resources, as they have technical collaboration, foreign directors on the boards, consultancy and marketing arrangements, trademarks, patent and managerial resource sharing and are associated with a higher degree of technology transfer and better business links (see Douma *et al.*, 2003) which influence a firm's performance positively. Shapiro (1983) also stresses that foreign subsidiaries possess advantages over local firms in terms of access to patents, trade-marks and brand names, technology and pools of managerial talent, as well as the ability to reduce transaction costs through market internalization. Willmore (1986) found that the foreign firms reached higher performance levels in many indicators than the local firms in Brazil because multinational corporations often had advantages in brand names, proprietary technology and links to overseas markets.

This study thus uses the SCP framework to compare performance levels of foreign and local suppliers linked to Proton, and to establish the determinants if statistically significant differences exist. Given the paucity of data the choice of proxies used to represent structure and conduct is not exhaustive.

Methodology and Data

This section presents the methodology used to examine the impact of structure and conduct of Proton's suppliers by foreign and local ownership patterns.

Data Collection

The economic and the financial ratio data used in this study were obtained from the Proton Vendors' Directory, 2005 and the Companies Commission of Malaysia respectively. This study assigned different categories of the suppliers with numerical coding of 1 for local suppliers and 2 for foreign suppliers. Such 'numeric ranking' was chosen just for easy data management or problem recognition and it had nothing to do with the order of importance or weight and scale of the two groups. The F-test is used to examine the difference between the following univariate null and alternative hypotheses for each discriminant variable:

$$H_0 : \mu_1 = \mu_2$$
$$H_1 : \mu_1 \neq \mu_2$$

μ_1 *and* μ_2 are population means for groups 1 and 2 respectively. In this connection, it was hypothesized that there is no significant difference (H_0) in the performance between the local and foreign suppliers. The H_0 for the variables will be rejected at the significance level of 0.05 per cent.

Model Specification

The performance of the local and foreign suppliers was evaluated using financial ratios and economic variables which formed the discriminant function between foreign and local suppliers. These variables were defined and constructed for the analysis as follows:

(1) Turnover (sales volume for the 2004 financial year);
(2) Martshar (market share is the share of each supplier in total sales of the industry which amounted to RM5.19 billion in 2004);
(3) 3 ... Pas (profit attributes to shareholders);
(4) Netdivid (net dividend);
(5) Ebitta (earnings before interest and tax);
(6) Gps (gross profit/sales);
(7) Curatio (current liability-current asset ratio);
(8) ROA (rate of return on assets)
(9) Profempl (profit per employee as a proxy of labour productivity); and
(10) Sizemplo (number of labour employed).
(11) The study does not make any prior assumptions, as to which is the best set of discriminant variables. Properties of the statistical test in discriminant analysis are derived by making a number of assumptions. The assumptions are multivariate normality, homoscedasticity and collinearity of the independent variables. The stepwise procedure employed the Wilks' Lambda (λ) as the basis to select variables that would form the discriminant function. Thus, the unstandardized discriminant function can be calculated as:

$$Z_1 = w_1{}^* X_1 + w_2 X_2 + w_3 X_3 + \ldots w_n X_n \quad (2)$$

Equation (1) represents a linear combination of the economic and financial ratio ($X_1 \ldots X_n$) for the suppliers. Thus, the objective of the analysis is to identify the weights of $w_1 \ldots w_n$, of Equation (1) that will also maximize Equation (2):

$$Z_1 = w_1{}^* \, Turnover + w_2 Martshar + w_3 Pas + w_4 Netdivid + w_5 Ebitta + w_6 Gps$$
$$+ w7Curatio + w_8 Profempl + w_9 Roa + w_{10} Sizeemplo$$

Based on Equation (2), a discriminant analysis is performed using groups (foreign and locally owned suppliers) as the dependent variables and the various economic and financial ratio performance indexes such as turnover, market share, total assets, fixed assets, net dividends and profit as the independent variables. At each step, the variable that minimizes the overall Wilks' λ is entered. A stepwise estimation method is used and under this procedure, the process of estimating the discriminant function is indicated when the independent variables are entered sequentially according to the discriminatory power and they add to the discriminant function(s) (Hall, 1981).

Consequentially, the objective of the analysis is to identify the minimum discriminant functions that will provide most of the discrimination among the groups (foreign suppliers and locally-owned suppliers). In this regard, discriminant analysis is used to predict the grouping of the two groups based on the specific features of the suppliers. The disciminant function is used as this technique can help the analysis in terms of: a) describing major differences among the two groups; and b) classifying subjects into groups on the basis of a set of performance measures (Stevens, 1986: 320). As such, the major differences among the groups are revealed through the use of uncorrelated linear combinations of the original values, that is, the discriminant functions. Since the discriminant functions are uncorrelated, they yield an additional partitioning between the groups (Stevens, 1986: 258).

Analysis of the Findings

This section discusses both the descriptive and inferential statistics making comparisons of the results between foreign and local suppliers.

Table 1. Proton's automotive suppliers by ownership, 2004

Ownership	Frequency	%
Local suppliers	78	78.8
Foreign suppliers	21	21.2
Total	99	100.0

Source: Based on data from the Proton Vendor's Directory (2005).

Descriptive Statistics

There were more local than foreign firms supplying Proton in 2004 (see Table 1) but there existed little statistically significant size differences between the two sets of firms (see Table 2). There were more large firms than small and medium firms among both local and foreign suppliers.

Inferential Statistics

As shown in Table 3 – which present the results of univariate analysis – the F-test reveals that all the variables but the Gps, Curatio Roa, Profempl & Sizemplo display significant differences between the group means. In other words, the null hypothesis (H_0) is rejected to indicate significant performance differences between local and foreign suppliers for the economic and financial indicators – including turnover, Martshar, Pas, Netdivid & Ebitta.

Table 4 shows that the first variable entering the model was PAS and it was sequentially followed by the other variables. Note that the Wilks' λ statistics decreased as each step was computed. Given this method, it generates one function which also indicates a high degree of significance, while the discriminant variables in Table 4 were Pas, Ebitta, Turnover, Curatio, Gps, Roa, Sizemplo & Profempl. Note that the criteria to enter or remove the variables from the function is based on Wilks'λ and the tolerance level of 0.001. The structure matrix gives the loading or the correlations between original variables and the discriminant score as shown in Table 5.

The empirical evidence from Table 4 is consistent with the SCP paradigm which emphasizes both the structure performance and efficient structure hypotheses as discussed by Shapiro (1983), Bahram *et al.* (1991), Gerard (1999), Keith (1997), and Kari *et al.* (2002). The performance indicators, such as turnovers (Turnover) and profits (Pas) are directly affected by the possible size of the larger market share and hence economies of scale or market efficiency as enjoyed by the foreign suppliers as they were predominantly involved in higher value-added (and hence higher prices) automotive parts production (Rosli, 2004).

The other financial ratios such as Roa, Curatio, Gps and Ebitta remain important in assessing the performance of the local and foreign suppliers.

Table 2. Ownership by firm size, 2004

Ownership	Small and medium	Large
Local suppliers	32	46
	(76.2)	(80.7)
Foreign suppliers	10	11
	(23.8)	(19.3)
Total	42	57
	(100.0)	(100.0)

Note: Small and medium suppliers are those firms with up to 150 full-time employees; and large suppliers are those firms with more than 150 full-time employees.
Chi-square is not significant, $p \leq 0.05$.
Source: Computed from data from the Proton Vendor's Directory (2005).

Table 3. Comparative performance of local and foreign suppliers

Variables	Local mean	Foreign mean	Total mean	Wilks' lambda	F	Sig.
Turnover	66.94	165.99	88.80	.914	8.687	.004
Martshar	1.29	3.19	1.69	.915	8.578	.004
Pas	1.73	8.62	3.18	.852	16.770	.000
Netdivid	0.82	5.03	1.71	.887	13.03	.000
Ebitta	0.07	0.230	0.01	.858	15.344	.000
Gps	0.04	0.088	0.05	.971	2.745	.101
Curatio	6.32	9.83	7.06	.999	.135	.714
Roa	0.07	0.05	.007	.995	.482	.489
Profempl	0.01	0.01	0.01	1.000	.002	.967
Sizemplo	1.58	1.55	1.57	.999	.085	.771

Source: Computed from data from the Proton Vendor's Directory (2005).

Similarly, all of these ratios represent the risk factors among the suppliers which eventually affect their profit margins. The mean for Curatio is relatively larger for the foreign suppliers than that of the locals. In other words, foreign suppliers are more likely to stay afloat when faced with a crisis when compared to the local suppliers. Based on the mean Curatio of 6.32 for local suppliers and 9.82 for the foreign counterparts, the latter are more able to pay up to 0.90 cents for every Malaysian Ringgit borrowed compared to only 0.60 cents for local suppliers. The same ratio could also indicate the short-term obligations of both supplier groups, especially their ability to pay up a short-term debt or interest rates on bank loans. Nevertheless, there is a significant difference in the means for the two groups in Ebitta, Netdivid, and Pas as shown in Table 3. As these financial variables were related to profits recorded by both sets of firms, it indicates that firm performance is strongly influenced by market shares as well as cost efficiencies of the firms (Bothwell *et al.*, 1984). Given that both foreign and local firms face similar markets with proton being the prime buyer the results obviously show that the former are either more efficient or engaged in production of higher value added

Table 4. Variables constituting the discriminant function

		Wilks' λ	
Step	Entered	Statistics	Significance
1	Pas	.854	.000
2	Turnover	.818	.000
3	Sizemplo	.776	.000
4	Ebitta	.759	.000
5	Curatio	.753	.000
6	Profempl	.738	.000
7	Gps	.736	.001
8	Roa	.748	.000

Source: Computed from data from the Proton Vendor's Directory (2005).

Table 5. Structure matrix

Variables	Function 1
Pas	0.692
Ebitta	0.672
Turnover	0.511
Gps	0.287
Curatio	0.064
Profempl	−0.051
Roa	−0.120
Sizemplo	0.007

Note: Pooled within-groups correlations between discriminant variables and standardized canonical discriminant functions. Variables are ordered by absolute size of correlation within function.
Source: Computed from the data from the Proton Vendor's Directory (2005).

components, or both compared to local firms. An empirical study on technologies used controlling for products is recommended to establish this point.

Higher performance of the foreign suppliers vis-à-vis the local ones could be related to the competitive advantages enjoyed by the former. According to Anazawa (1997), parent firms are eager to transfer technology to their wholly-owned subsidiaries. This is also true for the foreign suppliers in the Malaysian automotive industry which were appointed as new suppliers to Proton in order to fulfil the 60 per cent local content requirement imposed by the government at the end of the 1980s. This technology transfer was materialized when parent firms in the home country, Japan, sent their managers and engineers to their subsidiaries. On the contrary, there are claims that until recently the local automotive parts suppliers lacked company-specific capabilities to raise efficiency levels. They still lack design capability, manufacturing, engineering and skilled manpower and hence this explains that they spend little on quality control, automation and product testing.

Conclusions and Implications

This study compared the performance of foreign and local suppliers registered under Proton's supplier directory. The results allow the rejection of the null hypothesis that there are no significant performance differences between the local and foreign suppliers. It was found that the performance of the local suppliers fell short of the foreign suppliers both in the economic and financial variables. This empirical finding confirms the general belief that local suppliers lack the capabilities to compete effectively with foreign suppliers in the automotive industry in Malaysia.

From a practical viewpoint, the local suppliers need to give more attention to their market share, internal efficiency, and other firm-specific advantages in order to ensure their success when all preferential treatment is removed. Because it is more costly and difficult to acquire new production and process technologies from foreign firms efforts must be taken by local suppliers to either develop these machinery and equipment in-house or establish collaborative links with other local machinery and equipment suppliers to fabricate them for them (Rosli, 2004). In addition to absorbing best practice methods and technology local suppliers must establish strategic alliances to corner larger market shares to appropriate economies of scale and scope in their production runs to raise throughput efficiency levels

As the market dynamics represent a process that will affect the performance of the suppliers, it remains crucial for the suppliers to remain 'financially healthy' in order to sustain the economic objectives of the industry. While profitability, risk and liability factors continue to reflect supplier performance, these dimensions could be severely altered once other macroeconomic and trade-related factors change. Any assistance provided by the government, on the other hand, should gear towards increasing competitiveness of the local suppliers. The focus should be on shifting support to small and medium scale firms, and R&D expenditure so that these elements are compliant with WTO agreements and the AFTA process.

Local suppliers should also expect to face greater competition following further liberalization expected under the AFTA and WTO processes. The growing size of the automotive market in Malaysia and ASEAN is expected to attract more foreign suppliers. While the increased competition augurs well for the development of a wider range of automotive parts in ASEAN unless local suppliers upgrade foreign suppliers will become the prime beneficiaries of this expansion.

Last but not least, it needs to be stressed that some of the conclusions derived from this study should be interpreted with caution given the limitations of the secondary data used. Future research should employ primary data so that more focus could be given to the factors that contribute to the performance differences between the local and foreign automotive parts suppliers.

Notes

[1] National carmakers refer to the automobile companies initiated by the Malaysian government under the Heavy Industrial Policy launched in the early 1980s. Each project or company is a joint venture with foreign companies but dominated by the locals, particularly the government, through their majority shareholdings. Thus, non-national assemblers refer to the producers of vehicles other than the national.

[2] See the website for the Malaysian Industrial Development Authority, available at http://www.mida.gov.my.

[3] See the website for the Office of the Prime Minister of Malaysia, available at http://www.pmo.gov.my.

[4] The term Bumiputera refers to ethnic Malays who are Muslim by religion and the natives of Malaysia.

[5] See the website for the Malaysian Industrial Development Authority, available at http://www.mida.gov.my.

[6] Ibid.

References

Abdul Rahman, A. A. (1994) Nurturing of Bumiputera SMIs through PROTON's vendor scheme: a case of tracoma, in: H. Fujio (Ed.) *The Development of Bumiputera Enterprizes and Sino-Malay Economic Cooperation in Malaysia*, pp. 19–39 (Tokyo: Institute of Developing Economies).

Abdulsomad, K. (2003) *Building Technological Capabilities of Local Auto Parts Firms under Contrasting Industrial Policies: A Comparative Study of Malaysia and Thailand 1960–2000*, Lund Studies in Economic History, 27 (Stockholm: Almqvist & Wiksell International).

Abu Kasim, N. A., Minai, B. & Loo, S. C. (1989) Performance measures in Malaysia – the state-of-the-art, *Malaysian Management Review*, 24(3), pp. 3–9.

Anazawa, M. (1997) Technology transfer in the automobile industry in Malaysia: PROTON and vendors, *Economic Review*, 47(4), pp. 119–154.

Bahram, A., Chow, G. & Gritta, R. (1991) Market structure, profits in the airline industry, *Atlantic Economic Journal*, 19, pp. 98–102.

Bothwell, J. L., Cooley, T. F. & Hall, E. H. (1984) The new view of the market structure-performance debate, *The Journal of Industrial Economics*, 32(4), pp. 397–417.

Companies Commission of Malaysia, Commercial company data.

Coplin, L. C. H. (2002) Competitive advantages and the SMEs: The role of distinctive competences as determinants of success: are there differences across gender, sector, and size? Ph.D. thesis, Universitat Autonoma De Barcelona, Spain.

Douma, S., George, R. & Kabir, R. (2003) Foreign and domestic ownership, business groups and firm performance: evidence from a large emerging market. Available at the Social Science Research Network, http://papers.ssrn.com

Ferguson, P. R. (1993) *Industrial Economics: Issues and Perspectives* (Hong Kong: Macmillan).

Garrigos-Simon, F. J., Marques, D. & Narangajavana, Y. (2005) Competitive strategies and performance in Spanish hospitality firms, *International Journal of Contemporary Hospitality Management*, 17(1), pp. 22–38.

Gerard, G., Kamerschen, D. & Delorme, C. (1999) Market structure and price-cost margins in Philippine manufacturing industries, *Applied Economics*, 31, pp. 857–864.

Hall, P. (1981) On nonparametric multivariate binary discrimination, *Biomterika*, 68, pp. 287–291.

Kari, F., Jaafar, A. H., Allen, J. & Couvillion, W. (2002) Market structure, market share and profits in the surface freight industry. Paper presented at the 2002 Annual Meeting of the American Economics Association, pp. 28–31 (California: July Long Beach).

Kari, F., Jaafar, A. H. & Abdullah, F. H. (2004) Technology transfer and foreign direct investment: the Malaysian experience. Paper presented at the Malaysian-Egypt Annual Conference, Kuala Lumpur, 12–13 September.

Keith, H., White, R. & Chaudy, D. (1997) Government and industry performance: a comparative study, *Applied Economics*, 29, pp. 1227–1237.

Kiggundu, M. N. (2002) Entrepreneurs and entrepreneurship in Africa: what is known and what needs to be done, *Journal of Development Entrepreneurship*, 7(3), pp. 239–258.

MACPMA (1996) *MACPMA Directory 1996/97: Automotive and Component Parts Industry* (Kuala Lumpur: MACPMA).

McGahan, A. M. & Porter, M. E. (1997) How much does industry matter, really?, *Strategic Management Journal*, 18, pp. 15–30.

McNamee, P., Greenan, K. & McFerran, B. (1999) The competitive analysis model: a new approach to strategic development for small businesses, *Benchmarking: An International Journal*, 6(2), pp. 125–146.

Meyanathan, S. D. & Ismail, M. S. (1994) Malaysia, in: S. D. Meyanathan (Ed.) *Industrial Structures and the Development of Small and Medium Enterprise Linkages: Examples from East Asia*, pp. 23–66 (Washington, DC: World Bank).

MIDA (the Malaysian Industrial Development Authority) (n.d.) Report on the Automotive Industry in Malaysia, Kuala Lumpur.

MIDA (1998) *List of Promoted Activities and Products* (Kuala Lumpur: Malaysian Industrial Development Authority).

MIDA (2004) Report on the Automotive Industry in Malaysia, the Malaysian Industrial Development Authority, Kuala Lumpur (unpublished).

MIDA (unpublished) *The Automotive Industry in Malaysia* (Kuala Lumpur: Malaysian Industrial Development Authority).

MITI (The Ministry of International Trade and Industry) (1994) *The Ministry of International Trade and Industry Report 1994* (Kuala Lumpur: The Ministry of International Trade and Industry).

MITI (1996) *The Second Industrial Master Plan 1996–2005* (Kuala Lumpur: The Ministry of International Trade and Industry).

Mohd Shah, A. B. (1995) Peranan sistem vendor dalam pembangunan industri kecil dan sederhana Bumiputera (The role of vendor system in the development of Bumiputera's small and medium industries). Paper presented at Bengkel Kebangsaan Penglibatan Bumiputera dalam Industri Kecil dan Sederhana (National Workshop on Bumiputera's Involvement in Small and Medium Industries), Kuala Lumpur, September.

Neely, A. (1998) *Measuring Business Performance* (London: Profile Books).

Powers, T. L. & Hahn, W. (2002) Skill and resource based competitive methods: impact on firm performance, *Journal of Services Marketing*, 16(2), pp. 113–124.

PVA (Proton Vendor Association) (2005) *Proton Vendor's Directory* (Shah Alam: Proton Vendor Association).

Ramachandran, V. & Shah, M. J. (1999) minority entrepreneurs and private sector growth in sub-saharan Africa. Discussion Paper, No. 86, World Bank, Washington, DC

Rasiah, R. (2004) *Foreign Firms, Technological Capabilities and Economic Performance: Evidence from Africa, Asia and Latin America* (Cheltenham: Edward Elgar).

Rasiah, R. (2005) Trade-related investment liberalization: the Malaysian experience, *Global Economic Review*, 34(4), pp. 453–471.

Rogers, M. (2000) The role of diversification on firm performance, Melbourne Institute Working Paper, September.

Rogoff, E. G., Lee, M. S. & Suh, D. C. (2004) Who Done It? Attributions by entrepreneurs and experts of the factors that cause and impede small business success, *Journal of Small Business Management*, 42(4), pp. 364–376.

Rosli, M. M. (2004) Entrepreneurship, economic organization and the automobile industry: a study of the Asian model and Malaysia Experience. Ph.D. thesis, University of Malaya, Kuala Lumpur.

Schmitz, J. & Platts, K. W. (2003) Roles of supplier performance measurement: indication from a study in the automotive industry, *Management Decision*, 41(8), pp. 711–721.

Simons, R. (2000) *Performance Measurement & Control Systems for Implementing Strategy* (New Jersey: Prentice Hall).

Shapiro, D. M. (1983) The comparative profitability of Canadian- and foreign-controlled firms, *Managerial and Decision Economics*, 4(2), pp. 97–106.

Stevens, J. P. (1986) *Applied Multivariate Statistics for the Social Science* (Mahwah, NJ: Lawrence Erlbaum Associates).

Torri, T. (1991) Changing the manufacturing sector, reorganizing automobile assemblers and developing the auto component industry under the new economic policy, *The Developing Economies*, 29(4), pp. 387–413.

Tvorik, S. J. & McGivern, M. H. (1997) Determinants of organizational performance, *Management Decision*, 35(6), pp. 417–435.

Wijewardena, H. & Tibbits, G. E. (1999) Factors contributing to the growth of small manufacturing firms: data from Australia, *Journal of Small Business Management*, 37(2), pp. 88–95.

Willmore, L. N. (1986) The comparative performance of foreign and domestic firms in Brazil, *World Development*, 14(4), pp. 489–502.

Taiwanese Automotive Parts Suppliers in China

LIH-REN LI & YURI SADOI

Introduction

As a newly industrialized economy (NIE), Taiwan developed rapidly to achieve a high technological level in the manufacturing industry by the 1990s. The competitive advantage of the manufacturing industry in Taiwan is based on the flexibility of its supplier networks, having integrated capital and intensive technology, strong operations management capability and tie-ups in global value chains. In particular, Taiwan relied mostly on techniques of original equipment manufacturing and original design manufacturing to produce and export.

However, Taiwan as well as other Asian NIEs experienced falling export competitiveness due to a rise in labour costs from the 1980s and the rapid development of China. As a consequence, Taiwanese foreign investors relocated extensively in China from the 1990s to lower production costs. Taiwanese automotive manufacturers followed the same direction relocating labour- and scale-intensive assembly activities in China while retaining knowledge-intensive and small batch production in the country. Relocation in China also helped Taiwanese suppliers to take advantage of Chinese supply chain networks connecting with Japanese and American assemblers operating in the country.

This contribution attempts to examine technological issues in Taiwanese automotive suppliers in China. The rest of the study is organized as follows. The next section examines the nature of Taiwanese foreign direct investment (FDI) in the production of automobile parts in China. Drawing from interviews with 72 Taiwanese suppliers in 2004–05, we subsequently investigate the nature and extent of technology transfer from Taiwan to China that has taken place among Taiwanese suppliers. Finally, we discuss our research findings drawing implications for the position of Taiwanese suppliers in China in the division of labour with other automotive firms in China, Japan and Taiwan.

Theoretical Framework

Taiwanese industrial development has been studied from various perspectives. In the 1980s, the economic development of Taiwan was being studied as an Asia Newly Industrialized Economy (NIE). As Association of South East Asian Nations (ASEAN) economies develop, studies have focused on Chinese networks and the role of overseas Chinese. In particular, there are many studies on the development of the Taiwanese semiconductor industry and its competitiveness. Moreover, Taiwan's industrial structure and competitive advantages with its flexible supplier network has been emphasized.

After the economic reform of China in 1978, Taiwan has been playing an important role in the Chinese economy. Taiwan started investing in China in the 1980s and the pace of this accelerated between the late 1980s and the 1990s. Taiwanese investment in China has been studied in recent years, mostly focusing on the semiconductor industry and its production shift to China, with few studies on the automobile industry.

In the study of Taiwan's investment in China, recent research has focused on the theory of the division of labour among China, Japan, and Taiwan. When considering Taiwan's foreign direct investment (FDI) to China, we examined the direct and indirect involvement of Japan. Zhu (2005) claims that Japanese enterprises play four roles in Taiwanese investment in China. The first role is that of capital involvement. Japanese enterprises act as joint venture partners and are corporate in management and technical assistance. The second role is that Japanese joint venture firms in Taiwan transplant and set up production sites in China. In this case, the production plants in China maintain Taiwanese supplier networks in China. The third role is that Japanese firms in China and Taiwanese firms in China start business cooperation in China. Last but not least, the fourth role is the case that Japanese technology transferred to Taiwan is re-transferred to China. In this case, Taiwanese firms play the role of transferring Japanese technology to China.

The automobile industry is globally very competitive and requires high technology, high quality and reliability. Competitive multinational enterprises are seeking markets with huge potential and rushing to invest in China. However, many foreign firms face supply chain related difficulties in China. The automobile industry requires a highly developed supply chain. In China, there are difficulties in locating local qualified suppliers, an underdeveloped information technology and telecommunications infrastructure, an unreliable transportation infrastructure in many areas, and a high rate of damage/loss in transit (Jiang, 2002).

The automobile industry in Taiwan is not yet competitive globally. The alliance of two companies creates a new market, accumulation of innovation, realization of scale merit and reduction of risk (Pietras & Stormer, 2001). When investing in China, each player should maximize its comparative advantages. Taiwan automobile parts producers have competitive advantages on key parts and original equipment manufacturer (OEM) production, while the multinational automobile manufacturers have advantages in research and development (R&D) developing new models, and Chinese firms have advantages in producing common parts and service parts. A Taiwanese-Chinese-Japanese alliance might create a superior advantage and lower the risk than that of two parties (Chih-Tung *et al.*, 2000).

In the three-party alliance among Taiwan, China, and Japan, Taiwan would play a crucial role in transferring and spilling over (Taiwanese and/or Japanese) technology to the second tier local suppliers in China. In order to analyse this hypothesis, we researched parts procurement and technology sources of Taiwanese parts suppliers in China.

Taiwanese Direct Investment in China

The automobile industry in China has grown rapidly in the last two decades. Accordingly, the number of foreign parts and material suppliers is increasing. In this section, we discuss the status quo of Taiwanese suppliers in China and the role of those suppliers in the development of the Chinese automotive parts industry.

For the past 22 years, from 1983 to 2005, there have been 1,576 suppliers of automotive parts and material from various parts of the world investing in China, setting up production and manufacturing there (Fourin, 2005). At first, FDI by automobile suppliers to China was a result of requests from their customers who set up production in China. Among the total of 1,576 cases of FDI in automobile parts and material suppliers, 296 cases are from Taiwan. As shown in Figure 1, more than half of the cases (54.9 per cent) of investment came from Japan,

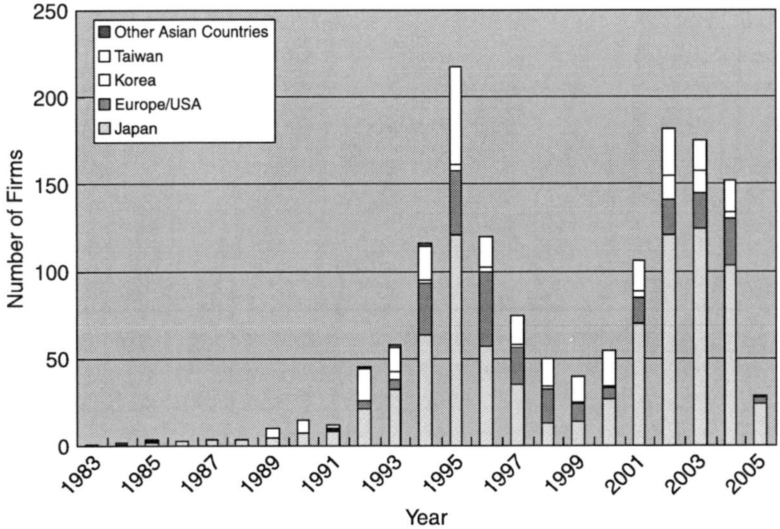

Figure 1. Number of parts suppliers established in China, 1983–2005. *Source*: Fourin (2005).

one-fifth of the cases (21.3 per cent) came from Europe and the USA, and 18.8 per cent, about the same amount as from Europe and the USA, came from Taiwan. Only 4.4 per cent of cases came from Korea. The percentage of automotive parts and material suppliers' investment from Taiwan is quite high compared to the size of the industry in the home countries.

The number of investments increased slowly from 1983 to 1993, but increased dramatically in 1994 and 1995, reaching 220 cases in 1995 alone as shown in Figure 1. One of the major reasons for such a sudden increase is that the Chinese government officially proclaimed its automobile industry development policy for the first time in 1994. The policy positions the automobile industry as a major industry to be developed in China. In order to solve the problems that China faced at that time, such as unfocused investment, small-scale inefficient production, and quality control, the policy also stated firstly a relaxation of regulation on foreign investment in mergers and alliances. The government is trying to introduce high technology, production know-how, and industrial organization of multinational enterprises (MNEs) to develop the automobile industry in China.

The investment of Taiwanese automobile suppliers started gradually from 1989. In October 1990, the Taiwanese government passed legislation permitting indirect investment and technology assistance to China via a third country. As a result, the number of investments from Taiwan increased rapidly and 18 suppliers set up operation in 1992. The investment accelerated after the statement of the official automobile industry development policy by the Chinese government in 1994, as stated above. In total, 57 suppliers registered in 1995. In the same year, China Motor Corporation (CMC) (Taiwan) established South East Motor Corporation (SEM) Automobile in China, a joint venture with Fujian Automobile in China. CMC in Taiwan was founded in June of 1969 and signed a technical collaboration with Mitsubishi Motors Corporation the following year (Mitsubishi Motors Corporation 14.61 per cent, Mitsubishi Corporation 5.01 per cent). Together with CMC, 35 of CMC's major suppliers invested in production plants in China. Yulon Motor Company (YL), in technical collaboration with Nissan Motor Japan, set up a joint venture Aeolus Automobile Co., Ltd in Guangzhou, China in 2000.

For Taiwanese automobile manufacturers, such as CMC and YL, investing in such a huge market is indispensable for surviving the international competition. CMC is the first example of a company making inroads into the huge Chinese market. In order to set up quickly and to form a supply chain in China, CMC and 35 major CMC suppliers launched simultaneously in China.

According to the Taiwan Transportation Vehicle Manufacturers Association (TTVMA), among 445 member firms of TTVMA as of 2004, 129 automobile parts suppliers (29 per cent) invested in production sites in China and started production there. In total, 296 cases of investment occurred between 1985 and 2004. Figure 2 shows the percentage of those FDI cases by parts category. Most investments went to body parts (34 per cent), followed by engine parts (18 per cent), electric parts (17 per cent), and chassis parts (7 per cent).

Figure 3a shows the percentage of FDI cases from Taiwan, Japan, the USA and Europe, and Korea by parts category. The number of cases exhibiting the same data is shown in Figure 3b. The ratio of body parts related investment is larger from Taiwan compared with that from Japan, the USA and Europe, and Korea.

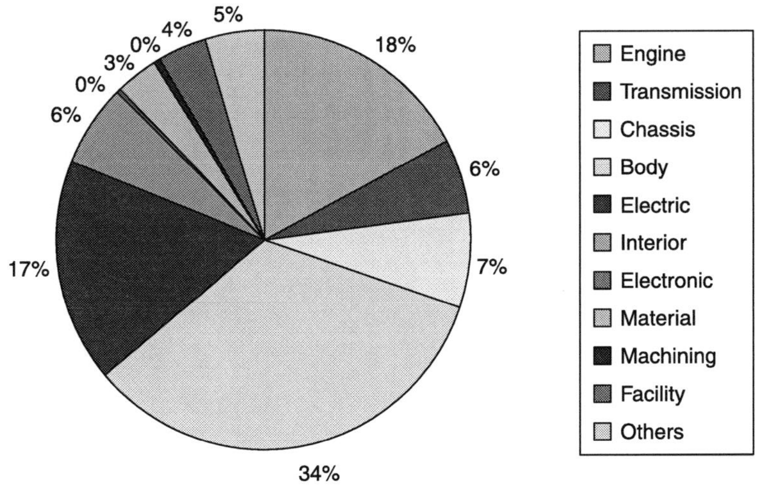

Figure 2. Taiwan Auto Parts Investment in China, 1985–2004. *Note*: In total, there were 296 cases of investment in China by Taiwanese companies (1985–2004). *Source*: Authors, based on data from Fourin (2005).

It is noteworthy that there was no R&D investment from Taiwan to China in the area of automotive parts production. On the contrary, nearly 8 per cent of US and European parts suppliers that invested in China have invested in R&D followed by that of Korean suppliers and Japanese suppliers.

As shown in Figure 3b, almost 900 Japanese automotive parts suppliers invested in China, which is about three times larger than that of Taiwan, while there are few Korean investments in China.

Another feature of Taiwanese suppliers in China is that of the location. Taiwanese automobile parts investment concentrates in Fujian and Jiangsu Provinces. Among 296 investments, 69 cases are located in Fujian, 61 are in Jiangsu, followed by 40 in Guangdong, and 25 in Shanghai. In Fujian Province, CMC has invested in China's South East (Fujian) Motor Corporation Ltd. (SEM) since 1995 together with 35 suppliers, as stated earlier. Jiangsu Province and Shanghai City form an industrial district for accumulated parts and material production for Shanghai Volkswagen and Shanghai GM. In Guangdong Province, Guangzhou City, YL Taiwan set up a joint venture, Aeolus Automobile Co., Ltd (Aeolus), with a technical agreement with Nissan to produce Nissan brand automobiles in Guangzhou in 2000. In addition, Nissan established an R&D centre for passenger cars.

Taiwanese Automotive Parts Suppliers

The parts localization rate can be used as a criterion for measuring the progress of technology transfer. An automobile consists of 30,000 or more parts. When developing countries start automobile production, initially, they start from completely knocked down production (CKD), which is mainly assembling imported parts. Then, gradually, they localize parts production in-house or use

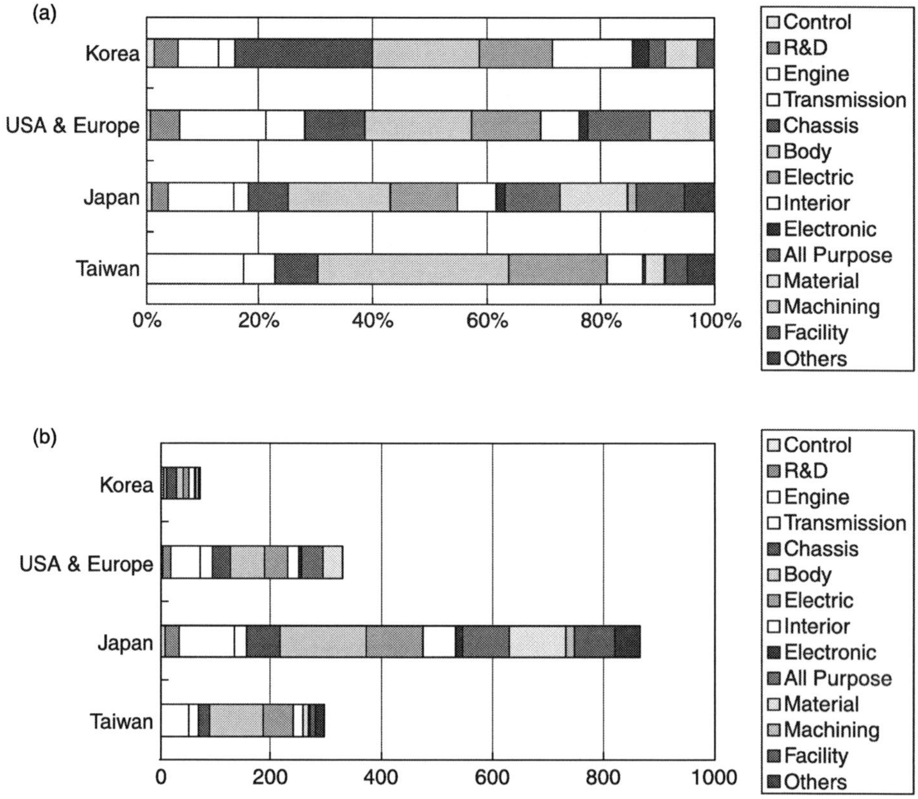

Figure 3. Percentage of investments in China by area and type of parts, 1985–2004. *Source*: Authors, based on data from Fourin (2005). Figure 3b. Number of investments in China by area and type of parts, 1985–2004. *Source*: Authors, based on data from Fourin (2005).

outsourcing. The progress of the parts localization is a criterion for measuring the transfer of technology to the host countries.

In the cases of Taiwan automobile suppliers in China, we looked not only at the rate of localization, but the role of three players, China, Taiwan and Japan. For this, we surveyed Taiwanese parts suppliers in China and researched their parts procurement sources.

In 2004 and 2005, we conducted a two-part survey involving questionnaires and direct interviews. Companies were selected as follows. First, we used the list of the *Overseas Taiwanese Vehicle Manufacturers Directory 2003–2004* published by the Taiwan Transportation Vehicle Manufacturers Association (TTVMA, 2004), which includes all the firms of automobiles, automobile parts, motorcycles, and industrial vehicles manufacturers in Taiwan. Among the 175 firms in the list, we surveyed 129 firms that produce automobile parts and have production plants in China. The number of firms was reported as 296 cases in the third section of this contribution. Many Taiwanese suppliers that invested in China have one or more plants in China, including the makers of motorcycles and industrial vehicles.

First, we explained the purpose of our survey to all 129 firms by telephone, and obtained their cooperation. Then, questionnaires were sent to the 129 mother companies in Taiwan. Among the 129 samples, 77 were collected. Except for five invalid replies, 72 samples (55.8 per cent) were collected. After collecting the questionnaires, we visited about one-third of the firms for detailed interviews. In the questionnaires, we asked mainly about the establishment of their Chinese plants, the part procurement sources in their plants in China, and their division of labour between Taiwan and China.

Our survey shows that most Taiwan parts suppliers established their plants in China in the period between 1995 and 1999. Nearly 60 per cent of those plants (42 plants) in China were established during the five years (1995–99). This indicates that many of the Taiwanese parts suppliers invested just after the Chinese government officially stated their automobile industry development policy in 1994. In addition, in 1995, the Taiwanese government permitted automobile makers to invest in China. About 20 per cent of the firms were established after the year 2000, when YL officially invested in Guangzhou. In total, 80 per cent of the investment from Taiwan was after 1995. However, it is noteworthy that 22 per cent (16 firms) of firms were established before 1995.

There were two main reasons for the investment in China: 1) because the carmaker (customer) started production in China (35 firms, 46.8 per cent); and 2) in order to access the potentially huge Chinese market (25 firms, 34.7 per cent). Those two reasons account for 83.3 per cent of the answers.

Among the 72 Taiwan parent firms, 21 firms are joint ventures with foreign firms, and 17 of them are joint ventures with Japanese firms. In the case of body and electric firms, all the joint venture partners are Japanese firms, while engine firms are a mixture of Japanese (3 firms), US (2 firms) and others (2 firms) (see Table 1).

On the contrary, in the case of subsidiaries in China, all the firms that have joint ventures with foreign firms are with Japanese firms. When we look at the parts categories, eight body firms have joint ventures with Japan, which is the highest rate among the parts categories. This trend is the same as the situation of those parent companies of Taiwan as stated above. Two electric firms and five engine firms have joint ventures with Japan.

Do those firms depend on foreign firms for their technology? As shown in Table 2, 35.6 per cent of Taiwan parent companies have technology agreements with Japan, while more than half of the firms have no technical agreement with foreign firms. In the case of body parts suppliers, 40 per cent of them have technology agreements with Japan. The ratio is the highest among all the categories, followed by engine parts suppliers (32.3 per cent) and electric parts suppliers (31.6 per cent).

According to the survey by TTVMA, among Taiwan parts suppliers who have technology agreements with foreign firms, over 95 per cent of them have the agreements with Japan (TTVMA, 2005). Our survey results show that the majority of technology agreement partners are Japanese firms as well.

As for Chinese subsidiaries, the majority of technologies came from Taiwan (79.3 per cent), followed by Japan (16.1 per cent), as shown in Table 2. Among the parts categories, body parts depend less on Taiwanese parent firms compared with

Table 1. Investment form, China sample

	Taiwan parent firm			Joint venture partner				
	Solely owned	Joint venture	Total	Japanese firm	American firm	Others	-	Total
Body	18	9	27	9	0	0		9
Electric	12	5	17	5	0	0		5
Engine	18	7	25	3	2	2		7
Tyre	3	0	3	0	0	0		0
Total	51	21	72	17	2	2		21
	China subsidiary			Joint venture partner				
	Solely owned	Joint venture	Total	Chinese firm	Japanese firm	American firm	Others	Total
Body	15	12	27	4	8	0	0	12
Electric	11	6	17	4	2	0	0	6
Engine	16	9	25	4	5	0	0	9
Tyre	3	0	3	0	0	0	0	0
Total	45	27	72	12	15	0	0	27

Note: Solely owned firm means a 100 per cent investment of the Taiwanese side.
Source: Author's survey, 2004–05.

Table 2. Technological agreement, China sample (firm numbers by country)

	Owned by oneself	Taiwanese parent firm	from Japan	from the USA	from others	Total (%)
Taiwanese parent firm	50 (55.6)	-	32 (35.6)	5 (5.6)	3 (3.3)	90 (100.0)
Body	19(54.3)	-	14(40.0)	0(0.0)	2(5.7)	35(100.0)
Electric	11(57.9)	-	6(31.6)	2(10.5)	0(0.0)	19(100.0)
Engine	17(54.8)	-	10(32.3)	3(9.7)	1(3.2)	31(100.0)
Tyre	3(60.0)	-	2(40.0)	0(0.0)	0(0.0)	5(100.0)
Chinese subsidiary	1 (1.2)	69 (79.3)	14 (16.1)	1 (1.2)	2 (2.3)	87 (100.0)
Body	0(0.0)	25(73.5)	8(23.5)	0(0.0)	1(2.9)	34(100.0)
Electric	1(5.3)	16(84.2)	2(10.5)	0(0.0)	0(0.0)	19(100.0)
Engine	0(0.0)	25(80.7)	4(12.9)	1(3.2)	1(3.2)	31(100.0)
Tyre	0(0.0)	3(100.0)	0(0.0)	0(0.0)	0(0.0)	3(100.0)

Note: Effective samples are 72 (multiple answers).

that of electric and engine parts firms. At the same time, the ratio of technology agreement with Japan is higher in body suppliers (23.5 per cent) than that of electric (10.5 per cent) and engine (12.9 per cent) suppliers. Overall, Japanese technology plays an important role in those Taiwanese subsidiaries in China, especially, in body parts technologies.

Survey on Parts Procurement

In order to survey the technological capability and the relationship between Taiwanese mother plants and their Chinese plants, questions on the parts procurement sources were asked in the questionnaires. First, the rate of locally procured parts was surveyed. Then, those locally purchased parts were identified if they came from the Taiwanese firms in China or other firms in China.

Furthermore, imported parts were categorized into four: imports from Taiwan, imports from Japan, imports from the US, and imports from other countries. Tracing back to the producers of the parts may show the linkage of those actors, division of labour and the process of technology transfer through Taiwan to China.

Procurement of Parts and Material (Non-key Parts)

Our survey shows, in the case of non key-parts, that most of the all-Taiwanese automotive parts firms in China purchase parts and materials from three channels: local Taiwanese firms, other local firms, and imports from Taiwan. Figure 4 shows the number of firms that indicated their source of procurement. While most of the firms import parts from Taiwan, it is noteworthy that in all body, electric, and engine firms, about half of them import parts from Japan. This is also the case to a slightly higher extent in the electric firms, but all the parts categories show the same trend.

In order to examine the weight of these sources, each firm was questioned about the share of each source. Figure 5 shows the average share each firm procured. The average was calculated only for companies that indicated their procurement sources in percentages. As shown in Figure 5, on average, body parts firms

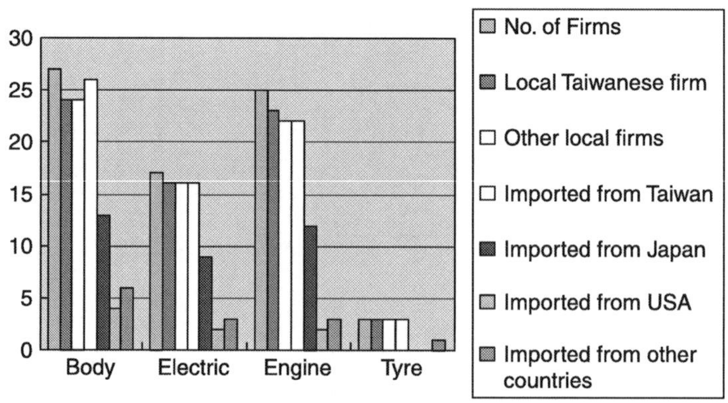

Figure 4. Procurement of Taiwanese automotive parts firms in China (cases). *Source*: Authors' survey, 2004–05.

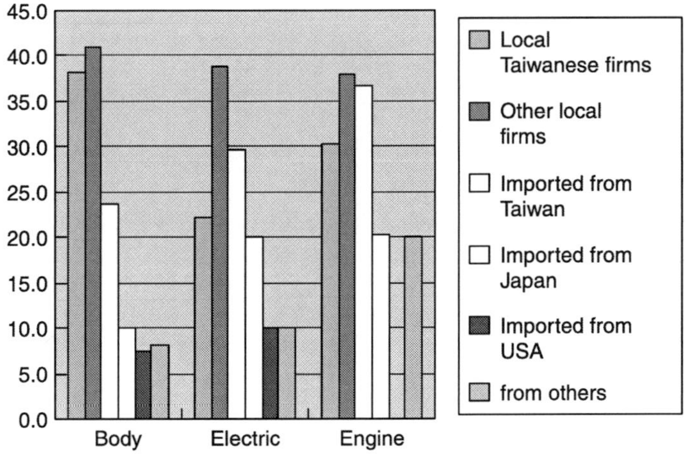

Figure 5. Average shares of parts procurement sources, China. *Source*: Authors' survey, 2004–05.

purchase about 38 per cent parts of their total purchasing parts from local Taiwanese firms. About 41 per cent of their procurement comes from local firms other than Taiwanese. Twenty three per cent of them are imports from Taiwan. Ten (or lower) per cent of them are imports from Japan, the USA and other countries.

In the case of electric parts firms, purchasing from local firms other than Taiwanese made up nearly 40 per cent, the highest source among all. Purchases from Taiwanese firms in Taiwan are higher than the Taiwanese firms in China. This fact indicates that some electric and electronic parts are less available locally. The category of automotive parts investment in China is relatively less when compared to others (as shown in Figure 2).

Engine parts firms show a slightly different trend. First, imported parts are higher in share than locally purchased parts. Second, most imports come from Taiwan. On average, 37 per cent of the total purchase of each firm depends on imports from Taiwan. Twenty per cent of the total purchases of each firm depend on imports from Japan. The rate is as high as that of electric parts firms. The rate of imports from other countries is the same as that of electric parts firms.

Procurement of Key Parts

On the contrary, our survey shows that the key parts for those Taiwanese parts firms in China are mostly imported. Figure 6 shows the number of firms and the procurement source of the key parts in the Taiwanese suppliers in China. The data is based on the numbers of firms who answered 'yes' to the question if they have key parts in their products. Forty-eight firms indicated their key parts production location. Including multiple answers, in total 60 cases were collected here. The numbers are shown in the table below Figure 6.

As shown in Figure 6, in the cases of body parts firms, exactly 20 per cent (4 firms out of 20) of Taiwanese body parts firms in China produce their key parts in-house. The percentage is the highest among all categories of the parts firms

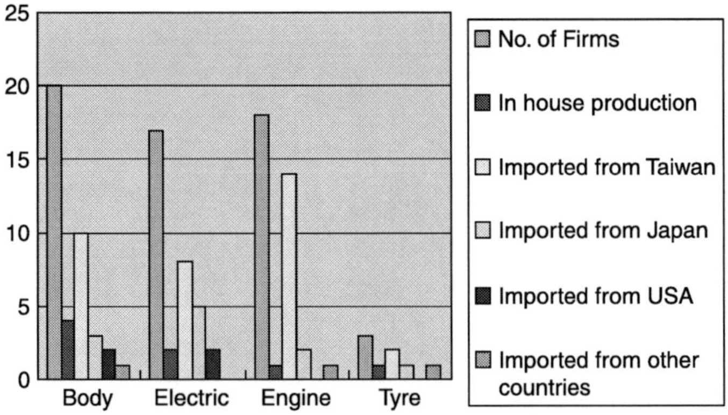

Figure 6. Key parts procurement in Taiwanese Suppliers in China. *Note*: 48 firms, multiple answers. *Source*: Authors' survey, 2004–05.

researched. The rate of body parts firms who are supplied from their mother company in Taiwan is 50 per cent (10 firms out of 20). About 15 per cent (3 out of 20) of them purchase parts from Japan.

In the case of electric and electronics parts, the rate of in-house production is slightly lower than that of body parts firms (12 per cent, 2 firms out of 17). And about 47 per cent (8 firms out of 17) of electric parts firms purchase their key parts from their mother companies of Taiwan. It is noteworthy that nearly 30 per cent (5 firms out of 17) of those firms import their key parts from Japan, which is nearly two times higher than that of body parts firms (and three times higher than that of engine parts firms, as stated below). These five firms are in the production of motors, distributors, air-conditioner (A/C) assys, centre door locks, and lamps. Three out of the five are joint ventures with Japanese firms.

In the case of engine parts, only one firm out of the engine parts firms produces their key parts in-house. Nearly 80 per cent of engine parts firms import their key parts from Taiwan. On the contrary, the rate of engine parts firms that import their key parts from Japan is low. Only 2 firms out of 18 (11 per cent) imported key parts from Japan. For example, firms which produce major engine and control parts such as crankshafts, connecting rods, and brake cylinders are sole Taiwanese firms, but receive technological support from Japan and import non-key parts from Japan.

Division of Labour

Our survey shows, as described above, that Taiwanese automotive parts firms in China purchase their parts and materials (non-key parts) from three channels: local Taiwanese firms, other local firms and imports from Taiwan. However, they mostly import key parts from their parent companies in Taiwan and from Japan as well.

Next, we consider how Taiwanese parts suppliers control the involvement of three parties and manage Taiwan's role in the division of labour. Our interview survey on samples reveals the division of labour in China, Japan and Taiwan. We use the three categories in parts, body (including tyres), electric, and engine parts and aim to identify the role and strategy of Taiwan in the division of labour.

Body Parts Suppliers

First, we consider the case study of a body parts firm (Firm A). In the previous section, the body parts category showed that parts localization in general parts has progressed most but is low in key parts. Here, we will consider the body firm; both the Taiwanese parent firm and the Chinese subsidiary are a joint venture with Japan and import key parts from Japan. Focusing on the division of labour in the three countries, the case study of the body parts firms is studied.

Firm A was established in Taiwan in 1969 as a joint venture of YL group (Taiwan) and NHK Spring (Japan). Firm A had a technological agreement with Johnson Controls Japan in 1991. Firm A produces leaf springs, coin springs, (electric) seats and head linings. The investment in China was made in 1995 when A was requested by CMC to become a member of the initial number of suppliers who set up plants in the suppliers' park of SEM in Fujian. A few years later, A and NHK Spring set up another joint venture plant in Guanzhou China, close to Aeolus.

When Firm A first set up its plant in China, production technology and machines were installed by Taiwan. Having technology assistance from Taiwan and Japan, Firm A achieved a high local content rate (80 per cent). In the case of key parts production, most of the sub-parts are imported from Japan, and material from Taiwan.

The technological division of labour on seats production in China is shown in Table 3. As the seats produced in China are an old model that was produced in Taiwan and transferred from Taiwan, all the R&D process is performed in Taiwan, except the technological evaluations assured by both Taiwan and Japan. On the production side, all the processes are performed in China.

The next case study of body parts (Firm B) is the manufacturer of tyres. Firm B is the oldest among three major tyre firms in Taiwan. Its predecessor, B Rubber Plant was established in 1940 to manufacture rickshaw tyres, rubber shoes, and so on. In 1959, Firm B was established to produce car tyres receiving technical cooperation from Yokohama Rubber Co. Japan.

In 1997, Firm B invested in the free trade zone (FTZ) of Zhangjia Gang in Jiangsu Province, aiming to expand its potential market, supplying tyres for local carmakers, and creating its production base for exports with a lower labour cost. Production started in 2003. The new Chinese plant depends on the Taiwanese side for its production technology and machinery. About 80 per cent of parts and materials are purchased in China, however, as far as key parts are concerned, many of them are imported from Taiwan and Japan.

Firm B in China is for export oriented production, exporting 90 per cent of products to service markets in the USA, and other countries, while 10 per cent is for the domestic market. As shown in Table 3, most of the R&D process and production process depends on the Taiwanese side.

Electric Parts Suppliers

Next, we consider the case of electric parts firms. The first case produces its key parts in China, which is the minor case in the category described in the previous section. The case study, Firm C, one of the initial members of the SEM supplier park, invested in China in 1995 (the same year as Firm A). Firm C is a leading

Table 3. Division of labour in China, Taiwan and Japan

		Firm A	Firm B	Firm C		Firm D		Firm E		Firm F	
	Parts	Seat	Tyre	Wire harness	Key parts	A/C Assys	Key parts	Piston ring	Cylinder block	Air cleaner catalytic converter	Key parts
R&D	Advanced development	T	T	T	T	T	T	C	T	C	C
	Specification planning	T	T	T	T	T	T	C	T	C	C
	Designing	T	T	T	T	T	T	J	T	C	C
	Prototype	T	T	T	T	T	T	J	C	C	C
	Evaluation	T·J	T	T	T	T	T	C	C	C	C
Production technology	Process Planning	C	T·C	C	C	T·C	T·C	C	C	C	C
	Process Designing	C	T·C	C	C	T·C	T·C	C	C	C	C
	Production Preparing	C	T·C	C	C	T·C	T·C	C	C	C	C
	Production equipment	T·C	T	T·C	T	J·T	J·T	T·J	T·J	T·C	T·C
Production	Production	C	C	C	C	C	C	C	C	C	C

Note: T·C indicated in Production Technology means that China cannot operate alone.
Source: Authors' survey in 2005.

producer of wire harnesses in Taiwan and produces fuses, seats and switches as well. Firm C was established in 1959 as an electrical appliances producer. In 1965 it expanded and started to manufacture various automobile parts, such as wire harnesses. In 1987, it established technological agreements with Kyohritsu Hiparts (a Nissan supplier), and, the following year, started to export parts to Japan. In 1993, Firm C established another technical agreement with Ryosei Denso, a MMC (Mitsubishi Motor Corporation) supplier.

The Chinese subsidiary of Firm C produces key parts in China, but local content is low, about 40 per cent. The remaining parts (60 per cent) are imported from Taiwan and Japan. Its major customer is SEM, but it also supplies to the Japanese manufacturers in China, such as Komatsu and Yanmar. In addition, it re-exports to Taiwan, although the volume is small.

As shown in Table 3, in Firm C, research and development are all performed in Taiwan, both the wire harness and key parts. On the production side, the Chinese plant is in charge of the whole process, including production planning, production preparation and production. The Taiwanese side has the initiative because the initial production line in China was transferred from Taiwan. The production line operated in a Taiwanese plant was transferred and installed to the Chinese plant. As the production volume of the Chinese plant increased, new production machinery for wire harness was purchased in China and installed there. As for key parts, new production machinery was purchased in Taiwan and installed in the Chinese plant.

Overall, in Firm C, although all the production processes were transferred and controlled by China, even in key parts, all R&D activities depend on the Taiwanese side. Initially, the Taiwanese side received technological collaboration from Japanese firms. This case shows the division of three parties: China, Taiwan and Japan. Based on the technology collaboration from Japan, R&D is performed in Taiwan, and then the final processes are performed in China.

The next case study is similar, but less transferred than the case study of Firm C. As in the case of Firm C, electric Firm D is a Taiwanese firm as a joint venture with Japan. However, the Chinese plant lags behind its parts localization and imports the majority of its key parts from Taiwan and Japan.

Firm D, an electric parts supplier, was founded in Taiwan in 1987 as a joint venture of Yungtay Engineering Co., Ltd. (Taiwan) and Calsonic (Japan). Its major products are air conditioner (A/C) assys, heater assys, condensers and evaporators. In 2002 as requested by a major customer YL, it set up an operation site in Guangdong Province in order to supply parts to Aeolus, a joint venture automobile manufacturer with YL in China.

The local content rate of the Chinese subsidiary is low, about 30 per cent. It imports the remaining parts including key parts and materials from Taiwan and Japan. Currently, Firm D is still at the initial stage of operation; three-years' operational experience in China. Therefore, all the R&D processes and most of the production planning and preparation are controlled by the Taiwanese side. Taiwanese engineers and managers advise and assist at the production site on a regular basis.

As explained in an earlier section of this contribution, Taiwanese suppliers seldom set up their R&D division in China. In Firm D, new product concepts, designing, testing, and evaluations are performed in the Taiwan R&D division. As the Taiwanese parent company is a joint venture with Japan, the production facilities and other technology are under technical agreement with Japan Calsonic, as shown in Table 3.

Engine Parts Suppliers

Next, we consider the case of engine parts suppliers. The engine parts category has the following features: 1) the ratio of localization of key parts is very low; and 2) most of the key engine parts are imported from their Taiwanese parent firms.

Firm E was established in Taiwan in 1968 as a joint venture of Riken Corporation (Japan) and Yuen Foong Group (Taiwan). Receiving technology from Riken Corporation Japan, Firm E produces major engine parts, such as camshafts, piston rings, exhaust manifolds and iron casting parts.

Firm E's sole investment in China started in 1989, one of the earliest investments from Taiwan, aimed at taking advantage of the potentially huge market. However, it was six years before production started in 1995. The initial production began with piston rings and cylinders for motorbikes. The engine parts production for motorbikes was transferred to its Chinese subsidiary, while the production of camshafts and exhaust manifolds for automobile engines remained in Taiwan.

The division of labour in the Taiwan and Chinese plants is active in Firm E. The Chinese plant concentrates on motorbike engine parts, while the Taiwanese plant produces major automobile engine parts. In the case of cylinder blocks for motorbikes, the development process and drawing are performed in the Taiwan R&D Centre. Based on the drawings, prototype and evaluation is performed in China. For production the casting process is performed in China. The casting cylinder blocks are partly exported to Taiwan and machined and finished in Taiwan. On the other hand, piston rings are half-processed in Taiwan and sent to the Chinese plant for machining and finishing. This division of production processes between Taiwanese and Chinese plants is practical. The range of division is expanded involving Japanese parts suppliers. Currently, the local content rate of the Chinese plant is about 50 per cent. The rest of the parts and pre-processed parts are imported from Taiwan and Japan.

Production technology and machining were initially introduced from Taiwan. Recently, machinery was installed locally from Japan or Japanese machinery subsidiaries in China. Therefore, as far as machinery is concerned, the Chinese plant introduces new technology from Japan directly, while it maintains ties with Taiwan on conventional machinery.

Firm F, was established in 1968 in Taiwan and developed as a leading producer of air cleaners, air cleaner elements, catalytic converters and fuel filters. In 1987, it obtained advanced technology on air cleaners through technical cooperation with Japan Tokyo Roki Co., Ltd, and in 1993, started production of catalytic converters with technical assistance from Yutaka Giken Co., Ltd (Japan).

Firm F's investment in China started in 1995 at the request of a major customer (CMC). At that time, Firm F had already absorbed advanced technology from Japan through technology agreements. Therefore, Firm F invested in China at the site of the CMC Supplier Park by itself.

As of 2004, the local content rate of the Chinese subsidiary was about 60 per cent, which is a relatively high rate compared with other cases. Key parts and materials are imported from the Taiwanese plant. Seventy per cent of products produced in the Chinese plant were supplied to carmakers in China, while 25 per cent of them are exported to Taiwan and 5 per cent to Japan. As shown in Table 3, most of the R&D and production process are performed in China. Product concept and designing are performed by the carmakers there. After receiving detailed drawing from the carmakers, Firm F is responsible for production technology, production planning, and production control. Taiwan's contribution is only a limited part, such as production facilities and machinery. The case study of firm F shows low dependency on Taiwan, in both R&D and production.

Analysis of Findings

The Industrial Technology Intelligence Service in Taiwan (ITIS, 2000) reported that key parts are mostly produced and controlled by the Taiwanese side. Our survey shows the same trend as in the report. We considered details of the sources and division of the labour in production of the key parts, and found that the rate of in-house production of the key parts is 10 per cent or lower depending on the parts categories. Even in the highest categories, the rate reaches only 20 per cent. This trend shows that it is inclined towards Taiwan in the international division of labour of the key part. An average of all categories, in-house production is 13 per cent, the rate is less than that (18 per cent) of imports from Japan, while the rate of imports from Taiwan is 57 per cent.

The Industrial Technology Intelligence Service in Taiwan (ITIS) (2000) reported the international division of labour of Taiwanese manufacturers in China in the production of key auto parts and other automotive parts. According to the report, key parts were controlled mostly by Taiwan except material purchasing and metal processing. As shown in Table 4, Taiwan controls design and development, heat treatment or coating, assembly, packing and marketing of key parts. Material and metal processing are not always controlled by the Taiwanese side. In the case of other non-key parts, the upper part of the production process, such as design and development, and marketing were performed in Taiwan or controlled by the Taiwanese side. Other than these two divisions, non key-parts were produced in both China and Taiwan, and not always under Taiwan's control.

Table 4. International division of labour, Taiwan and China

	Key parts	Other parts
Material	□	□
Design & development	○	○
Metal processing (forging, casting, drilling, grinding, etc.)	□	□
Heat treatment or coating	○	□
Assembly (QC included)	○	□
Packing	○	□
Marketing	○	○

Note: ○ = Manufactured in Taiwan(controlled by Taiwan).
□ = Manufa.
Source: ITIS (2000).

Our research revealed similar results to the ITIS report, but found diversity in the individual cases and differentiation in the parts categories. In addition, we examined the division of labour including Japan's direct and indirect role.

From the technology transfer perspective, we traced back the transferred production technologies from Taiwan to China to determine what kind of production processes and parts were transferred from Taiwan automotive parts firms to their plants in China and who is the major player for each processes among the three: China, Taiwan or Japan.

Among the list of firms we researched, we chose six firms for further research. In all six cases, the technological division of labour among the three parties – China, Taiwan and Japan – was surveyed and the results are summarized in Table 3. Those divisions of labour were researched in three major areas: research and development processes, production preparation processes and production.

As shown in the six investment cases above, Taiwanese firms maintained their controls in the R&D division over their subsidiaries in China (Firms A, B, C, D and E). Although all six Taiwanese firms are joint ventures or technological corroborations with Japan, the Japanese involvement in the R&D process has weakened. Only Firm E is involved in R&D. During the years of technical cooperation with Japan, Taiwanese firms obtained and absorbed advanced technologies. In some cases, the Chinese side provides drawings and prototypes (Firms E and F).

In many cases, the Chinese side manages the production preparation and planning. Most cases show that the initial production lines in China were installed by the Taiwanese side. Two cases transferred their conventional lines which operated in Taiwan to their Chinese plants (Firms B and C). In the two other cases (Firms D and E), some production lines and machine tools were transferred from Japan. Thus, it is clear that Japan also plays a crucial role in supporting core technologies for automotive parts production.

However, many cases show that after production volume increased, they purchased machinery in China. As the number of machine tool firms investing in China increases, machinery is more likely to be locally available.

In the case of parts and material procurement, many import their key parts and material from Taiwan and Japan. The rate of imports is lower in firms with longer operational experience in China. We observed practical use of the division of production processes in engine parts (Firm E).

Conclusions and Implications

This contribution examined technology transfer issues involving China, Taiwan and Japan of Taiwanese automotive parts suppliers in China. China's automobile development policy of 1994 and the Taiwan government's approval of investment into China in 1995 were instrumental in the accelerated relocation of Taiwanese automotive suppliers in China. Hence, most firms reported operational experience of less than ten years.

The percentage of the automotive parts and material suppliers' investment from Taiwan is quite high (18.8 per cent of the investment from the world) compared to the size of the industry in their home countries. The main reason for Taiwanese auto suppliers to invest is that the two leading Taiwan automobile manufacturers,

CMC and YL set up a joint venture in China and requested that their suppliers set up production sites in their supplier parks at the same sites. Another reason for suppliers to invest is the huge potential market in China, benefiting from their advantages in communication and cultural background.

Our research shows that Japanese body parts suppliers are playing an important role in both Taiwanese firms and their Chinese subsidiaries. As Japanese joint ventures with Taiwanese firms are the highest among the body parts suppliers, as a consequence, the number of body suppliers investing in China is high.

Taiwanese subsidiaries in Chinese imports made up quite a large percentage of parts from Taiwan. In the case of key parts, the most average of all the categories, in-house production is 13 per cent, while 18 per cent of them are imported from Japan and 57 per cent are imported from Taiwan. Thus, it is clear that Japan as well as Taiwan plays a crucial role from the viewpoint of supporting the core technologies for automotive parts production.

On the contrary, in the case of non-key parts, most Taiwanese automotive parts firms in China purchase parts and materials from three channels: local Taiwanese firms, other local firms and directly from Taiwan. While most firms import parts from Taiwan, it is noteworthy that about half of them import parts or material from Japan.

The two main findings of the survey and case studies are as follows. Firstly, Taiwanese suppliers have been accumulating advanced technologies from Japan through technology collaborations and capital involvement over many years. Such technology accumulation was upgraded through competition and cooperation with Japanese partners to expand parts exports overseas and established strong relationships with major automobile makers in Taiwan as well as in Japan. Active technological ties among Taiwanese suppliers with Japanese suppliers resulted in quick accumulation of technology and an expansion in the number of customers. The rush of investment in China after 1995 was a result of high technological capability and strong relationships with automobile manufactures. It realized the synchronous investment of CMC and 35 suppliers to Chinese SEM.

Secondly, there has emerged a technical division of labour among the three parties, that is, Taiwanese firms, subsidiaries in China and Japanese technical partners. As shown in the case studies, half the cases are joint ventures with Japanese suppliers and the other half are technological collaborations with Japan. As a result, the Chinese subsidiaries receive direct and indirect technology transfers from Taiwan and Japan in the most effective way. The Chinese subsidiaries have better choice of technology, key parts procurement sources and production processes. Taiwan provides conventional technology to China and cultural and communicational advantages to Japan, while Taiwan receives brand value and advanced technology from Japan.

It is noteworthy that no Taiwan parts supplier has set up R&D centres in their Chinese subsidiaries. From the strategic perspective, Taiwanese suppliers seem to prefer to maintain their competitive advantage in R&D by confining their location to Taiwan. The implications are clear for Chinese policy makers that Taiwanese suppliers may only be interested in participating in low technology activities in China. Policy efforts to attract R&D offshoring among Taiwanese suppliers may require a revision to their incentive framework to include grants, and also complementary upgrading in Chinese firms. Further research is necessary to examine these possibilities.

References

Chih-Tung, H., Chun-Wen, Y. & Po-Young, C. (2000) Collaboration of automobile industries study, *Tunghai Management Review*, 2(1), pp. 119–130.

Fourin (2005) *List of Parts Makers in China 2005* (Nagoya: Fourin).

ITIS (Industrial Technology Intelligence Service in Taiwan) (2000) Interaction of the automobile and motorcycle industry between Taiwan and China. ITIS Report, 20 November (in Chinese).

Jiang, B. (2002) How international firms are coping with supply chain issues in China, *Supply Chain Management*, 7(4), pp. 184–188.

Pietras, T. & Stormer, C. (2001) Making strategic alliances work, *Business & Economic Review*, 47(4), pp. 9–12.

TTVMA (Taiwan Transportation Vehicle Manufacturers Association) (2004) *The Overseas Taiwanese Vehicle Manufacturers Directory 2003–2004* (Taipei: TTMUA).

TTVMA (Taiwan Transportation Vehicle Manufacturers Association) (2005), The Report of the Development of the Taiwan Automobile Industry, March, (Taipei: TTMUA).

Zhu Y. (2005) *Learning from Taiwan Firms' Success in China* (in Japanese) (Tokyo: Toyo Keizai Shinposha), (in Japanese).

Table A1. Surveyed Data of Taiwan Automobile Suppliers in China

No.	Company Name	Established Year	Main Products	Investment Form I * 1	Partner of JV I * 2	Investment Form II * 3	Partner of JV II * 4	Technical Grant I * 5	Technical Grant II * 6	Local Content (%)	Intra Firm Trade (%)	Procurement of Key Parts f * 7	Procurement of arts and material											
													Local Taiwan-ese firm		Other local firm		From Tai-wan		From Japan		From USA		Other country	
													R	%	R	%	R	%	R	%	R	%	R	%
Bo 05	Nak Sealing Technologies Corp. / Kun Shan Mao Shun Sealed Piece Industry Co., Ltd	'00	Oil Seal, Washer, Rubber Parts	1		1		1	1	80					1	60	2	40						
Bo 09 ?	Y-Teks Co., Ltd/ Y-Teks (Fuzhou) Automobile Interior Industrial Co., Ltd	'98	Door Trim, Sunvisor	2	1	2	2	2	2	20	10	2	2		1		3		4					
Bo 12 ?	Uni Auto Parts Manufac-ture Co. Ltd/ Fuzhou Lanhong Motor Parts Company Ltd etc.	'98	(*Leaf Spring, Coil Spring*) (Electric)Seat, Headlining	2	1	2	2	2	1,2	80		3	1		3		2		4					
Bo 17	Tsu Tah Elastomerics Co., Ltd/ Xiamen Good Will Elastomeric Co., Ltd	'98	Valve Guide, Cylinder Liner, Air Intake Tube, Intake Manifold	1		1		1	1	60		2	2				1							
Bo 20	Ensure Co., Ltd/ Shanghai Alloy Wheel Co. Ltd	'95	Wheel Disk	1		2	1	1	1	95	20		2	5	1	90	2	5						
Bo 22	Chu Chang Rubber Co., Ltd / Chu-Shin(Fuzhou) Rubber Co., Ltd	'95	Silencer, Garnish/Trim, Rubber Parts	1		1		1,2	1	50		2,5	3	20	2	30	1	50						
Bo 25 ?	Fehrer Enterprise Corp. /China Hanquan Hi-Tech Textile(Pinghu)Ltd	'02	Floor Mat, Rear Trunk Trim	1		2	2	1	1,2	90			2	20	1	60	2	20						
Bo 30	Lih Feng Jing Enterprise Co., Ltd / Shanghai Fengya Fireproof Insulation Materials Co., Ltd	'98	Exhaust Muffler, Exhaust Pipe, Silencer, Heat Insu-lator	1		1		1	1	70	35		2		3		1		5		6		4	
Bo 33	Zeeman Industry Co. / Zeeman Fuses Mfg,(Xia-men)Corp. etc.	'89	Fuse Seat, Fuse	1		1		1	1	30	20	3,4	2	20	1	30	2	20	4	10	4	10	4	10

Table A1. *Continued*

No.	Company Name	Established Year	Main Products	Investment Form I * 1	Partner of JV I * 2	Investment Form II * 3	Partner of JV II * 4	Technical Grant I * 5	Technical Grant II * 6	Local Content (%)	Intra Firm Trade (%)	Procurement of Key Parts f * 7	Procurement of arts and material: Local Taiwanese firm R	Local Taiwanese firm %	Other local firm R	Other local firm %	From Taiwan R	From Taiwan %	From Japan R	From Japan %	From USA R	From USA %	Other country R	Other country %
Bo 38 ?	Tatung Precise Meter Co., Ltd / Changzhou Shan Chih Precise Machine Co., Ltd etc.	'95	Gauge Fuel Tank, Instrument Panel	2	1	1		2	1	50	30	2			3		1		2					
Bo 40	Kaifa Industry Co., Ltd / Hunan Kaifa Industry Co., Ltd etc.	'95	Shock Absorber	1		1		2	1	50	20	2	2		3		1		4					
Bo 46 ?	Tai Yue Rubber Industrial Co., Ltd / Fujou Fu-Yue Rubber & Plastic Industrial Co., Ltd	'95	*(Water/Radiator/Brake Hose)* Weatherstrip, Moulding, Rubber Parts	2	1	2	2	2	1,2	75			3	8	4	7	1	74	2	11				
Bo 47	Seng Ton Transportation Implements Co., Ltd / Xiamen Sengyen Transportation Implements Co., Ltd	'95	Air Cleaner, Air Cleaner Element, Catalytic Converter, Fuel Filter, Plastic Parts	1		1		1,2	1	60		2	1	60			2	40						
Bo 50 ?	GSK Steering Wheel Co., Ltd / Liao Yang Jinxing Automobile Decorations Co., Ltd etc.	'97	*(Parking Brake Lever, Air Bag)* Steering Wheel, Knob, Instrument Panel	2	1	2	1	1	1	80	10		2		1		3		4		5		6	
Bo 54	Three Brothers Machinery Industrial Co., Ltd / Ximen Three Brothers Machinery Ind. Co.	'95	*(Door Panel, Roof, Frame, Bumper)* Engine Hood, Die, Fixture, Jig	1		1		1	1	90	20		1	70	2	20	3	10						
Bo 56 ?	Chung Kwang Rubber Goods Mfg. Co., Ltd / Tianjin Star Light Rubber & Plastic Co., Ltd	'94	Side Protector, Bumper Pad, Weatherstrip, Plastic Parts, Rubber Parts	2	1	2	2	2,4	1,2,5	90	5	2,3	1	65	3	10	2	15	3	10				

Bo 57	Shiuan Yue Industry Co., Ltd / Fuzhou Shiuan Yue Metal Co., Ltd	'99	Engine Mounting, Chassis &Parts, Bumper, Stamping Parts, Cross Member, Shift Lever, Knob, Pedal	1		1		1	1	85		1	1	60	2	40								
Bo 59	Asset Trading Co., Ltd / Liuzhou Liuxin Auto Stamping Co., Ltd etc.	'98	Engine Hood, Car Body Door Panel, Fender, Roof, Frame, Bumper	1		2	1	2	1	45	10	2	3		4		2		1				5	
Bo 60	Kian Shen Corporation / Fu Shiang(Fuzhou)Motor Industrial Co., Ltd	'95	Engine Mounting, Frame, Stamping Parts	1		1		1,2	1	80	15	1			1	80	2	10	2	10				
Bo 61	Her Sheen Enteprise Co., Ltd / Fuzhou Hersheen Auto Parts Co., Ltd	'95	*Bumper, Stamping Parts, Cross Member, Pillar, Brake/Shift Lever,* Fender Trim, Mud Guard, Spoiler, Floor Mat	1		1		1,2	1,2	90	5	2	1	60	2	35	3	5						
Bo 62 ?	Wuu Shang Industrial Co., Ltd / Fu Zhou Fu Shiang Motor Industrial Co., Ltd etc.	'97	Radiator Mounting, Engine Mounting, Car Body, Door Panel, Chassis & Parts, Frame, Bumper, Stamping Parts	1		2	2	1	1	90	10	1	3	5	1	85	2	10						
Bo 63	Chao Long Motor Parts Corp.	'01	Gauge Fuel Tank, Meter, Fuel Gauge	1		1		1,2,4	1	70	50	5	1	60	2	20	3	10	3	10	5	5	5	5
Bo 64 ?	Ta Yih Industrial Co., Ltd / Fuzhou Ta Yih Industrial Co., Ltd	'95	Lamp, Die, Fixture, Jig, Checking Gauge	2	1	1		1	1	90		1	1	70	2	20	3	10						
Bo 66	Ren Chen Industrial Co., Ltd / Ren Chen(Shanghai)Industrial Co., Ltd	'00	Samping Parts, Die, Fixture, Jig, Checking Gauge	1		2	1	1	1	35	5		1				2							
Bo 67 ?	Fuchi Textile Co., Ltd	'94	Door Trim, Roof Lining	2	1	2	2	1,2	1,2	80	10		2	20	1	50	3	10	3	10			3	10
Bo 69	Eurocharm Innovation Co., Ltd / Allied Machineries (Shanghai) Co., Ltd	'95	Fuel Pipe, Stamping Parts, Die, Fixture, Jig, Checking Gauge	1		1		1	1	80	10	2	2	30	3	20	1	50						
Bo 70 ?	Hsin Chong Machinery Works Co., Ltd / Chong Qing Yan Feng Industry Co., Ltd	'98	Steering Wheel, Door Trim,(Electric), Seat, Heading	2	1	2	2	2	2	70			1		2		3							
El 01 ?	Mabuchi Taiwan Co., Ltd / Mabuchi Motor Jiangsu Co., Ltd	'95	Motor	2	1	2	2	1,2	1,2	50	5	2,3	3	20	4	10	1	30	2	30			5	10

Table A1. *Continued*

No.	Company Name	Established Year	Main Products	Investment Form I *1	Partner of JV I *2	Investment Form II *3	Partner of JV II *4	Technical Grant I *5	Technical Grant II *6	Local Content (%)	Intra Firm Trade (%)	Procurement of Key Parts f *7	Procurement of arts and material: Local Taiwan-ese firm R	%	Other local firm R	%	From Tai-wan R	%	From Japan R	%	From USA R	%	Other country R	%
El 03	Safety Control Cable Ind. Co., Ltd /Hsu Suey Hsing(Fuzhou)Auto Part Co.	'89	Control Table	1		1		1	1	90			3		1		2							
El 07	Just Auto Accessories Co., Ltd / Guang Shin International Co., Ltd	'98	Lamp, Spoiler, Exterior & Interior Parts	1		1		1,3	1	50	30	4	2	30	3	20	1	40			4	10		
El 13	Tai Yue Electric Co.., Ltd / Fuzhou Shin Yue Electric Co., Ltd	'95	Wire Harness, Fuse Seat, Switch	1		1		2	1	40	20	1	5	5	1	35	2	30	3	20			4	10
El 14 ?	Tong Yee Industrial Co. Ltd, / Tianjin Tong Yee Industrial Co. Ltd,	'93	Battery	2	1	2	2	2	1,2	99	50		2	7	1	90	3	2	4	1				
El 15	Universal Scientific Industrial Co., Ltd / Usi Electronics(Shenzhen)	'00	(*Combination Meter, Instrument Panel*) Regulator, Rectifier, Ignition Module	1		1		1	1	20		2	2	8	3	2	1	90						
El 16	Toh Fon Machine Co., Ltd / Jiang Yin Yuan Feng Communication Equipments Co., Ltd	'96	Control Cable	1		2	1	1	1	90	20	2	3	20	1	50	2	30						
El 21 ?	Toyo Jiann Tsang Electric Co., Ltd / Changzhou Toyo Jiann Tsang Electric Co., Ltd	'95	Switch	2	1	1		2	1	90		2	2	10	1	80	2	10						
El 27	E-Lead Electronic Co., Ltd / E-Lead Electronic Technology (Jiang Su) Co., Ltd	'00	(*Car Audio, Car Navi, Car Security*) Electrical Parts, Car Hand-Free, Mobil Phone	1		1		1	1	50		2	1	45	1	45								

El 36	Dainty Electric Industries Co., Ltd / Gemmy Electronics Co., Ltd etc.	'94	Horn, Car Audio	1		1		1	1	95			1	60	2	35	3	5				
El 37	Shin Chin Industrial Co., Ltd / Shin Chin Ind.(China)Co., Ltd	'95	Distributor, Fuse Seat, Ignition Cable, Ignition Coil, Battery Charger	1		1		2	1	50		2,3			1	50	2	30	3	20		
El 39 ?	Taiwan Calsonic Co., Ltd / Hui Zhou Dong Feng Yi-Jin Industrial Co., Ltd	'01	A/C Assy, Heater Assy, Condenser, Evaporator	2	1	2	1	2	1	30	20	2,3	4	10	1	30	1	30	1	30		
El 43 ?	Tung Thih Enterprise Co., Ltd / Xiamen Tung Thih Electron Co., Ltd	'94	Central Door Lock, Car Burglar Alarm, Reverse Sensor	2	1	2	1	1	1	50	20	3	1	30	3	20	1	30	3	20		
El 48	T.Y.C. Brother Industrial Co., Ltd / Changzhou Tamao Lighting Co., Ltd	'97	Lamp	1		1		1	1	80		2	2				1		3			
El 52	Taiwan Kou Mu Industrial Co., Ltd	'96	Switch, Door Lock, Lock	1		2	1	1	1	45	15		1		2		3		4			
El 55	Jenn Feng Industrial Co., Ltd / Shaghai Jenn Feng	'95	Lamp	1		1		3	1	30	5	3,4	1		2		3		5		4	6
El 68	Kaisers International Corp.	'00	LCD Car TV, Car Rear View	1		1		1	4	60	2	1	1		2		3					
En 02 ?	Shihlin Electric & Engineering Corp./ Changzhou Shihlin Electric & Engineering Co., Ltd etc.	'95	Engine Parts, Distributor, Motor, Ignition Coil	1		2	2	2	1	30	4.4	2	2	30	2	30	1	38	4	2		
En 04	United Alloy-Tech. Comp. / United Alloy Tech.(-Shenzhen)Co. Ltd	'92	(*Casting Parts*) Forging (Processing)	1		1		1	1				1	60	2	40						
En 06	Yung Jen Industry Co., Ltd / Yung Jen Enterprise Co., Ltd	'03	Radiator Mounting, Engine Mounting, Chassis & Parts	2	3	1		1	1	100	10		1		2							
En 08	Ying Ming Industry Co., Ltd / Ying Ming (Fuzhou) Industrial Co., Ltd	'95	Nut, Bolt, Forging Parts (Processing)	1		1		1	1	75		2	3	20	2	30	1	50				
En 10	Ghon Zu Industrial Corp. / Fuzhou Dongchang Machinery Model Ltd etc.	'96	(*Connecting Rod, Torsion Bar, Shift Lever*) Die, Fixture, Jig, Checking Gauge	1		1		1	1	85	40		1	40	2	20	1	40				
En 11	ROC-Spicer Ltd / Fujian Spicer Drivetrain System Co., Ltd, Shenyang Spicer Driveshaft Co., Ltd	'94	Rear Axle Assy, Propeller Shaft	2	2	1		3	1	70	10	2	1				2					

Table A1. *Continued*

No.	Company Name	Established Year	Main Products	Investment Form I * 1	Partner of JV I * 2	Investment Form II * 3	Partner of JV II * 4	Technical Grant I * 5	Technical Grant II * 6	Local Content (%)	Intra Firm Trade (%)	Procurement of Key Parts f * 7	Procurement of arts and material											
													Local Taiwan-ese firm		Other local firm		From Tai-wan		From Japan		From USA		Other country	
													R	%	R	%	R	%	R	%	R	%	R	%
En 18 ?	Shye Shyang Mechanical Industrial Co., Ltd / Shye Shyang(Fujian)Mechanical Industrial Co., Ltd etc.	'96	(*Air Cleaner, Catalytic Converter*) Fuel Tank, Exhaust Muffler, Steering Column, Clutch Assy	2	1	2	2	2	1,2	80		2	3	5	1	75	2	20						
En 19	Jui Li Enterprise Co., Ltd / Hainan Jui Li Industry Co., Ltd	'02	(*Fuel Tank, Chassis &related Parts, Die, Fix-ture, Jig, Checking Gauge*) Engine Hood, Door Panel, Fender, Trunk Lid	1		1		1	1	10	20	2					1	100						
En 23 ?	Full Wei Industry Co., Ltd / Foshan Shi Quanhui Auto Parts Co., Ltd	'00	Fuel Tank, Exhaust Muf-fler, Exhaust Manifold, Exhaust Pipe, Oil Filter, Frame, Bumper, Die, Fix-ture, Jig, Checking Gauge	1		2	2	1,2	1	70			2	25	3	15			1	60				
En 24	Heng Tong Auto Parts Inc. / Heng Kuo Machinery Co., Ltd etc.	'93	Brake (Master) Cylinder, Drum/Disk Brake Assy	1		1		1,2,3	1	70	2	2,3	1		2		3		4					
En 26	Right Way Industrial Co., Ltd / Right Way Auto Part(Fuzhou)Co. Ltd	'96	Piston, Connecting Rod	1		1		1	1	72	5.5	2	1		2		3							
En 28	Sing Yung Machinery Co., Ltd / Wu Han Sing Yung Brake Co., Ltd	'94	(*Brake (Master) Cylinder, Clutch (Master)* Cylinder) Brake Cylinder	1		2	1	1	1	84	4	2	1	84			2	16						
En 29	Zenith Troop Industrial Co., Ltd / Shanghai Da Tong Co., Ltd	'93	Piston. Piston Pin, Piston Ring	1		2	1	1	1	80	40		2	10	1	80	2	10						
En 31	Hentry Factory Co., Ltd / Xiamen Jing Heng Hard-ware Industry Co., Ltd	'95	Nut, Bolt, Screw, Stamp Parts	2	3	1		1,4	1,5	80	15		3	15	1	65	2	20						

En 34 ?	World Known Mfg. Co., Ltd / Changle Anderson Machine Hardware Co., Ltd	'03	(*Camshaft, Crankshaft, Flywheel, Exhaust manifold*) Brake Cylinder, Brake Master Cylinder, Brake Drum /Disc	2	1	1		1	1	60	7		1		2		3		4				
En 35	Hota Industrial Mfg. Co., Ltd / Wuxi Hota Precision Gear Co., Ltd	'96	(*Mainshaft/Countershaht, Propeller Shaft*) Camshaft, Gear Shift Parts ,Gear (Motorcycle)	1		2	1	1	1	60	1		1		2		3						
En 42	Je-Ee Industry Co., Ltd / Shenzhen Yibao Industry Co., Ltd	'94	Engine Parts, Intake Manifold, Fuel/Oil /Water Pump, Forging /Casting Parts (Processing)	1		1		1	1	5	10	5	2		1		3		4		6	5	
En 44 ?	Taiwan Riken Industrial Co., Ltd / Xiamen Riken Industrial Co., Ltd	'89	(*Camshaft,Exhaust Manifold, Casting Parts Processing*) Piston Ring ,Cylinder	2	1	1		2	1	50	10				1	40	2	30	2	30			
En 45	San Yes Automotive Technology Co., Ltd / Fuzou San Yes Automotive Industry Co., Ltd	'96	Intake Manifold, Brake (Master) Cylinder, Clutch (Master) Cylinder, Casting Parts (Processing)	1		1		1	1	80	12	2	3		1		2						
En 49 ?	Fu pen Rubber Industrial Co., Ltd / Fu Zhou Fu Chuan Rubber Co., Ltd etc.	'95	Engine Gasket Kits, Cylinder Liner, Piston Liner, Connecting Rod, Air Intake Tube	1		2	2	1,2	1,2	95	5	1	2		1		4		3				
En 51	Cheng Shing Piston Co., Ltd / Changzhou Cheng Shing Piston Co., Ltd etc.	'95	Piston	1		1		1,2	1,2,3	15	15	2	3	20	2	25	1	50	4	5			
En 53	Goshen Industries, Inc. / Goshen(Fuzhou)Industries, Inc.	'97	(*Stabilizer Bar, Torsion Bar*) Brake Tube, Drum/-Disc Brake Assy. Brake Drum/Disc	1		1		2	1	85		2	3		4		1		2				
En 58 ?	Lioho Machine Works Ltd / Hujiwa Machinery Industry Co., Ltd etc.	'92	Engine Parts, Fuel Tank, Exhaust Manifold, Intake Manifold, Power Steering Pump, Drum/Disc Brake	1		2	2	2	1	80	20	2	2	20	2	20	1	30	5	10		2	20
En 71	Shinnfu Corporation / Shinn Chia Machinery & Foundry(Kun Shan) Co., Ltd etc.	'94	Crankshaft, Connecting Rod, Drum/Disc Brake Assy. Brake Drum/Disc	1		1		2	1,2	75	3	2,3	1	35	3	15	1	35	3	15			

Table A1. *Continued*

No.	Company Name	Established Year	Main Products	Investment Form I *1	Partner of JV I *2	Investment Form II *3	Partner of JV II *4	Technical Grant I *5	Technical Grant II *6	Local Content (%)	Intra Firm Trade (%)	Procurement of Key Parts f *7	Procurement of arts and material: Local Taiwan-ese firm		Other local firm		From Tai-wan		From Japan		From USA		Other country	
													R	%	R	%	R	%	R	%	R	%	R	%
En 72	Zoeng Chang Industry Co., Ltd / Rongtai (Wuxi)Casting & Forging Co., Ltd	'99	(*Engine Parts, Crankshaft, Gear Shift Parts, Clutch, Forging/Casting Parts Processing*) Propeller Shaft	2	2	2	1	3	1	65	14	2	3		1		2		6		4		5	
Ti 32	Nankang Rubber Tire Co., Ltd / Nankang Rubber Industry Co., Ltd	'97	Tire	1		1		1,2	1	80	0	2,3	1		2		4						3	
Ti 41	Federal Corporation / Federal Tire(Jiang Xi)Ltd	'96	Tire	1		1		1,2	1	65	10	1,2,5	1	40	3	10	3	10					1	40
Ti 65	Kenda Rubber Industrial Co., Ltd / Kenda Rubber(-Shenzen)Co., Ltd etc.	'94	Tire	1		1		1	1	70	15		1		2		4						3	

Note:(1)*1: (Taiwanese parent firm) 1 = Solely owned, 2 = Joint venture
*2: (Taiwanese parent firm) 1 = Japanese firm, 2 = American firm, 3 = Others
*3: (Chinese subsidiary) 1 = Solely owned, 2 = Joint venture
*4: (Chinese subsidiary) 1 = Chinese firm, 2 = Japanese firm, 3 = American firm, 4 = Others
*5: (Taiwanese parent firm) 1 = Owned by oneself, 2 = from Japan, 3 = from American, 4 = from Others
*6: (Chinese subsidiary) 1 = Taiwanese parent firm, 2 = from Japan, 3 = from American, 4 = Owned by oneself, 5 = from Others
*7: 1 = owned by oneself, 2 = from Taiwan, 3 = from Japan, 4 = from USA, 5 = from others

(2) ?R?means the firms who replied by ranking; ?%?means the firms who answered by percentage.

(3) ???is a subsidiary company or joint enterprises of the Japanese company (there are 23 companies in total).

(4) The former company name is Taiwanese parent company name, and the latter are the Chinese subsidiary company names (when the English name is not available, we show the parent company's name only).

(5) An italic type character in the parentheses of Main Products means that they are produced only in Taiwan, the others are produced in common.

Source: Author's survey, 2004–05.

Technology Transfer in Automotive Parts Firms in China

YURI SADOI

Introduction

The automobile industry in China has developed rapidly in the last two decades following increased flows of FDI into the country. Economic reforms allowed foreigners to establish joint ventures legally with Chinese companies on Chinese territory, on the principle of equity and mutual benefit since 1979. The large domestic market has been a key driver of the automobile sector: China became the fourth largest producer and third largest seller of automobiles in the world in 2004, reaching 4.44 million cars per year. China's strategic relations with foreign investors – including through effective technology, transfer initiatives – have been important in the development of local firms within a short period of time.

This contribution aims to analyse the development of the automotive parts industry in China with a focus on the impact of foreign direct investment on the technological capability of local suppliers. It examines in detail upgrading strategies in the core technology of engine and transmission parts, which is pertinent for China to move up the technology ladder in the automotive industry. The rest of the contribution is organized as follows. The next section analyses FDI inflows into the automotive industry, followed by automobile development policies and strategies used to promote technology transfer from foreign to local firms in China. The subsequent section draws on company-level interviews in Shanghai and Shenyang to evaluate the technical capability and skill formation strategies in metal engineering firms – for example, forging, casting, machining, and welding – which are key components in the assembly of completely knocked down (CKD) automobile parts. The localization experience of Chinese suppliers are compared throughout with that of Malaysia's Proton since both China and Malaysia started automobile manufacturing in the 1980s using national industrial development policies. The primary research information used in this study was gathered by the author over the period 2004–05 in Shanghai and Shenyang, and 1996–99 in Malaysia (see Sadoi, 2003).

Foreign Direct Investment and Technology Transfer

The impact of foreign direct investment on economic development has been a subject of study for many years, more actively since the 1970s. The economic rise of Asian NIEs in the 1970s and development of South East Asian countries since the late 1980s has been attributed to the increase of FDI from Japan. Following the Plaza Accord, the trend accelerated due to the high appreciation of the yen. After the Asian financial crises of 1997, FDI was re-evaluated as an important and a more secure source of finance than other forms of private capital flows of portfolio equity. FDI fulfils domestic capital needs and allows technology transfer to recipients.

The three basic ways for countries to acquire technology are: export, licence, and FDI. FDI is one of the means available for a firm to transfer technology outside its home country, or that a host country can use to acquire technology. A firm may export products that embody the technology, a firm may license its technology to an agent abroad who then uses the technology to upgrade its own production, and a firm can set up a foreign establishment using FDI to exploit the technology itself (Maher & Christiansen, 2001).

FDI in China has been increasing since the 1990s. Multinational enterprises (MNEs) make decisions concerning FDI based on factors, such as ownership advantages, location advantages and internationalization advantages (Dunning, 1993). There are six main location advantages (Lee & Houde, 2000). These are market size and growth prospects, natural and human resource endowments including the cost and productivity of labour, physical financial and technological infrastructure, openness to international trade and access to international markets, the regulatory and policy framework and policy coherence, and investment promotion. In the case of China, using the absolute advantage in terms of its location, China has attracted FDIs and has even been able to control the FDIs in order to facilitate technology transfer.

The three key elements that can be identified in the operation of a joint venture are MNEs, the indigenous firm and the host government. Securing a joint venture with an MNE appears an efficient means of acquiring advanced technology as well as capital investment (Zhang & Taylor, 2001). In China, the joint venture between a Chinese firm and a MNE is the dominant form of technology transfer (Chen, 2000).

The Chinese strategy of technology transfer can be described by the following principle (Wang, 1999): to attract large MNEs to invest in China since MNEs are the major source of technology, and to revise regulation on foreign investment in which the foreign funded enterprise sector is to be encouraged, including high-technology industries.

This strategy is typically observed in the automobile industry development policies by the Chinese government. For example, the policy in 1994, which was the policy in which the government officially stated the automobile industrial development policy, as one of five pillar industries: the machine-building, automobile, electronics, petroleum and construction sectors. The policy requires MNEs to regulate an advanced level of products, production facilities, machine tools, and the requirement of research and development facilities.

The automobile production technology is regarded as difficult to transfer because it requires more coordination processes than the electric and other industries (Fujimoto & Shintaku, 2005). Therefore, the state required high technology for MNEs, using its absolute location advantages.

Wang (1999) pointed out the other strategy about the reform of state-owned enterprises. That is, the reform of state-owned enterprises to upgrade the level of industry concentration which provides a new investment niche for foreign investors. China has decided to sell off a lot of small state-owned enterprises. Foreign investors are permitted to merge, lease or buy out medium-sized and small state-owned firms, whereas previously they could only form joint ventures or cooperate with state-owned enterprises or establish wholly-owned subsidiaries to balance the industrial structure. Thus, China depends primarily on technology transfer from developed countries to facilitate their technology upgrading.

A major pattern of setting up joint ventures with MNEs and indigenous firms in developing countries is illustrated in Figure 1. The automobile industry consists of a layered structure of firms, with the final assembler at the top, the next layer of the first tier suppliers, then the second tier suppliers, and so on. In most cases, the final assemblers are joint ventures of MNEs and indigenous firms. Then, when the final assembler proceeds to localize its supplied parts, the common practice seen in many developing countries is that the final assembler acts as a go-between and helps to set up joint ventures of its supplier in its own country with a local firm. When the first tier firms promote their localization, the first tier firms act as a go-between for the second tier. Similar practices are seen in each layer of the industry.

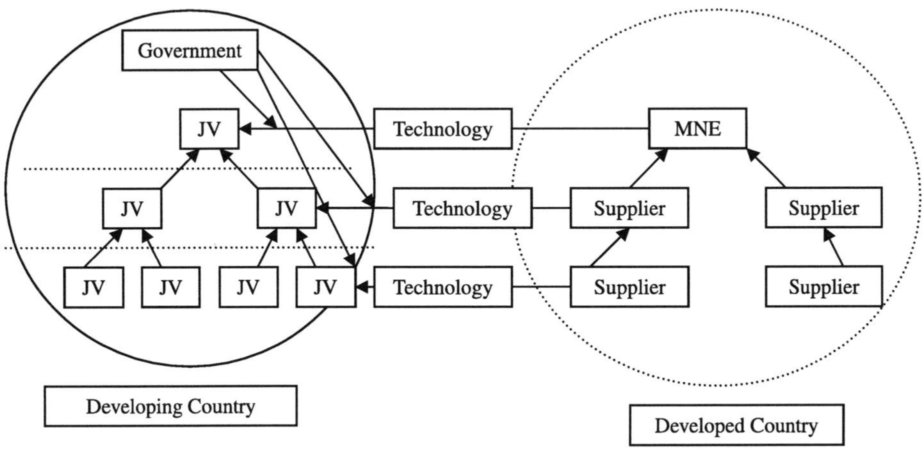

Figure 1. Technology transfer in the automobile industry. *Notes:* JV = Joint Venture; MNE = Multinational Enterprise.

As noted above, the automobile industry in China has developed by achieving high technology largely from the technology transfer of MNEs. A hypothesis arises here that if the Chinese automobile industry achieved a high technology level by technology transfer from MNEs, is the situation the same for the final assembler and the first and second tier suppliers?

Historical Backdrop

This section examines the development process of the automobile industry in China and the effects of industrial policies for development. China launched its automobile industry in 1956, with the cooperation of the Soviet Union, and established the First Automobile Works to produce the Jiefang ('Liberation') line of middle size trucks. The production technology transferred from the Soviet Union was the Ford production system in the 1920–30s. This particular technology transfer set was simply a re-transfer of Fordism via the Soviet Union (Lee, 1995).

Until 1978, the industry was organized according to a strict centrally planned system in which each province had one major industry. The largest automobile manufacturers were the First Automobile Works, now First Automobile Works (Group) Corp., (FAW) in Changchun, Jilin Province established in 1956, and the Second Auto Works (Dongfeng Motor Corp., or DMC) in Shiyan, Hubei Province, established in 1969.

At the time of the opening of the Chinese economy in 1978, a total of 55 automobile manufactures were producing 150,000 vehicles, of which only 5,000 were passenger cars. There were a great many small-scale automobile manufacturers in China. The number of automobile firms continued to grow, with a total of over 100 in 1985 and a production volume which exceeded 440,000 (Maruyama, 2001). However, the sector still included too many small-scale firms with low productivity.

In 1986, the leading automobile manufacturers in China were reorganized in terms of both production capacity and the types of vehicle produced, and consequently referred to as the 'Big Seven'. In addition to FAW and DMC, they included Beijing Automotive Industry Group Corp. (BAIC), China National Heavy-duty Truck Corp. (CNHTC), Shanghai Automotive Industry Group Corp. (SAIC), Tianjin Automotive Industry Group Corp. (TAIC), and Yuejin Automobile Group Corp. (YAGC).

The passenger-car market was dominated by eight firms, six of which were China-foreign joint ventures and two of which were the result of technological collaborations with Japanese firms. These assembly facilities are referred to as the 'Big Three' (DMC, FAW, and SAIC), the 'Little Three' (BAIC, Guangzhou Peugeot, and TAIC), and the 'Two Minis' (Chang An Automobile Co., Ltd. and Guizhou Aviation Industry Corp.).

The central government's Ministry of Machine-Building Industry (MMI) is responsible for supervising the country's automobile industry. MMI is responsible for industry-related investment, project approval, production planning and overall policy decisions. Except for CNHTC, DMC and FAW, which are under the direct authority of the State Planning Commission (SPC), all of China's carmakers are under direct control of a ministry or a provincial or municipal government. BAIC,

SAIC, and TAIC, for example, are under the jurisdictions of the respective municipalities of Beijing, Shanghai, and Tianjin. The Guangzhou city government oversees Guangzhou-Peugeot. Chang An and Guizhou are under the control of the ministerial-level entities China North Industries Corp. (NORINCO) and China National Aviation Industry Corp. (AVIC).

In 1994, the government officially formulated an automobile industry development policy. The policy forced on FDI regulations for engine and complete car manufacturers in order to acquire upgraded technology, and to improve R&D capabilities and productivity (Fourin, 2005). This policy was the first official statement which included guidelines for FDI in automobile sectors. Following the inception of this policy, investment increased substantially.

The number of FDI contracts in China between 1986 and 2003 is shown in Figure 2. The investment contracts increased slowly until 1991. Hong Kong was a major source of investment until 1991. The investment figures from Hong Kong include investments from Taiwan, Europe and other areas. The year 1992 shows a dramatic increase in FDI cases. Following a peak in 1993, the number of investments started to decline. After 2000, the number of investments from Taiwan, Japan and Korea increased steadily. For a long time, Hong Kong was responsible for a majority of FDI in China, but its share has now decreased to almost one-third of total FDI in China. Most of the investments concern the manufacturing industry, followed by service and trading sectors. In manufacturing industries, the highest investment came from Hong Kong and accounted for nearly US$250 billion in 2003, followed by investments from the Virgin Islands, Korea and Japan. In service and trading sectors, most of the investments came from Hong Kong (Seike & Ma, 2005).

Ever since China officially opened its doors in 1978, the automobile, and parts and material industries have become attractive sectors for foreign investors. In the 20 years spanning the period from 1983 to 2004, the total number of automotive cooperative (including parts and components) projects, joint ventures and wholly foreign-owned ventures reached 1,449 (Fourin, 2005).

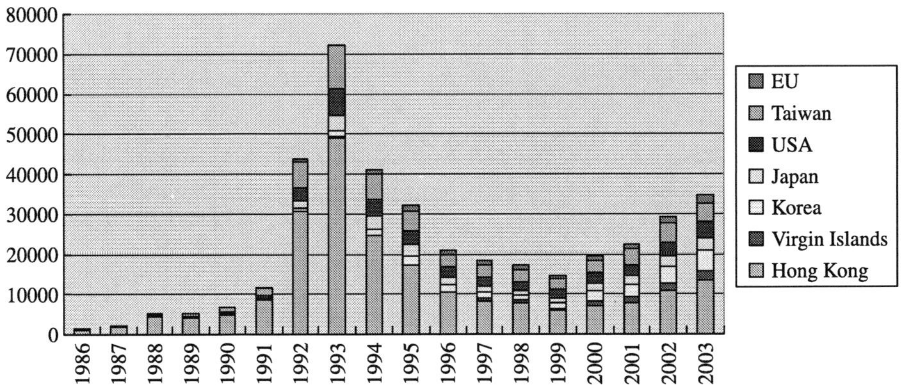

Figure 2. Number of FDI contracts in China. *Source:* (Seike & Ma, 2005).

A joint venture between Ford Motor Co. and Jiang-ling Motors Corp. in Nanchang, Jiangxi Province produces transit vans. Ford has also set up four automobile component joint ventures. Other van or light-bus joint ventures include Fuzhou-China Motors Corp. (China Motors is a Taiwan-based affiliate of Mitsubishi Motors Corp.), Jinbei-Hiace, Nanjing-Iveco (a joint venture with Iveco, a unit of Italy's Fiat S.p.A.), and Sanjiang-Renault. In addition, Nissan Motor Co. has a 5 per cent equity interest in the Zhengzhou-Nissan Automobile Co. to produce Nissan pick-up trucks. Chrysler Corp.'s joint venture, Beijing Jeep Corp., has been producing its multi-purpose vehicles since the mid-1980s. The Two Minis have both recently announced joint-venture deals with Japanese technology providers. Chang An is working with Suzuki Motors to produce the 0.8-liter Alto, and Guizhou with Fuji Heavy Industries Ltd. to produce the 0.54-liter Skylark. As the result, the production volume of passenger cars in China has increased in the 1990s and grew drastically from 2000 as shown in Figure 3. The production volume of Malaysia is shown in the figure as a reference and will be discussed in a later section.

The growing number of foreign automobile manufacturers in China has stimulated the world's leading automotive parts firms rushing to set up their China subsidiaries. Figure 4 shows automotive parts and material suppliers' investment operations in China from 1983 to 2004. Among these, the number of investments by Japanese parts suppliers is highest. The investments began around the mid-1980s, and were at first limited in number. The investments began to increase starting in 1992, culminating in 1994 and 1995. In 1995, Japan alone was responsible for 120 instances of investment in automobile parts industry. Following this period, investments slowed down for a couple of years. From 2000 onwards, however, investment from Japan has again dramatically increased, with over 120 cases per year after 2002.

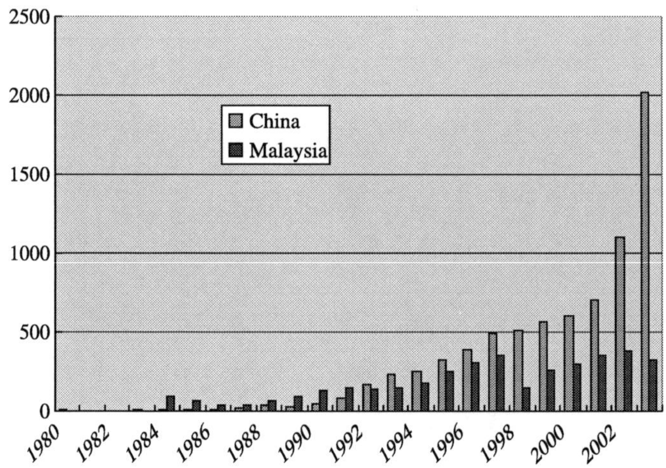

Figure 3. Production volume of passenger cars in China and Malaysia. *Source:* Malaysia data: MAA, China data: Fourin, 2005. Unit: 1,000 vehicles.

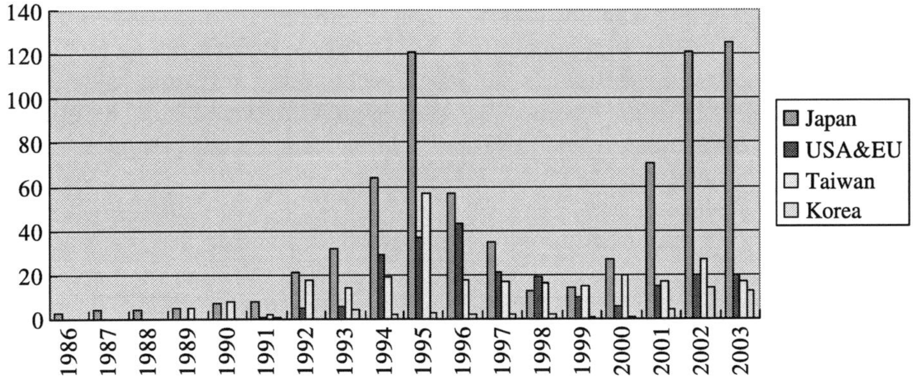

Figure 4. Number of FDI cases of the automobile parts and material suppliers in China. *Source:* (Fourin, 2005).

Most American and European leading parts suppliers are involved in parts and components joint ventures in China; examples of these are Robert Bosch, Cooper, Dana Corp., Delphi Automotive Systems, ITT, Lucas Varity Inc., Rockwell, Siemens, TRW Inc., Tenneco Inc., United Technologies Corp., Valeo, AlliedSignal Inc. Delphi alone has formed more than a dozen joint ventures, and developed one wholly owned enterprise for the production of engine-management systems, wire harnesses, electric systems, drive shafts, brake systems, steering gears and columns, and generators and batteries (Delphi, 2005).

Methodology and Data

In order to examine the hypothesis of this contribution – that if the Chinese automobile industry achieved high technology level by technology transfer from MNEs, have the final assembler, the first tier supplier, the second tier suppliers acquired their technical capabilities from their foreign joint venture partners? – this section describes the empirical research on the automobile industry in China.

The methodology used here is as follows. The automobile industry is divided into three layers of firms. They are: final assembler, the first tier supplier (especially core technology) and the second tier suppliers (especially core technology). For the core technology, we have selected an engine supplier for the first tier, and clutch disk and oil tank suppliers for the second tiers, as the engine and its parts are regarded as key parts because they require the highest precision, durability, reliability and technology. Then, for the three layered research objects, establishment background, development process, products and their production technology, as well as localization rate and process are surveyed. In addition, interview research with managers and engineers, was carried out by the author in 2004, 2005 and 2006.

Final Assembler Survey

First, a major automobile manufacturer in China located in Shanghai – Volkswagen Automotive Co., Ltd. (SVW) – was chosen and researched by the author to survey the technology levels and localization rates of a Chinese automobile manufacturer. FDI generally helped upgrade its technology levels and localization rate. In this section, technology levels and localization rates of the Chinese automobile and automotive parts manufacturers are examined. The production site research and interviews with managers and engineers were carried out by the author in August 2004.

Shanghai Volkswagen Automotive Co., Ltd. (SVW) was established in 1985, a China-German joint venture automobile manufacturer, the Chinese shareholders owning 50 per cent and the German shareholders owning the other 50 per cent, on a 25-year contract. SVW is located in Anting International Auto City in the north-west of Shanghai, covering a total area of 3.218 million square metres and employing 15,000. SVW currently has the largest production scale and the widest product variety in China, covering models such as Santana B2, Santana 3000, Passat, POLO and GOLF. SVW holds a 52 per cent share of the domestic sedan market with its 1.8-litre Santana. Its has an annual production capacity of 450,000 units. In 2003, it achieved 215,547 units of sales. Currently, SVW has four major production plants, three car plants and one engine plant. SVW also has a technical centre with a prototype-making and testing base, and a proving ground.[1]

The production volume and localization rates of SVW are shown in Figure 5. As shown in the figure, during the first ten years of the production, the volume remained low. However, the localization rate increased from the beginning of the 1990s. By June 1995, 281 parts suppliers were supplying parts to SVW, and 167 of them (59.4 per cent) were located in Shanghai city (Ikeya, 1997). Among the 281 suppliers for SVW, 183 firms completed their localization, purchasing their sub-parts 100 per cent locally. Out of the 183 localized firms, 64 were joint

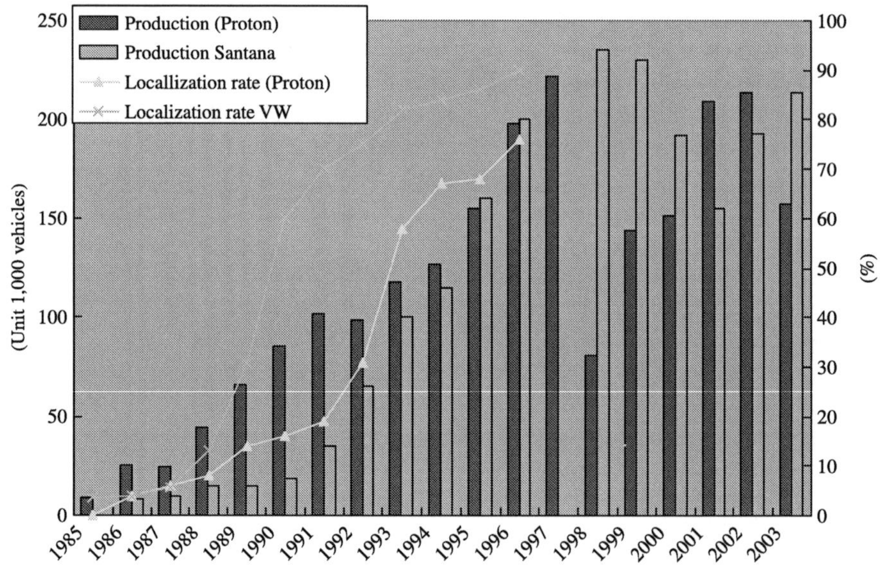

Figure 5. Production volume and localization rate in Proton and Shanghai VW. *Source:* Proton data: (Sadoi, 2003), Shanghai VW data: Fourin (2005), Ikeya (1997), Chen (2000).

ventures with foreign automotive parts suppliers, 45 were involved in technical collaboration or testing equipment from foreign countries and 28 imported their production lines from abroad (Ikeya, 1997).

Although in the early phase, SVW displayed a high localization rate where parts were concerned, the situation might have been different in the other areas. In order to examine the localization status and technological capability closely, the following section surveys and analyses key parts suppliers in China.

Engine Firm Survey (First Tier)

In the study of technical capabilities, casting, forging, and machining technologies in key parts play an important role in improving the national technological base (Sadoi, 2003). In this section, to examine the hypothesis of the contribution, the role of FDI partner and the capabilities in engine and transmission parts suppliers are discussed. To this end, Shenyang city has been chosen for the research, since it is the area in China where heavy industry was first developed.

Shenyang Aerospace Mitsubishi Motors Engine Manufacturing Co., Ltd (SAME), and its local suppliers were surveyed and interviewed with directors, managers, engineers and workers by the author in 2005 and 2006 in order to analyse localization practices and the capabilities of local producers. SAME was founded in 1997 as a joint venture between the state aerospace engine manufacturer producing military aircraft engines and Mitsubishi Motors. The Chinese government wanted to privatize its state military engine manufacture through association with a foreign partner. In 1994, the government of China proposed a joint venture to Mitsubishi Motors and, in 1996, the joint venture project was officially signed. The joint venture was established in 1997 with the Chinese partner controlling 51 per cent of the capital (China Aerospace Manufacture controlled 30 per cent and Shenyang automobile 21 per cent). The other partners controlled respectively 25 per cent (Mitsubishi Motors), 14.7 per cent (Malaysia CIC), and 9.3 per cent (Mitsubishi Corporation).

The initial production, consisting of semi knocked down production, began in 1999. The engine plant had at its disposal all production processes required for casting, aluminium die-casting, machining and assembling. The installed machine tools were state of the art and brand new, which meant the equipment was superior to that of the Mitsubishi engine plant in Kyoto Japan, which had been operated for 15 years. In order to accelerate technology transfer and improve the technology level in China, the Chinese government introduced a system of regulation for the installation of new production lines. New production lines had to contain facilities or machine tools which had to have been designed or produced within the last eight years.[2] As a result, brand new upgraded machine tools were installed in the Shenyang plant. More than 80 per cent of machine tools came from Japan, nearly 15 per cent from Germany and the rest from Chinese machine tool companies.

Instruction concerning the production lines was carried out in its entirety by the Mitsubishi partner. Production technology staff from Japan were sent to speed up the installations. First, an assembly line was installed and semi knocked down production began in 1999. The initial installation of cylinder block casting lines and cylinder heads die-casting lines took longer than Mitsubishi Motors Corporation

(MMC) expected because of the differences in the level of technology available to the state aerospace manufacturer and the technology required for the new plants. In addition, production staff and workers working with aerospace engines were not used to setting up new production technology; nor were they used to the working attitudes in the new joint venture system. Among the 800 workers in the new plant, 400 workers, approximately half of all employees, came from the aerospace engine manufacturer. Another 400 employees were newly hired. The president and two vice-presidents came from MMC. In total, 11 Japanese occupied management and advisory positions.

Once the casting lines for cylinder blocks and the die-casting line for cylinder heads were completed, completely knocked down production began. In the following year, 2000, machining lines for cylinder blocks and cylinder heads were completed and full production began. In 2005, the joint venture produced 150,000 engines and built a new plant to increase its production capacity to 300,000 engines by the end of 2005.

Most of the engine and transmission parts are produced in SAME or purchased from SAME's local suppliers. Table 1 shows a list of major engine and transmission parts. The list indicates the production location of those major parts. They are divided into in-house, local suppliers, imported from Japan, and imported from other countries. Cylinder blocks, cylinder heads, cam shafts, con-rods, crankshafts and intake manifolds are produced in-house by SAME. Other parts are purchased from local suppliers or imported from Japan. As shown in Table 1, all 24 major parts are produced locally, either in-house or by local suppliers. Twenty parts are either produced locally or imported from Japan, depending on the type of engine. It seems that the division of labour between China and Japan is determined on basis of the type of engine and transmission. For instance, one type of cylinder block is produced by SAME and exported to Japan because of the scale merit. Because it is imported from Japan does not always mean that SAME is not able to produce the part. It is noteworthy that as far as engine and transmission parts are concerned, practically all parts can be purchased from local suppliers. In addition, four parts are only produced locally. What is more, the majority of local suppliers are 100 per cent Chinese owned. There were no subsidiaries of major foreign parts manufacturers in the list of suppliers.

Second Tier Suppliers Survey

What is the status of the technology level and technical capability of the local suppliers? How did the parts suppliers in China obtain the production technology required for major engine and transmission parts? Two SAME suppliers, a clutch disk supplier and a fuel tank supplier, were surveyed in 2005 in order to study their development processes and current technical capability

The clutch disk firm. Shenyang Yidong Quadruple Ring Clutch Co. Ltd. (SYQ), a joint venture specializing in the production of clutches, was formally founded in Shenyang in April 2000 by two state corporations, Changchun Yidong Clutch Co. Ltd and the Shenyang General Factory of Frictional and Sealing Materials. Before

Table 1. Major engine and transmission parts list and localization status in China

		China			
	Major parts	In-house	Local suppliers	Import Japan	Import others
Engine	Cylinder head	○		○	
	Cam shaft	○		○	
	Intake/exhaust valve	○	○	○	
	Cylinder block		○	○	○
	Piston		○	○	
	Timing belt cover		○	○	
	Con-rod	○		○	
	Flywheel		○	○	
	Crankshaft	○		○	
	Oil pump		○	○	
	Oil seal		○	○	
	Fuel injector		○	○	
	Fuel pump		○		
	Fuel tank		○		
	Intake manufold	○	○	○	
	Exhaust manifold		○	○	
	Catalytic converter				
	Turbo charger				
	Ecu		○	○	
	Sensors		○	○	
	Water pump		○	○	
	Fan		○	○	
	Radiator		○		
Transmission	Clutch disk		○	○	
	Clutch disk cover		○	○	
	Clutch housing		○		
	Gears		○		
	Gear box housing		○		
	Drive shaft				
	Differential shaft		○		

Source: Author's survey in 2005.

the economic revolution, these two companies worked as state enterprises and produced clutches for trucks.

SYQ was founded to produce clutches for passenger cars and adopted the advanced technology for clutch disks without any technical collaboration with foreign manufacturers. Since SYQ knew that Shenyang state would set up SAME for the production of engines for passenger cars in 2000, their aim was to begin producing clutch disks for these cars.

The first target of SYQ was to acquire qualifications for supplying clutches to SAME. In order to qualify as a SAME supplier, the production of one of the parts, that is, the disks, received technical support from AP, a UK clutch manufacturer, and SYQ also imported one type of disk from Valeo, based on technical advice from SAME. Other parts were all produced in-house. Forging, machining, stamping and assembly processes were all carried out in-house. Only screws and bolts were purchased from local suppliers.

SYQ produces clutches of the diaphragm-spring type for its automobile engines. They began supplying the clutch to SAME in 2001 and adapted production in order to produce various types and specifications of Mitsubishi models. These clutches are mainly used in car models such as Shenyang Shonghua, Changfeng Cheetah, Southeast Delika, Southeast Fulika, Fengxing of Liuzhou Automobile Factory, Shenyang Gold cup, Jiangling, Beijing Pajero and others.

All machine tools, forging, pressing and machining, were made and installed by Chinese machine tool makers. It is noteworthy that all the metal moulds were made in China and maintained and modified by SYQ. SYQ qualified for QS9000 authentication and ISO 9001 in 2003, and is preparing for upgrading the quality systems to ISO/TS 16949.

The president of SYQ has much varied experience with the production process in this former state enterprise. He began his career as a simple worker and was promoted first to the position of manager in a production section, then a purchasing manager, a general sales manager, and finally the president of the parent plant of Shenyang. All four SYQ executives came from parent companies. Three of them, the president, the vice-president in charge of production, and the purchasing director, came from Shenyang, and the vice-president in charge of finance came from Changchun.

SYQ has 110 employees and 20 temporary workers. One quarter of the staff consists of engineers and university graduates and the other three-quarters are high-school graduates or graduates from technical schools such as the Toyota training school. The average age of the employees is 32.

SYQ introduced a new evaluation system for all managers and workers in order to motivate employees and increase productivity. All managers are evaluated based on their meeting a yearly target which they set themselves. Assistant managers evaluate section managers and workers every month. Each section consists of four to five workers. There is no grading system for evaluating workers; instead they are evaluated by performance related to their wage system. The workers' wages consist of a basic wage and a performance evaluation. Wages vary greatly, with a ratio of 1 to 4 between maximum and minimum wages. In addition, SYQ also introduced a reward and punishment system. For example, a 25,000 yuan reward (equivalent to 30 months' salary) was offered to a worker who completed a new irregular production in a short period of time. On the other hand, a manager was fined 3,000 yuan for a problem in production management.

This evaluation system has improved SYQ's productivity. For instance, the net sales of the former state clutch firm were 20 million yuan for each 1,400 employees. At the moment, 30 million yuan net sales are produced for each 100 employees, a 20 times higher rate of productivity.

The fuel tank firm. Shenyang Automobile Filter Factory (SAF), a state enterprise, has been producing fuel tanks for trucks for nearly 40 years. In 1998, SAF started to issue stocks and renovated the factory to produce parts for passenger cars. From 2003 onwards, SAF started to produce parts for passenger cars. These were mainly presswork and welding parts, such as air filters, gas tanks, engine suspension beams, instrument board cross beams, engine rocker arms, compartment feeds, and air condition presswork. SAF supplies to SAME, Shenyang Jinbei Automobile Manufacturer, Harbin Dongan Automobile Engine Manufacturing and others. It includes more than 100 sets of large-type cold pressing equipment, machinery processing equipment and automatic welding equipment, as well as three production lines of electrostatic painting. In 2001, the factory acquired a QS-9000 quality authentication certificate.

SAF was never involved in any technical collaboration with or capital investment from foreign manufacturers. Production lines and machine tools were all made in China. The vice-president of SAF designed and built the electrostatic painting lines. For presswork, SAF uses hundreds of metal moulds. These metal moulds are mostly made and modified in-house. SAF bought a hundred old metal moulds from a Japanese electric manufacturer for a very low price and used them in the factory. Ninety five per cent of steel and aluminium materials are supplied from local steel companies and the remaining 5 per cent are from Nippon Steel Corporation, Japan.

SAF products are produced on the basis of drawings by customers. The production procedure is as follows: first, SAF receives drawings of parts from customers. Based on these drawings, the SAF engineering division plans the production process. Some parts require a combination of over 100 metal moulds for pressing. SAF products are subject to high safety standards because they are used for fuel tanks and fuel-related parts. In order to form steel sheets into fuel tanks, the steel must undergo hundreds of pressing processes to expand steel and form it into parts. The metal moulds used in these processes are manufactured and modified by in-house technicians. All finished parts are tested twice since fuel parts require high safety standards.

As of July 2005, SAF employs 80 executive staff (university graduates), 210 workers (high school graduates), and 120 contract workers. The executive staff is classified into two categories: manager and assistant manager. An assistant manager is in charge of several section managers who each manage 10 to 40 workers.

The wage system for workers is based on production output. There is no basic wage. All wages are calculated on the basis of completed items and performance. There is no grading system among workers. Evaluation is based purely on output. The wages differ by a ratio of 1 to 3, from 500 yuan to 1,500 yuan.[3] A worker can be promoted to the position of section manager, as a result of an evaluation and assignment by the relevant managers.

The president of SAF, 52 years old, has been working for the company since 1975. Before entering the company, he was sent to the countryside to work on a farm during his university years under the Cultural Revolution. In 1975, he was sent to Shenyang as a worker of the fuel tank factory for trucks. Starting as a worker, he was promoted to section manager and then to assistant manager in 1980, all in just five years. In 1981, he was promoted to the position of production manager, and in 1983, to the position of secretary to the president of the factory. The following year, he became vice-president of the factory. Since 1997, he has been the president of the factory. He recalls that even under the planned economy system in China, he worked twice as hard as others did and did overtime, even though his pay was the same as that of others who worked much less than him. SAF carries out training for its employees, but only introductory training for new employees, such as safety and regulations. On-the-job training (OJT) is the only source of training.

In sum, the localization of engine parts production in Shenyean has progressed. Due to the strong historical background of the metal industry in Shenyean, and despite the low level of quality and productivity, local parts manufacturers were able to produce major engine parts without technical collaboration from abroad. They mostly installed local machine tools; they created and modified local metal moulds, and produced parts without any help from foreign advisers or engineers.

Analysis of Findings

The findings of the research are summarized as follows. Firstly, the final assemblers in China are joint ventures with MNEs and largely receive their technology from the MNEs. A high localization rate has been achieved in the final assembler since the 1990s. Secondly, the situation is about the same for the engine manufacturer. The engine manufacturer, a joint venture with a MNE, received technology from the MNE and achieved a high localization rate. Thirdly, on the contrary, the second tier suppliers for the engine firm were privatized state enterprises, but are not a joint venture with MNEs or receive technical assistance from MNEs.

Here, we would like to examine the first finding in comparison with Malaysia. Malaysian automobile development case studies are used to determine the technological capability of China. China and Malaysia both started automobile production in the 1980s. Both governments carried out their national industrial development policies by focusing on the development of their automobile industries. In the last 20 years, both China and Malaysia have increased their automobile production volume and improved their production technologies. Malaysia's national car policy, which started in 1985, developed automobile production technological capabilities in Malaysia and succeeded in designing and producing Malaysia's own cars. A study of localized production process and supplier's capability in Malaysia (Sadoi, 2003) is used here.

First, a final assembler's case is examined. The production volume of SVW is compared with that of Proton Malaysia, which started passenger car production in the same year as SVW. Figure 5 shows the progress of the production volume of SVW and Proton. At the beginning, the production volume of SVW was much lower than that of Proton. From the year 1995, after ten years of operation, the production volume of SVW has increased rapidly and has exceeded that of Proton. In 2003, SVW and Proton produced about the same volume of passenger cars.

When we look at the localization rate of SVW and Proton, although the production volume of SVW was lower than that of Proton until 1995, the localization rate of SVW reached a higher level than that of Proton in 1988 and increased the rate higher and faster. In 1990, the SVW localization rate reached over 60 per cent, while that of Proton was lower than 20 per cent. In 1995, Proton reached over 60 per cent and SVW continued to increase localization rates to nearly 90 per cent. As far as the research result is concerned, the final assembler in China achieved a high localization rate from the early phase.

How did SVW manage to achieve such a high localization rate earlier than Proton? This is of particular importance since both China and Malaysia introduced localization policies to upgrade automotive parts suppliers.

In the case of Shanghai, both the central and the Shanghai government prioritized the increase of localization rates in the early phase. In 1987, the Santana parts localization project began and both the central and the Shanghai government began investing in localization projects and developing a number of protective policies for local suppliers involving tax reductions and other measures (Chen, 2000). The development of the automobile industry in Shanghai has been promoted both by the central government and the Shanghai government, resulting in a concentration of investments in the Shanghai area.

In 1994, the state of China officially presented its automobile development policy. In this policy, a parts localization rate of 40 per cent was required in order to qualify for tax exemption. The Chinese government developed many regulations for joint ventures with foreign automobile makers in order to speed up the transfer of foreign technology. For example, the Chinese partner must control over 50 per cent of the capital in a joint venture with a foreign automobile and engine manufacturer. In addition, joint ventures must produce car models from the 1990s or later, they must have an internal R&D division, and give priority to local parts suppliers.

Next, we would like to discuss the second finding of the contribution. Thus, that the situation in the first tier engine firm was about the same as the final assembler. That is, the engine manufacturer is a joint venture with MNE and received technology and achieved a high localization rate.

As shown in the findings from an engine firm in China, the majority of engine parts – metal processing parts – were locally available in 2005. The reason for this can be described as the same as in the case of the final assembler. It depends largely on technology from MNE as a joint venture partner. As described in the earlier section, managers and engineers from MNEs were playing an important role in the localization process in production.

However, the third finding, that is, the second tier suppliers which produce core engine and transmission parts are not joint ventures or receiving technical agreement from MNEs, shows a different pattern, in contrast with the Malaysian case. When we conducted the research at the clutch disk firm and oil tank firm in Shenyang, both were privatized ex-state enterprises. The directors in both firms were long experienced engineers, who started their careers as blue-collar workers. Although their technological level was not advanced at the beginning, they seemed to have improved, learning while working through trial and error.

In Malaysia, the localization process of clutch disks was organized differently. The clutch disks were localized in Malaysia in 1999, a process carried out by Excedy, a joint venture between a Japanese clutch maker and Malaysian capital. The same types of clutch disks were supplied to Proton. When Excedy invested in Malaysia, three Japanese suppliers of Excedy, a forging process supplier, a machining process supplier, and a heat treatment process supplier, all of whom supply parts to Excedy Japan, set up a production site in Malaysia, as requested by their major customer Excedy. All three Excedy suppliers invested in Malaysia at the same time (Sadoi, 2003).

Malaysia has undergone a different process of parts localization from that of SYQ in Shenyang. Historically, Malaysia did not have a local metal industry basis. Therefore, for each clutch disk production process, four suppliers took charge of the process and combined their investments. Compared with the Malaysian case, SYQ shows an advanced process of localization in clutch disk parts production, with the advantage of a strong local metal industry basis, human resources, machine tools, local metal moulds, and all the forging, stamping, and machining processes taking place in-house.

Conclusions and Implications

Attracted by the huge domestic market the volume of foreign direct investment has expanded rapidly to accelerate the development of the automotive sector in China. Government policy requiring joint venture and technology transfer conditions has played an important role in stimulating localization in the industry

Chinese Automotive engineering and parts suppliers have been one of the big beneficiaries of government-led technology transfer and localization strategies. The successful implementation government policy helped automotive firms achieve localization in China at a rate much faster than in Malaysia. Even key technologies related to engine and transmission parts have been rapidly localized in China. The greater success achieved by Chinese firms compared to Malaysian firms goes beyond simply differences in market size. Government policy in China also focused directly on the development of technological capabilities in local firms whereas in Malaysia the emphasis has been limited largely to incentives.

Human capital development has also been important in driving technological capability building in local firms in China. Most presidents of supplier companies in China have had long careers in engineering in the field, which have been instrumental in driving upgrading in human resource management systems. Recognizing that automobile manufacturing is a knowledge-intensive activity, the captains of Chinese supplier firms created environments to motivate workers to raise productivity. Although enterprise training is not very developed in most of the small and medium-sized enterprises, the merit system introduced in them has encouraged workers to improve their knowledge by attending technical colleges. Many of the employees from these firms have undergone a three-year casting training programme in Japan. Indeed, government institutions, the enterprises and individuals are all aware of the importance of technical training.

The government's focus on local capability building – in product and process technology as well as the requisite human resources to drive it – has been central in explaining rapid technology transfer and localization in the automotive industry in China. A strong domestic foundation in the metal industry helped supply human resources (especially in executive and management levels), as well as, training to help improve local automotive parts suppliers' technological capabilities. The evidence shows that attempts to impose localization conditions on foreign assemblers had to be met with commensurate capability development in local suppliers to ensure rapid absorption of technology from foreign firms.

Notes

[1] Author's survey, August 2004.
[2] Shenyang state regulation (from an interview with a production process manager of SAME).
[3] 8.1 yuan = 1 US$ (as of August 2005).

References

Chen, J. (2000) *Growth Strategies of the Chinese Automotive Manufacturers* (Tokyo: Shinzansha Press) (in Japanese).

Delphi (2005) Delphi Company Information. Available at http://www.delphi.com (accessed August 2005).

Dunning, J. H. (1993) *The Globalisation of Business* (London: Routledge).

Fourin (2005) *The Automobile Industry in China* (Nagoya: Fourin) (in Japanese).

Fujimoto, T. & Shintaku, J. (2005) *Architecture-based Analysis of Chinese Manufacturing Industries* (Tokyo: Toyo keizai shinpousha) (in Japanese).

Ikeya, K. (1997) Development of Shanghai automobile industry, in: M. Seki & K. Ikeya (Eds) *The Automobile Industry in China and Japanese Firms* (Tokyo: Shinpyoron) (in Japanese).

Lee, C. (1995) Adoption of the Ford system and evolution of the production system in the Chinese automobile industry, 1953–93, in: H. Shiomi & K. Wada (Eds) *Fordism Transformed: The Development of Production Methods in the Automobile Industry* (London: Oxford University Press).

Lee, H. L. & Houde, M. F. (2000) Recent trends and main characteristics of foreign direct investment in China, *Financial Market Trends*, No. 77, October (Paris: OECD).

MAA (Malaysian Automotive Assoication) (n.d.) Summary of sales & production data (Kuala Lumpur: MAA).

Maher, M. & Christiansen, H. (2001) Growth, technology transfer and foreign direct investment. Paper presented at the OECD Global Forum on International Investment, Mexico City, 26–27 November.

Maruyama, Y. (2001) *Development and Technical Transfer of the Automobile Industry in China* (Tokyo: Tsugeshobo) (in Japanese).

Sadoi, Y. (2003) *Skill Formation in Malaysian Auto Parts Industries* (Bangi: UKM Press).

Seike, A. & Ma, S. (Eds) (2005) *Chinese Enterprises and Management* (Tokyo: Kadokawa Gakugei) (in Japanese).

Wang, X. M. (1999) A new strategy of technology transfer to China, *International Journal of Operations & Production Management*, 19(5/6), pp. 527–538.

Zhang, W. & Taylor, R. (2001) EU technology transfer to China – the automotive industry as a case study, *Journal of the Asia Pacific Economy*, 6(2), pp. 261–274.

Conclusions and Implications: The Role of Multinationals in Technological Capability Building and Localization in Asia

RAJAH RASIAH

Introduction

This collection analyzed several critical issues concerning multinationals, technology and localization in the development of the automobile and automotive component firms in East Asia. Among the selected economies, China, India, Japan, Korea, the Philippines, Taiwan, Thailand and Malaysia have been major platforms for automotive manufacturing. Either directly (through foreign direct investment) or indirectly (through licensing, the absorption of tacit knowledge embodied in human capital or imports of components and parts) MNCs have been important in at least the initial growth of the industry in all these economies.

Local firms have been important in Japan, Korea and China. Foreign MNCs have been important either as totally owned affiliates or as joint ventures with local capital in automotive manufacturing in China, Malaysia, Thailand, the Philippines and India. National car development policies drove automotive manufacturing growth in Japan, India, Korea, China, Malaysia, and briefly in the Philippines and Indonesia. Along with the United States and Germany, Japan and China are the third and fourth largest manufacturers of automobiles in the world. The latecomers of the Philippines, Indonesia and Thailand have managed to expand operations in automotive manufacturing despite the lack of local brand names, and all three have implemented the conditions relating to the Trade-related Investment Measures (TRIMs) agreement by 2003, which requires the abandonment of localization policies (see Rasiah, 2003). Foreign direct investment has been the critical driver of automobile manufacturing in Malaysia, the Philippines and Thailand.

Differences in government policies, effective demand in domestic markets and company-level strategies facing different historical specificities, localities and insertion in global markets have produced a wide range of technological capabilities and performance among automotive firms in the seven economies. The findings provide valuable evidence for both policy and theory. The wide geographical space and issues covered offer significant implications for addressing some of the topics involving the role of MNCs in developing economies.

Appropriating Benefits – Potential and Actual

Dunning (1958) had argued over the benefits local firms can extract from the operations of MNCs relocating from superior parent sites, pointing *inter alia* to financial, managerial and market access benefits that American firms could potentially bring to United Kingdom firms. To this list one may add specific technologies – both process and product – starting with the acquisition of simple operative technology to process and product adaptation, and export market orientation, creative duplication to eventually novel innovations (see Kim, 1997; Rasiah, 2004).

Foreign firms in the automotive industry in Rasiah & Kumar's study show statistically significant higher labour productivity, export-intensity and technological means than local firms. The contributions by Busser, and Peter Wad and Rosli & Kari also showed that foreign firms are also technologically superior and more competitive than local firms among suppliers in Thailand and Malaysia (Proton). These greater advantages suggest that foreign firms have deployed higher technology – human resources (HR), process and research and development (R&D) – than local firms. This advantage and higher wages can provide the positive effects associated with efficiency-driving competition and the demonstration effects as argued by Caves (1974). The exposure of local employees to better technology in foreign firms can also raise the pool of tacit and experiential knowledge embodied in human capital for the development of the industry in India, Thailand and Malaysia. Further research is essential though to ensure that the foreign firms are not 'poaching' skilled workers from local firms.

Interestingly, where the relocation involves home and host sites that are technologically at the frontier, the nature of benefits appropriated may be horizontal in nature. Merieke Stevens had argued convincingly using the Renault-Nissan link-up that strategic alliances can provide mutual benefits. This alliance brought to the negotiation boardroom one firm endowed with strong financial and management capabilities (Renault) and the other with strong technological and manufacturing capabilities (Nissan). Of importance here is also the capacity of two informed partners to negotiate benefits horizontally, suggesting a clear need to distinguish such agglomerations from defensive takeovers involving asymmetric partners.

Where asymmetric relationships are involved the success of government strategy in China (as shown by Lih-Ren Li & Yuri Sadoi, and Yuri Sadoi) and Korea (as demonstrated by Peter Wad) in stimulating significant technological upgrading in local firms demonstrates the significance of effective government coordination of localization and domestic policies to drive technological capability building. Local suppliers in Malaysia (as shown by Peter Wad, and Mohamad Rosli & Fatimah Kari), Thailand (see Rogier Busser's study) and the Philippines (as demonstrated by Rene Ofreneo) have appropriated less benefits from foreign MNCs than in Korea and China owing to ineffective government policies and a lack of technological catch-up strategies. The provision of financial incentives and captive markets alone is not enough to drive technological catch-up in local firms, which is paramount to the survival of these firms in the long run as they will eventually have to face external competition. Chinese firms have enjoyed rapid localization through strong capability building to quicken technology absorption.

Government and Company-level Strategies

The Asian experience also shows that governments promoting national champions such as Proton or firms seeking ambitious growth paths should place emphasis on strategy and contingency plans with the objective of benefiting both partners rather than simply employing short-termist milking and asset-stripping strategies that in the long run could lead to the collapse of one or both partners. Clearly local firms in the Philippines and Malaysia lack a dynamic set of strategies to learn and benefit from the operations of MNCs in the automotive industry. Whereas Rene Ofreneo has already classified the Filipino experience as a disaster, the account by Rosli and Kari is only less categorical in their conclusions, providing evidence to show that local firms' performance falls significantly short of foreign firms. Peter Wad provided the rationale behind the poor performance of local suppliers in Malaysia arguing that these firms have not upgraded effectively to move up global value chains. Successful upgrading and integration in global value chains have helped Korean firms to move up the value chain.

Strategic technology management with an emphasis on upgrading in HR practices, and process and product technology should become an inherent part of both government promotion as well as company-level strategy to drive company-level competitiveness in the automotive industry. Participation in technology-intensive activities (especially in R&D) appears to rise in Indian automotive companies when skills intensity levels are higher. It is not enough to simply introduce mandatory training instruments such as the Human Resource Development Act enacted in 1992 in Malaysia when the actual intensity and content of training carried out in firms is low. More stringent monitoring of company-level strategies in Korea and China has helped drive greater technological capability building among suppliers in these countries. Automotive parts firms in India and Malaysia reported serious institutional failures that have restricted company-level learning and innovation. Although the cross-sectional regressions in the contributions by Rasiah and Kumar and Rosli and Kari on automotive parts in India and Malaysia respectively did not provide time trend and panel effects, the results support the view that governments in these countries should emphasize skills development to promote technological upgrading.

Global Value Chain

Exposure to competition and scale from global markets through export-orientation has played a key role in driving upgrading in the more export-oriented Asian economies. Integration in global value chains has been instrumental in Korean and Chinese firms in particular, and Thai, Filipino and Malaysian firms in expanding exports. Although export-intensities have been low in the Indian sample – 7.3 per cent among foreign firms and 5.5 per cent among local firms – the statistical results produced by Rasiah and Kumar show that export-orientation is strongly correlated with technological intensities.

Integration in global markets is greatly enhanced when firms participate in R&D activities as demonstrated by automotive parts firms in India. Export-oriented automotive firms showed higher intensity of participation in R&D activities than inward-oriented firms in the Indian sample. The same can be said of inward-oriented local suppliers in Malaysia whose performance as reported by Rosli and Kari has been way below foreign firms. Policy makers in India and Malaysia should not only view the experience of automotive firms in China and Korea, but also simply examine the strong and positive relationship produced in Rasiah and Kumar to dismantle India's and Malaysia's overly protected automotive sector. Despite tariff and quota liberalization initiatives since especially 1991 India has still remained fairly closed to competition from abroad. Malaysia's automotive sector is much more liberal than that of India but the application of localization policies to meet particular elites ethnically has denied the industry of effective upgrading (see Jomo *et al.*, 2003). Government policy in India and Malaysia can then be targeted to promote particular components and technologies on the basis of scope. Global integration of this nature on the basis of simultaneous coordination between government and markets to reduce failures in both can ensure that final assemblers receive the highest quality of components at the cheapest price and just in time.

Local automotive firms in Thailand, the Philippines, India and Malaysia show fairly low levels of upgrading in value chains led by MNCs in automotives. Clearly, government policy in these countries need to put in place an effective framework to drive upgrading so that local automotive firms can upgrade in order to participate in creative duplication and innovation to catch the forces of competition. The successful trajectories demonstrated by local firms such as Hyundai in Korea may suggest that Kim's (1997) argument on the importance of control and strategies centred on creative imitation as opposed to duplicative imitation may be important for driving upgrading and catch-up in the automotive industry. Kim (2003) also showed – using the examples of Daewoo (joint venture between General Motors and local capital) and Hyundai (local capital) – that the latter through strong local strategies but learning creatively from access to foreign technologies through both reverse engineering and licensing agreements managed to acquire and develop far more than the former.

The failure of local suppliers to achieve significant forays into the value chains of automotive assemblers in the face of more efficient expansion of foreign suppliers calls for a review of automobile support programmes in Malaysia and Thailand. Rosli and Kari on Proton and Rogier Busser on supplier firms in Thailand supplied enough evidence to suggest that local firms may even be costing the competitiveness of car assemblers in their respective countries.

Conclusions

The Asian automotive manufacturing experience on driving upgrading and competitiveness through links with MNCs demonstrates the importance of the coordinating roles of government and company-level strategies, and connecting in global value chains to stimulate the appropriation of advantages, including financial, managerial and technology. Where alliances are involved between horizontal firms with complementary advantages, their effective coordination can drive synergistic improvements in local partners. Where local firms are endowed with low capability levels – technology, exports and management – strategic government policy should take on a dual but coordinated focus of imposing spillover conditions in MNCs and at the same time technological capability building in local firms alongside increased integration in global value chains.

Whereas the Nissan-Renault merger shows that a mutually beneficial alliance can be established when the partners involved enjoy similar powers and complementary relative capabilities, the experience of supplier development in Korea and China demonstrates a pervasive role by governments but with strong coordination with markets, MNCs and global value chains. Local automotive parts firms in India, Thailand, Malaysia and the Philippines can learn from the Korean and Chinese experiences to raise their technological capabilities and the competitiveness of local firms. One may extend this policy lesson to other countries enjoying automotive parts manufacturing in Asia such as Indonesia, Pakistan, Iran and Turkey.

References

Caves, R. (1974) Multinational firms, competition and productivity in host-country industries, *Economica*, 41, pp. 176–193.

Dunning, J. H. (1958) *American Investment in British Manufacturing Industry* (London: Allen & Unwin).

Jomo, K. S., Rasiah, R., Rokiah, A. & Jaya, G. (2003) Industrial policy and the emergence of internationally competitive manufacturing firms in Malaysia, in: K. S. Jomo & T. Ken (Eds) *Manufacturing Competitiveness: How Internationally Competitive Nations Firms and Industries Developed in East Asia* (London: Routledge).

Kim, L. (1997) *From Imitation to Innovation* (Cambridge, MA: Harvard Business School Press).

Kim, L. (2003) The dynamics of technology development: lessons from the Korean experience, in: S. Lall & S. Urata (Eds) *Competitiveness, FDI and Technological Activity in East Asia* (Cheltenham: Edward Elgar).

Rasiah, R. (2003) Transnational corporations, learning and innovation: implications of the TRIMs agreement. Technology Policy Brief, Maastricht, UNU-INTECH, 2(1).

Rasiah, R. (2004) Technological capabilities in East and Southeast Asian electronics firms: does network strength matter?, *Oxford Development Studies*, 32(3), pp. 433–454.

INDEX

Page numbers in *italics* represent tables. Page numbers in **bold** represent figures.